Ageing and Co
Female Musici

Ageing and Contemporary Female Musicians focuses on ageing within contemporary popular music. It argues that context, genres, memoirs, racial politics and place all contribute to how women are 'aged' in popular music.

Framing contemporary female musicians as canonical grandmothers, Rude Girls, neo-Afrofuturist and memoirists settling accounts, the book gives us some respite from a decline or denial narrative and introduces a dynamism into ageing. Female rock memoirs are age-appropriate survival stories that reframe the histories of punk and independent rock music. Old age has a functional and canonical 'place' in the work of Shirley Collins and Calypso Rose.

Janelle Monáe, Christine and the Queens and Anohni perform 'queer' age, specifically a kind of 'going beyond' both corporeal and temporal borders. Genres age, and the book introduces the idea of the *time-crunch*; an encounter between an embodied, represented age and a genre-age, which is, itself, produced through historicity and aesthetics. Lastly the book goes behind the scenes to draw on interviews and questionnaires with 19 women involved in the contemporary British and American popular music industry: DIY and ex-musicians, producers, music publishers, music journalists and audio engineers.

Ageing and Contemporary Female Musicians is a vital intergenerational feminist viewpoint for researchers and students in gender studies, popular music, popular culture, media studies, cultural studies and ageing studies.

Abigail Gardner is Reader in Music and Media at the University of Gloucestershire, UK and writes on ageing, temporality and marginality, particularly in relation to women and popular music. Her publications include *Popular Music and Aging in Europe* (2019), *PJ Harvey and Music Video Performance* (2015) and *Rock On: Women, Ageing and Popular Music* (2012). She is a founder member of http://wamuog.co.uk, has led Erasmus + media and storytelling projects and produced 'In My Own Right', a documentary short (Zinder and Gardner, 2019) about two women's relationship in a small Orthodox community.

Interdisciplinary Research in Gender

Actresses and Mental Illness
Histrionic Heroines
Fiona Gregory

Cultural Production and the Politics of Women's Work in American Literature and Film
Polina Kroik

Masculinities and Desire
A Deleuzian Encounter
Marek Wojtaszek

Feminism, Republicanism, Egalitarianism, Environmentalism
Bill of Rights and Gendered Sustainable Initiatives
Yulia Maleta

Ungendering Technology
Women Retooling the Masculine Sphere
Carol J. Haddad

Ageing and Contemporary Female Musicians
Abigail Gardner

Sexual Violence and Humiliation
A Foucauldian-Feminist Perspective
Dianna Taylor

Gender, Sexuality and the Cultural Politics of Men's Identity in the New Millennium
Literacies of Masculinity
Robert Mundy and Harry Denny

https://www.routledge.com/Interdisciplinary-Research-in-Gender/book-series/IRG

Ageing and Contemporary Female Musicians

Abigail Gardner

Routledge
Taylor & Francis Group
LONDON AND NEW YORK

First published 2020
by Routledge
2 Park Square, Milton Park, Abingdon, Oxon OX14 4RN

and by Routledge
605 Third Avenue, New York, NY 10017

First issued in paperback 2021

Routledge is an imprint of the Taylor & Francis Group, an informa business

British Library Cataloguing-in-Publication Data
A catalogue record for this book is available from the British Library

Library of Congress Cataloging-in-Publication Data
Names: Gardner, Abigail, author.
Title: Ageing and contemporary female musicians / Abigail Gardner.
Description: Routledge, London; New York: Routledge, 2019. |
Series: Interdisciplinary researches in gender | Includes bibliographical references and index. |
Identifiers: LCCN 2019013068 (print) | LCCN 2019014708 (ebook) |
ISBN 9781315170411 () | ISBN 9781138048065 (hardback: alk. paper)
Subjects: LCSH: Women musicians. | Older musicians. | Women in music. |
Aging–Social aspects. | Popular music–Social aspects.
Classification: LCC ML82 (ebook) | LCC ML82 .G3 2019 (print) |
DDC 781.64082–dc23
LC record available at https://lccn.loc.gov/2019013068

ISBN 13: 978-1-03-209153-2 (pbk)
ISBN 13: 978-1-138-04806-5 (hbk)

Typeset in Baskerville
by codeMantra

Contents

Preface

At supper in the overheated summer of 2018, my mother-in-law asked me what this book was about. When I told her it was about ageing and music, she replied 'What on earth has ageing got to do with music? I'm 74 and I play the violin'. Sure enough, she performs in an amateur orchestra when her health allows her to, and has been playing and consuming classical music all her life. But her question stayed with me as often, at popular music conferences or media seminars in HE in the UK, there is a kind of shrugging of the shoulders when talking about age and music. Ageing is the preserve of Health and Social Care studies, perhaps, for gerontologists, and, yes, for feminists working on representation within visual culture (Dolan, 2017; Woodward, 2006; Jermyn and Holmes, 2015). Indeed, work at the Centre for Women, Ageing and Media at the University of Gloucestershire, where I have been based, has spearheaded this feminist approach to unpacking ageism within contemporary popular culture. What can be said about getting older and pop music? Well, it seems increasingly that a lot can, and is, being said about it. As pop matures, as it becomes museumified, as its fans refuse to give up their idols, so research is being carried out on fan allegiances (Vroomen, 2004; Harrington and Bielby, 2010; Driessen, 2015; Bennett, 2009, 2012, 2013, 2016), on pop heritage (Roberts and Cohen, 2015; Leonard and Knifton, 2015; Long and Collins, 2012) and on ageing voices (Elliott, 2015). More scholars across fan studies, sociology, anthropology and cultural studies are mapping out disciplinary spaces where the relationships between discursive and representational practices and audience experiences of popular music across a life course are being examined. This book is part of these multidisciplinary trajectories.

It is also trying to do something different with 'age' by asking whether it is always aligned to the body, or to chronology, whether it has specific generic functions and what myths it engenders. This needs to be done now because ageing needs to be unpacked, dismantled and interrogated; we cannot just say 'ageing' and agree we are thinking the same thing (getting old); we cannot assume that by saying 'getting old' we mean decline. These questions need to be asked and to ask them of the bodies, voices and performances of 'contemporary female musicians' is to centre the discussion on an arena within popular culture where age and ageing are complex and contradictory. The world of popular music is itself, subject to weird time shifts. It is both cyclical and retromanic; it catalogues itself, archives itself, goes back to itself, reliving the 1980s, playing 'Golden Oldies'. It is a space where time is elastic, shifting, exacerbated. Women in it age against this backdrop, are subject to discourses of renaissance, resurgence and of the market realities of reissue culture. They age accompanied by their youth: what they sounded like, what they looked like, who they hung out with. So yes, this book is about 'what on earth has ageing got to do with music' and it's about time.

Acknowledgements

Thanks to the following:

For talking about music. Richard Elliott, Ian Biddle, Adam Behr, Emily Baker, Sarah Hill, Matthew Lovett, Kai Arne Hansen, Martin Cloonan, Paul Long, Sara Cohen, Gerry Moorey, Ben Wardle, Jasmine Taylor, Justin Williams, Justin Crouch, Gideon Capie, Simon Turner, Pete Chambers, IASPM UK and Eire conferences.

For talking about ageing. Lizzie Adshead, Gerri Frame, Laura Snapes, Jude Rogers, Anna Pointer, Carol Scott, Helen McCookeryBook, Martine McDonough, Sharron Kraus, Mandy Parnell, Fran Malyan, Aby Vulliamy.

For the Sound Girls. Rochelle Smith, Signe Miranda, Lindsay Martin, Aliyah English, Claire Murphy, Claire Marie Lim, Vanessa Lucca.

For answering cold calls. Tim Plester, Jean-Michel Gilbert, Andy Franks.

For support. Anne Dawson, Ros Jennings, Melanie Ilic, Nigel McLoughlin, David James, Maria Quinn, Pili Luna.

This book is for my family, Charles, Josh, Letty and Louis, and my great friend, Anne.

Introduction

This book is about ageing but it is not only about getting old. It is about a process that happens in time and it is about times that are remembered as particular ages. It is about music and women and the stories they sing, the memories they narrate. It is about the places they play, the 'whens' and the 'wheres'. It is about age as texture and as memory, about musical ages and musical markers of age. It is about women in music, their pasts and presents; their lives lived in time and the times as they change. It is about marking time and being marked in time; it is about ageing and contemporary female musicians.

It deals with age and ageing across three connected areas of female creative practice in contemporary popular music: the recent wave of women's rock memoirs, the continuing performance of women in their middle and late middle ages and of young female musicians. The focus takes us across Britain, France, Trinidad and Tobago and America, a mostly Anglo-American tranche of musicians. Its main theme is that age's diverse impact on gender and sexuality informs the memories, articulations and performances of female experience across popular music. The book argues that 'age stages' (youth and old age in particular) are embodied, voiced, performed and represented in multifarious ways that both support and subvert expected trajectories of femininity in relation to ageing. It has two core objectives when looking at these trajectories. The first is to seek to establish thinking with age as a positive methodology with which to approach women's popular music practice across the life course. What this means in practice is that age is the primary determinant and focus. I am interested in how it manifests, how it is represented, how it makes itself present or absent, what function it has, how women are placed within age and age is placed within narratives of popular music. *Ageing and Contemporary Female Musicians* argues that age is often, but not always, linked to femininity and sexuality for women working in popular music. Age matters, but the matter of age – its materiality, configuration, articulation and representation – is complex. Taking this as axiomatic, the book seeks to investigate the issue of ageing across popular music in a novel way, in that it is not only about 'older' women. It looks, in turn, at women across the lifespan. Its analysis pulls together a diverse set of literary and musical interventions to suggest that the early part of the twenty-first century is a contradictory space for women across the many spaces of popular music, where female experience is both valorised, canonised or marginalised and even ignored (or denied) altogether. It does this by focusing on a range of musicians, some of whom are in their early 20s to some in their early 80s, and, in the final chapter, on women working in the contemporary industry aged from their late teens to their early 60s.

Second, and possibly to complicate the first focus, it problematises age as a chronological certainty. It argues for more fluid understandings of the term, whilst acknowledging the continuing nexus of youthfulness as/and desire within the broad arena of 'popular music'. These approaches are founded upon broader feminist contexts within which music and performance are positioned. Ageing is a feminist issue. And looking at this issue within the world of contemporary popular female musicians allows for questions to be raised around creativity, (sexual) subjectivity and identity to be addressed. The book uncouples 'age' from 'time'. Whilst acknowledging how far ageing has been related to chronology, it opens up age to query it as a temporal category, as a fixed date. So what this means here is that 'age' – youth, middle and old – can appear in bodies that are not chronologically young, middle-aged or old. Age is 'staged' through accepted vocal and gestural performances that are not always aligned to numerical age. Age can also be understood as a vocal texture that emerges; it can be a material or an aesthetic quality; it can be a reference to a subcultural moment that has been defined as youthful; it can be allied to sonic geographies. I am interested in thinking about time as it is played out by women and on women who work in popular music and in so doing, I take age away from time as it is marked out on the body, to age as a space marked out in a variety of differing ways across and within popular music culture. Opening up 'age' in this way allows it to be framed as connected to temporality through materiality, sonic texture and historical alliance, and as both disarticulated from and redolent of the body. This approach uses age as a contested space from which and within which to consider fresh angles on women, ageing and popular music. My contention is that there is a broader shift around conceptualising temporality (Baars, 2012; Keightley, 2012; Port, 2012), which upsets ageing as a linear process whilst concurrently continuing to cement youth as an ideal. In short, temporality's certainties are being confounded whilst youth remains the touchstone against which older women are mapped. The book does not buy into a broader decline ideology that has marked the representation of ageing and which is now being critiqued by ageing studies scholars. These 'conventional accounts of ageing locate it within the body where it is expressed as a universal, intrinsic, non-reversible and ultimately deleterious process of decline' (Strehler, 1962 in Gilleard and Higgs, 2014, p. 1). This ageing body initiates disgust, shame or empathy because of its descent towards the abject, irrational body: leaking, demented, out of control (Grosz, 1998), which is in need of care. This narrative embodies the 'deep resistance towards old age that is located in our collective consciousness' (Pickard, 2018), crystallised, as Pickard notes, by Rodin's hag. The decline narrative is premised on a unidirectional route from youth (good) to old age (bad) and this book seeks to uncover different processes at play within the broad realm of 'popular music' that subvert such a narrative. It is mindful of a wider push from ageing studies to 'present ageing in a more positive light focused on its less "corporeal" aspects, through concepts such as "seniority", "integrity", "wisdom" or "longevity"' (Gilleard and Higgs, 2014, p. 1). It does not, however, buy into either of these narratives, the decline story or the renaming and refocusing of age through different categories of accumulated life course experience. Rather, it looks at both of these narratives as being alive in the stories of and about women of all ages who are performing in popular music.

For the past ten years I have worked with the Women, Ageing and Media Research Centre at the University of Gloucestershire. The research undertaken there has investigated the representation of older women across media and my work, some with Ros Jennings, has focused on older women and popular music. PhD students are beginning to come to us to work on ethnographic studies of older punk women, ageing vocality and other age-related topics. The idea that kick-started this book was to think about age as a process unhitched to oldness, and to think about age on youth, youth on age and all possible combinations thereof. It was in part a reaction against the idea of age as decline (Pickard, 2018), and, instead, to consider ageing as the living in different temporal places. The premise is that age appears on bodies and in texts, in music and in representations in complex ways that require an intervention. Travelling through musical lives, represented in audiovisual texts and encountered by ageing audiences, ageing for female contemporary musicians is a place that yields exciting avenues to explore around how we might think with ageing. And I was also tired of colleagues and friends thinking that ageing and music was a bit, well, boring, a bit sad, a bit obvious. I was becoming known as the colleague who wrote about old ladies and music. I wanted to say both that this is OK, it is worth researching and writing about, and that it's not always about old ladies (but if it is, then what's wrong with that). This book says that ageing, as it appears on the bodies and in the narratives of women in popular music, is the opposite of obvious.

Within the book, the term 'popular music' is deployed to encompass a number of genres, with chapters focusing on women in folk, electronic pop, post-punk, Grime, alt-rock and ska. It makes sense for me to establish how I am using the term throughout the book, and to make clear statements as to where I am writing from. This sets the parameters of the enquiry and allows for an understanding of both context and aim. Popular music is, if not almost meaningless, then determinedly slippery and mutating. Shuker argues that it is a 'shifting topography' (2013, p. 6) that is historically contingent and consistently changing. Shuker's notion sets the benchmark for an understanding of what popular music is for this book, as it did for the co-written book on ageing in Europe with Ros Jennings (Gardner and Jennings, 2019) where we dealt with the idea of ageing through travel and borders. Shuker's description, in particular, acknowledges a flexibility within the term itself, suggesting its contingency. In that respect, it is much like 'ageing', which, as Gullette (2004) has argued, is culturally determined. This book spotlights the specifics of that cultural determining, arguing that is generically, locationally, spatially and visually apparent.

Popular music is not always popular. Indeed, as we noticed in our work together, Ros Jennings and I tended to see and hear very different musicians when we considered the term. We wondered whether across many debates on the subject, written and at conferences, the 'popular' side of popular music has been somewhat overshadowed by work on rebellion and marginality (Reynolds and Press, 1995; Whiteley, 2000; Burns and LaFrance, 2002). Many of the works on the subject have underplayed the 'mass-ness' that is inscribed into the word 'popular', with its historical and ideological traces of low, 'canned' art (Keightley, 2016) that reflect a debate whose origins go back to Adorno. However there is, in counterpoint to this, a substantial body of work on 'pop' (Driessen, 2015; Hawkins, 2002, 2016a,b; Hawkins and Niblock, 2011) that has looked at how such a 'mainstream' format has allowed for experimentation around gender and sexuality. Pop, as a mainstream 'genre' has, it should be remembered, long acted as a vehicle within which deviance might very well be positioned. Indeed, this history of 'pop' has a veritable roll call of acts that have queered proceedings (Little Richard, Madonna, Boy George) through camp performance (see Robertson, 1996; Hawkins, 2016a).

The book moves between popular music forms, focusing less on taxonomical generic differences (although it does look at genre and age) and honing in, instead, on the potential for interesting 'takes' on age and ageing that are visible within and across popular music genres. The book is about women performing age across different musical traditions, and whilst acknowledging that the term is under continual debate, both for the technological developments that see increasingly diverse labelling practices (Beer, 2012) and from music journalists too like Ben Ratliff (2016), who has argued for affective groupings of genre rather than musicological ones, I have chosen musicians whose output and representation add to the overall theme of ageing *differently*. Whether outside of a linear heteronormative ageing, illustrative of ageing as hitched to genre, race or place, refusing to age or ageing within a specific canon, all of the 'female' musicians here age in ways that matter. They matter because they upset a one-way line of thinking about ageing, they upset because they are present as older women in a pop world whose very nascence and mythology was and has been hitched to youth and that is just coming to terms with its own ageing. Fran Malyan, interviewed in November 2018, is in charge of the 'legacy' and 'heritage' acts for EMI, Sony ATV. That popular music should collect its ageing acts and package them up as part of a specific heritage speaks to the way in which the industry itself is adjusting to its own ageing process. 'Old' age within popular music emerges in the representative mechanisms of UK Music and mainstream media discourses as 'heritage' (Empire, 2011). 'Heritage' rock positions the ageing musician as a cultural icon, similar to an 'event' or a 'listed building', part of a national landscape marked by reverence and acceptability. In a similar fashion to the rock memoir, it collects up the past in the body of the present performer and their recollections, as part of a broader popular cultural process of reflection, reification and recognition.

Why women, why ageing, why now?

In 2007, Marion Leonard's book on gender in the music industry discussed the problematic term 'women in rock' (2007, p. 32). Leonard noted that since it was not the default setting, not a 'band' but a 'female fronted band', it demarcated women as not the norm and 'peculiarise[ed] their presence' (Leonard, 2007, p. 32). Music papers have often, she noted, run 'periodic' (2007, p. 34) features on women rock performers. 'In September 1992, the British weekly music paper Melody Maker ran a three-page feature (Joy, 1992, p. 44–46) assessing the visibility of women rock performers' (2007, p. 33). She wrote of how:

> The expose-style coverage often afforded to female rock performers tends to erase the history of women how have spent many years working in the music industry as practicing musicians. The periodic articles on 'women in rock' in the music press present female performer as both notable and a topic for debate.
>
> (Leonard, 2007, p. 34)

Leonard notes that this has happened in 1992 (Melody Maker), and in 1973, in the NME in 1980 and 2002 and in Spin in 1997 (Leonard, 2007, pp. 34–35) and in other non-music press (Everywoman magazine, 1995; The Independent in 2005). 'Such articles, which regularly "rediscover" women performers, work against the normalisation of women working within rock' (2007, p. 35).

Female bands and musicians still make up a fraction of the industry (Sisario, 2018; Paier, 2018; prs foundation.com), and there remain concerns over a lack of presence in certain live areas, such as festival line-ups (in 2016, 9 out of 65 acts were female, Orr, 2015). Women in production make up 5% of sound engineers, 6% of producers and 30% of senior executives (Larsson, 2017). As some of the first women in key management roles gravitate towards retirement age and notable female musicians (such as Kate Bush) get folded into the heritage/legacy portfolio, so gender disparities in how they age and are aged by the cultures within which they move become apparent.

Ageing and popular music: the field

Age and ageing has not been ignored in popular music studies, but it has not been a significant strand of scholarly enquiry. With the increasing ageing demographics across advanced nations with well-developed music industries, the issue of ageing in relation to music consumption and production has begun to make small inroads into popular music studies (Driessen, 2015; Little, 2018, Hansen, 2020). Some of this work has built on the social care centred studies of Barbara Marshall (2014) and Stephen Katz (2005). Katz's (2014, 2018) work in particular on 'zoomers', baby boomers whose music preferences remain fixed on their youthful tastes, opened up a space for researchers. This work has been gerontologically focused and is largely concerned with older people's experiences and memories of music. Popular Music studies on ageing coming from a more Cultural Studies and musicologically driven agenda, such as Richard Elliott's 'Late Voice' (2015), track the vocal textures of musicians such as Joni Mitchell and Bob Dylan. My work with Ros Jennings collected differing feminist views on ageing women and discussed representations of older women, ageing and fandom and ageing audiences (Jennings and Gardner, 2012). Our more recent work on popular music and ageing across Europe has, we hope, opened up questions around ageing and the technological body, and youthful palimpsests on the ageing body (Gardner and Jennings, 2019). A lot of the research being conducted on ageing women and music is driven by memory work, which has its roots not only in Garde-Hansen (2011) and Keightley (2012) but in sociological investigations into ageing punks and Goths (Bennett, 2006; Bennett and Hodkinson, 2012). This book is not attempt to overwrite these endeavours; indeed, it benefits along the way from them. But it does seek to query age as a clearly delineated marker and does not sit within a sociologically driven tradition where it is concerned with lived experience. It is also not a book couched within memory studies, although it does use some of that work to consider memoirs of punk and indie-rock. Rather it seeks to throw 'age' about a bit, mess with it, see it as much of a mutable concept, which itself sits within an increasingly fractured and temporally discontinuous topography. This reworking of age is not a revisiting of postmodern articulations of time and experience and its discontinuous present. It does not deny the narrative arc whereby age might sit at one end but it does understand it as a specifically modernist construction and looks to queer theory, especially, for more fluid notions of approaching time as something other than a linear course through an expected trajectory (Halberstam, 2005).

Halberstam's work on 'queer' time discusses the interventions that non-normative models of being and desire have proposed. She refers to the Foucault of *The History of Sexuality* (1978), for whom queerness was not just about upsetting heteronormative conceptions of sex but of being in the world. Her work is an attempt to carve out a space that is not the flattened out formless space and time of postmodernity's Harvey and Jameson, nor is it to collude with 'Marxist geographers, for whom the past represented the logic of the present and the future represents the fruition of this logic' (2005, p. 11). Navigating a passage through these different conceptions of time, the book is positioned from a foundational perspective that time, like youth and age, is actively constructed through discourse and reiterated within popular culture, of which popular music is a part. How then these different conceptions of time become articulated and represented, how they appear within female contemporary musicianship and, crucially, how they intersect with articulating desire is where the book is focused.

Method

The methods used here are geared towards highlighting how age is performed: on stage, in video, in memoir and in and on the body. This mix of approaches and case studies, from the analysis of cultural trends in memoir publishing, through performance analysis to interviews, is broad but connected by the core theme of 'age stages'. Because the book is interested in how ageing appears, both in and about contemporary female musicians, so it looks at the places where those appearances occur. Stan Hawkins talks about the 'specific localities within which music is realised and contextualised' (2011, p. 105) and I extend this idea of 'locality' to the places of music video (performance), journalist reviews, biographical film, album cover art, memoir and memorials. This is a metatextual approach that is an amalgam of work coming out of Music Video Studies, Film Studies and Media Studies (Goodwin, 1992; Dyer, 1993; Lewis, 1993; Vernallis, 2004, 2013; Gardner, 2015) which focuses on text and discourse. Driving this analysis is the concern for how age(ing) appears in bodies and places. If 'musicianship is defined by performing, song writing, dance, acting and dramatized rituals' (Hawkins and Niblock, 2011, p. 4) then this book focuses on how ageing appears both in those spaces and others that I argue are related to them: film, music video and reviews, the 'extramusical props' (ibid, p. 37), where performing is staged, encountered and discussed.

The methods are mixed for a reason. The subjects they are addressing are different and range from memoir through video to interview. Chapter 1 is a critical reading of the memoirs of Viv Albertine, Kim Gordon and others; Chapters 2–5 are performance analyses afforded through close textual analysis of music video (and live) performance. Chapter 6 presents the findings of 19 interviews and questionnaires from a ten-month period (April 2018–January 2019) and the methodological approach to those participants is discussed in detail in that chapter. A degree of discursive musical analysis is provided in Chapters 2–5 with respect to how age might be heard. However, this is done not from a musicological position, as I am not trained in that discipline, and so does not use notation or score reading. It is a method of approaching music that is intertextual (De Nora, 2000, p. 28) whereby music needs to be decoded within a broader tapestry, because it 'is not possible to speak of and decode "music itself"' (p. 28). It is motivated more by a desire to *hear* age and how it might resonate 'as' an ageing voice; how 'age' might be produced.

For work on ageing and later age, Richard Elliott's (2015) book is key, and Apolloni's (2016) piece on Marianne Faithfull has concentrated on the change in vocals between the ingénue and the ageing singer. I am not focusing on the difference between youth and old age, on narratives of decline and disrupture. Indeed I think it is important to note that I am new to a number of these musicians, not having listened to their work before thinking about this book. I therefore approach and consider women like Shirley Collins, Calypso Rose and The Breeders 'as' contemporary female musicians, not as ageing performers trying to match the vocals of their youth. And in the case of Pauline Black, whom I listened to in the early 1980s, I am more focused on where she is *placed* than how she sounds.

I want to distinguish here how I am using the terms 'space' and 'place' since they come with a history (Lefebvre, 1991 in particular). In his work on space and place in hip-hop, Murray Forman cites Lawrence Grossberg's distinction of the two in terms of a 'structured mobility', stating that 'places are the sites of stability where people can stop and act, the markers of their affective investments,' and 'spaces are the parameters of the mobility of people and practices' (1992, p. 295 in 2002, p. 25). Places are 'being', spaces are 'becoming'. Places are filled with histories, belongings are marked, bounded, locatable in both space and time. Spaces are about potential. I use the term 'space' in Chapter 3 to argue how three gender fluid and/or queer performers carve out spaces in order to speak and I use 'place' in Chapter 5 to argue that it can both locate and constrict the work of British Black musicians.

Spaces and places appear throughout the book as important locations for a contextualisation of ageing. Women like Shirley Collins and Calypso Rose are placed within their musical traditions, canonical. Women who write memoirs are placed 'as' authors. Women make music in specific generic and subcultural places (The Breeders, Pauline Black, Helen McCookeryBook) and women open up new spaces from where they might speak (Monáe, Anohni, Letissier). Context is all and these locational threads appear throughout the book as the relationship between age(ing) and place becomes apparent.

Map of the book

Chapter 1 argues that the female rock memoir is an age-appropriate survival story which reframes the histories of punk and independent rock music. Memoirs by eight women including Viv Albertine, Tracey Thorn, Carrie Brownstein, Cosey Fanni Tutti and Patti Smith illustrate the Anglo-American neo-liberal emphasis on individual resilience (James, 2015). Narratives of overcoming the odds are not the sole preserve of female rock memoirs; male musicians and band memoirs pack the shelves of high street bookshops. However, there are two things to note about the timing of these accounts: one is that their presence indicates an acceptability of the ageing female authorial voice when it is couched within a literary, rather than a musical tradition. The second is that they function as a kind of retrospective 'settling of accounts' (McRobbie, 1991) because they insert distinctive female experiences into the popular myths of recent popular music history. They flesh out the popular histories of punk and post-punk from the sidelines that age has afforded them. They reset those histories by revealing the recollected stories from the private spheres: how music was encountered, how first guitars were purchased, how sex was negotiated, how abortions were had. The chapter teases out some of the differences between 'memoir' and 'confession' to look out how they both situate the ageing female musician as a singular survivor and what these accounts do in Anglo-American contemporary popular culture.

The memoirs are all written by white women predominantly from Anglo-American indie or punk traditions that are wrapped up in discourses of independence, rebellion, authenticity and auteurship (Bannister, 2006). These often occlude the communities and matrices within which they were fomented which research on punk allegiance and remembrance (Bennett, 2006) is going some way to uncover and valorise these collective histories. The memoir is individual however, and exists as testimony to the auteur, the singular, the exceptional. This ageing white female literary voice is then mobilised to re-present a popular cultural nostalgia for the youthful 'age' of punk and post-punk that is mirrored by contemporary cultural reflections on the era from the world of art and media.

Later in the book, I use Pauline Black's own memoir 'Black by Design' (2011), to think about place. My setting her apart from the memoir chapter is more by accident than design as initially it did not appear in searches for 'rock memoir' (because it is ska perhaps?) and I was not thinking of using her as a focus when the book was initially proposed. It was, however, a visit to the Coventry Music Museum where her imprint on that place and on the Two Tone movement became apparent. And her memoir, whilst admittedly still a 'struggle' narrative, also places her within a broader social context, one of racism and multiculturalism. It is, a review published in the book says, a 'valuable social commentary' (Abrahams, 2011, in Black, 2011). She ends it with the sentence 'The Selecter continues to gather speed on its musical journey. *Made in Britain* might not be kicking out the jams, but I like to think that we are putting a dent in the wishes of the far right'. This statement confirms her role as being part of a band that has a continuing progressive anti-right wing politics at its core, folding her into contemporary politics and place, less 'auteur' and author, more continuing band member.

Chapter 2 is about old age and its functional and canonical 'place'. It focuses on the English folk musician Shirley Collins and on the Trinidadian, Calypso Rose, who are in their late 70s and early 80s, arguing that they have a function as postmenopausal matriarchs. They are 'grand-maternal' figures within their genres, generating a sense of historicity and so valorising their musical canon. Their longevity 'as' older women within a specific familial network cements this functionality. They both appear in film and in promotional music video 'in place'; that is, they are situated within specific geographical locations that work to underscore their generic positioning. In particular, the critical literary work of Adam Scovell (2017) on folk horror is used to read Collins as a figure of English folk, locating her as a fixture within a specific generic landscape. Collins and Rose have both recorded albums of traditional and new material in their 'old' age, one (Collins) after having had a 35-year hiatus. These recent albums are the result of their creative alliances with younger male producers: Collins by David Suff, Ossian Brown and Stephen Thrower and Rose by Manu Chao. Their work is funnelled through the male producers' lens, and into their markets. This producerly pattern offers up these two female musicians 'anew'. By presenting the 'old' as new, this is a marketing strategy that serves to present classics, or 'legacy' artists to established and newer audiences (Gardner and Moorey, 2016). These two interrelated processes, their canonical function and their production at the hands of younger men deliver the postmenopausal matriarchal Collins and Rose 'as' grandmothers within the accepted traditions of folk and Calypso.

Chapter 3 focuses on the elasticity of gender and ageing in the music video performances of Janelle Monáe, Christine and the Queens and Anohni. It argues that these performances foreground performances of 'queer' age, specifically a kind of 'going beyond' both corporeal and temporal borders. Music video has arguably provided a space for 'an active politics of representation' (Hawkins and Niblock, 2011, p. 104, see also Hawkins, p. 107; Lewis, 1993; Vernallis, 2004, 2013; Railton and Watson, 2011) and these three contemporary acts use music video to experiment with bodies, space and time in exciting ways that arguably 'conjure new worlds' (Halberstam, 2013, p. 12). This focus on their visual rhetoric and performance tactics suggests that travel across ages and bodies and the experience of temporality is not always and ever linear. It interrogates the stability of the terms 'female' and 'ageing', the title of the book, to see how they can be unsettled. I suggest that Monáe is an Afrofuturist who performs queer futurities (Halberstam, 2005; English and Kim, 2013; Womack, 2013; Hawkins, 2016b), that Héloïse Letissier (the 'Christine' of 'Christine and the Queens') performs future nostalgias and that Anohni foregrounds 'trans-ageing' through the 'double address' or 'ventriloquist' music video mode, where she uses older women to lip sync (Moglen, 2008). This concept of 'trans-ageing' is not to do with the transness of gender, but with the subject's ability to experience different modes of ageing: to travel between and across age.

Chapter 4 is about ageing within genres. It introduces the idea of the *time-crunch*; an encounter between an embodied, represented age and a genre-age, which is, itself, produced through historicity and aesthetics. It takes The Breeders, The Askew Sisters and The Rheingans Sisters and suggests that there is something going on in the discourses within which they are positioned and which in turn position them: that mean their ages are wrapped up into, and around 'genre'. Chronological age and generic age jostle in the bodies of these musicians. The Breeders work ostensibly in 'alt-rock' which has its roots in grunge, rock and punk. All these factors work to promote it, despite its longevity, as a 'young' genre, within which The Breeders, 56 years old at the time of writing, are positioned. Folk is positioned as an 'old' genre, one that reifies its lineage and heritage. The chapter investigates how two 'young' bands, The Rheingans Sisters and The Askew Sisters, are represented 'as' folk acts, to foreground the collision of generic age within their younger bodies. The Rheingans and The Askews are, as their names testify, sisters, The Breeders are twins. Underpinning the idea of a collision of generic age and embodied age, the chapter also discusses the 'agelessness' of sisters and sisterhood, to assess how that plays out with the idea of 'timelessness', a notion that comes up in reviews and comments of The Breeders especially.

Chapter 5 positions Pauline Black, Lady Leshurr and Lava La Rue, as 'Rude Girls' and argues that their work is framed by the real and symbolic 'city'. This fixes them to a specific 'place' ('*lokalszeit*', Schütze, 1922), or to a 'sonic footprint time stamp' (Charles, 2019). How that then restricts their voices 'as' Black British artists speaking from somewhere, and what that somewhere might be, is at the centre of the chapter. It is therefore an examination of race and place, geographic, subcultural and temporal. Referencing work on hip-hop and place (Forman, 2002; Williams, 2014), it visits the Two Tone museum in Coventry, and analyses Lady Leshurr's series of music videos, The Queen's Speech and Lava LaRue's 2018 *Letra*. It argues that Black's role as a 'Rude Girl' works to generate her as always allied to 'youth' (and by extension, to a Jamaican diaspora and rebellious or even deviant subculture). It extends this idea of the 'Rude Girl' to Leshurr and LaRue in relation to their positioning within urban or city spaces and then asks how that folds them into a specific (colonial and racist) discourse. It revisits Halberstam's (2013) idea of 'going gaga' to ask how these three artists are involved in a process that enables them to vocalise a discomfort with 'England's colonial dreaming' (2013, p. 129). It is perhaps the most challenging subject for a middle-class, middle-aged white female academic to write about, and I am mindful of the problems of doing so. But it is written from the perspective of an old ska fan, myself, who is aware of the complexities about writing about race and place from a white perspective. Again, I do so with the emphasis on age, here with the particularities of place written into it.

Chapter 6 draws on interviews and questionnaires with 19 women involved in the contemporary British and American popular music industry: DIY and ex-musicians, producers, publishers, music journalists and audio engineers. It offers a snapshot of how age and gender might matter (or not) within the business of making popular music. Its methodology is qualitative and it searches for the stories of its subjects to reveal narratives of experience by women working in the music industry and its associated professions (such as music journalists). The motive for this chapter is to contrast the women who work 'behind the scenes' with those who perform, to offer some degree of a counterbalance to the textual thrust of the book. It also serves to spotlight how unwieldy the term 'music industry' is, where it is many, and how diverse the experiences and expectations of ageing might be from a small number of women who work within it.

'Afterthoughts' is a short addendum that sums up why ageing matters and how the matter of ageing in popular music is both something marked and feared, avoided and ironised. 'People don't really want to talk about being old' was one of the comments made and notes by an interviewee for the book. And why should they? In this refusal or reluctance lie narratives of decline that the book attempts to circumvent by decoupling ageing from being old and by disarticulating ageing from the body.

There are gaps to this book, and this is inevitable since it is the subjective product of one person writing from their perspective at one time. Many other female musicians could have been included. Marianne Faithfull released an album in 2018, as did Francoise Hardy. Both women are in their 70s and they could be examined as icons of the 1960s. Chrissie Hynde and Debbie Harry are not in here, nor is Tina Turner. Siouxsie and the Banshees, too, not in. Joni Mitchell was 70 in 2018 and 'the veteran' (Kellaway, 2019) Joan Baez's self declared 'last' tour is running across the globe throughout 2019. Some of them have had academic spotlight on their recent work (Faithfull discussed by Apolloni, 2016; Hynde by Coates, 2012 in Gardner and Jennings; Mitchell by Charnock, 2018; Petula Clark and Shirley Bassey by Jennings, 2016; Grace Jones by Gardner, 2016). But old age was not the determining criteria for inclusion. Rather, it was more about how ageing might be understood in relation to other ideas, such as genre, place, race, sexuality and canon. Some women who have appeared in the book are a surprise, to me more than anyone else. The proposal did not include Pauline Black, but seeing that she has released a record every two years since 2011 and that The Selecter are touring a '40th anniversary tour' made her an interesting and relevant subject to research. She too has published a memoir and towards its end, she has a lot to say about ageing and her role as an older woman. Similarly, the chapter on genre and ageing with The Breeders, The Askew Sisters and The Rheingans Sisters is one that could be written with any number of other component parts. Research is always a process of filtration and discarding, of dead ends and new destinations.

Ageing and Contemporary Female Musicians argues that age matters in nuanced and diverse sets of ways; the testimonies, memories and articulations of female experience in popular music are bound up in age and its impact on gender and sexuality. The emergence of recollections, returns, revivals and continuing performances alongside of a number of young female (and female identified) fronted bands begs analysis, since it suggests a richness of creative practice in an industry where the status of women continues to be a salient topic. Focusing on the extent to which these practices are inflected by age offers a perspective on women in popular music that argues for a more fluid understanding of age whilst acknowledging the continuing nexus of youthfulness as/and desire. *Ageing and Contemporary Female Musicians* plays with the idea of 'stage', as platform and phase, as location and temporal marker, with 'stages' of ageing that, in turn, are 'staged' through performance and representation. Margaret Gullette has argued that we are 'aged by culture' (2004; see also Pickard, 2016). This book I hope adds to that proposition by suggesting that women working in different areas of contemporary popular music are aged by genre, by race and by place. These practices serve to frame age as functional (as grandmothers) or as restrictive (as Rude Girls), as exceptional (as 'timeless') and as something to fear (for young tech crew). Simultaneously, some female and gender fluid musicians are involved in performance practices that carve out new spaces, third spaces and future places that give them room to act. These are the stages where age appears.

1 More than music

Female rock memoirs

Girlhood and growing up, clothes and sex, boys and music, being in a band: these are the standout themes from the titles of ten memoirs published between 2010 and 2017. Some of these include:

> 'Girl in a Band: A Memoir' (Gordon, 2015), 'Hunger Makes Me a Modern Girl: A Memoir' (Brownstein, 2015), 'Clothes, Clothes, Clothes, Music, Music, Music, Boys, Boys, Boys' (Albertine, 2014), 'Just Kids' (Smith, 2010) and 'M Train' (Smith, 2015), 'Bedsit Disco Queen: How I Grew Up and Tried to Be a Pop Star' (Thorn, 2013) and 'Naked at the Albert Hall' (Thorn, 2015), 'The Rise, the Fall, the Rise' (Smith-Start, 2016), 'Art, Sex, Music' (Fanni Tutti, 2017), 'Rat Girl' (Hersh, 2010).

They are written by eight American and English rock women musicians who, at the time of writing, were in their 40s and older: Kim Gordon of Sonic Youth, Patti Smith, Viv Albertine of The Slits, Tracey Thorn, Carrie Brownstein of Sleater-Kinney, Kristin Hersh of Throwing Muses, Brix Smith of The Fall and Cosey Fanni Tutti of Throbbing Gristle. Singers, bass players, guitarists, front women and backline: they are the recollections of some of the key figures on the Anglo-American punk, post-punk, grunge and 'independent' music scenes from the late 1970s to the early 1990s. These titles speak of belonging and appearances, and most importantly for this book, they view youth and girlhood from the vantage point of older age.

The second decade of the twenty-first century has witnessed a mini 'boom' in publications like this, and I am interested in why this might be and what they add to an understanding of the interplay between the punk pasts they narrate and the ageing presents from which they are narrated from. The female rock memoir is an age-appropriate survival story which reframes the histories of punk and independent rock music. They shed light on experiences and narratives of creativity, whose dominant themes centre on the matrices of domesticity, sexuality, trauma and musical creativity.

These memoirs narrate tales of trauma and belonging, family and sex and flesh out the histories of punk and independent rock. These survivor stories involve the documenting of the emotional journeys undertaken by the authors, as they flesh out the interior lives in retrospect. They feed into a neo-liberal conception of the individual that maps onto myths of 'rock 'n' roll' and underplays structural or systematic sexism and misogyny. They also build into a Romantic discourse of the individual creative auteur and continue a discursive (and problematic) trajectory of the 'confessional' singer-songwriter (Williams and Williams, 2016), whereby we expect the musician/author to divulge their inner lives through their art. And this is what we get in these memoirs, which though they are sold as 'rock memoirs' do not have music as the central theme. Rather, there is a focus on the intimate and on the domestic (McRobbie, 1991). They narrate mental anguish (Hersh), health traumas (Albertine, Tutti) and sexual confusion (Brownstein) as they seek to work out what music meant to them. They function as a kind of retrospective 'settling of accounts' (McRobbie, 1991) because they insert distinctive (traumatic, visceral, private) female experiences into the popular myths of recent popular music history.

This ageing female literary voice is part of a popular cultural nostalgia for the youthful 'age' of punk and post-punk that is mirrored by contemporary cultural reflections on the era from the world of art and media. This is, in part, due to an alliance between the contemporary cultural gatekeepers, the curators, publishers and journalists, who share similar life courses to the authors, but it is also about a need to reflect on times that are recalled as rebellious and to consider how memoir works to augment this historicising process. These rock memoirs not only focus on different versions of recent cultural history but feed into the mythologies of punk, grunge and indie in complex ways, both mythologising and canonising the periods of the late 1970s and early 1980s in punk and post-punk, whilst adding into it rich textural detail of the worlds behind the band and off stage. They write gendered subjectivities into that history, spotlighting the relationships, motives, fears and achievements of their times as musicians (see Edgar et al., 2019). Might it be too that there is an acceptability of the ageing female authorial voice when it is couched within a literary, rather than a musical tradition? These tales of trauma, sexual confusion, loss and illness emerge from the pens of older women, most of whom are still performing and recording. And so there is something here to consider around ageing pens writing youthful traumas and desires, and hitherto unvoiced youthful lives being folded into the widening histories of punk and independent Rock music.

Rocking memories

Rock memoirs are an established literary genre that functions as part of a broader ecosystem of popular music. They extend the reach of the musician and make them a cultural player in a broader cultural landscape. With an already identified audience, they make up part of a metatext of music, images and words that are the cultural configuration of that artist. They function as one element in the star making economy which popular music has, like the film industry, been reliant on. These tales of stardom are usually characterised by early struggles (with musical ability, with drugs, alcohol, and family), rejections (both by the industry and in relationships) and ultimate survival. There is, in them, a degree of familiarity as we know their stories already, but the memoir offers us the inside perspective. They take us off stage, behind the scenes and function in a similar fashion to the pseudo-documentary music video that Railton and Watson (2011) described. They allow us, the fan, an interested audience, a glimpse into the off-stage stories and offer an 'access-all-areas' account. They offer, like the documentary video, an authenticity that shores up ideas of the star and memories of performances; they are an authenticating narrative. The story of the struggling artist is a Romantic trope that has endured into the rock memoir, and tales of dissolution (Motley Crüe's 2002, *The Dirt: Confessions of the World's Most Notorious Rock Band*) and drug addiction (Nick Kent's 2010, *Apathy for the Devil: A Seventies Memoir*) only serve to perpetuate such a narrative. There is, in these narratives, an aura of the confessional tale, one that audiences perhaps knew already but are laid out on the pages for us to read. The memoirs of the women in this chapter share something of the confessional, in so far as all is laid bare, we are witness to events that were being enacted off stage. But they are more than this, and Radstone's analysis of the distinction between the two forms offers a platform from which to gauge how far these memoirs are not only individual confessional tales from the female rock star but that they are a rewriting of history. They feed into the mythology of the radical creative outsider (Negus and Pickering, 2002), and so might be understood as individual accounts of women in punk and post-punk, but we might also see them, as memoirs, as carving out, in retrospect, a history of women in rock that includes trauma, the body, sex and relationships: the matrix of their creative life.

These memoirs fit into a popular music industry that is part of a broader retromanic (Reynolds, 2011) culture which is defined by the urge to repackage, reunite and revive acts from its past (Driessen, 2015). The return of musicians from the 1970s and 1980s not only on stage, but in museums and exhibitions across Europe, the UK and the USA, and as part of interactive exhibitions (Gardner and Jennings, 2019) illustrates the veracity for such repeated encounters across different platforms. How then might we read the 'return' of younger women through the written memoirs of their older selves?

Catherine Strong, who has written on grunge and memory, writes in 2011 that 'Women are generally written out of historical accounts of music in order to reinscribe the creative dominance of men in this field' (Strong, 2011b, p. 398). These women are writing themselves back in. There are key themes that run through these selected female rock memoirs published between 2010 and 2017 that speak to an ongoing reluctance to claim young women as creative controllers with respect to popular music. All of the memoirs position music as part of a complex interwoven landscape across which personal relationships – emotional, sexual, parental, familial – are core. The women all sit at the centre of this network of relationships, and for rock memoirs, across many of them, music – how it is made, recorded, produced and performed – is not pre-eminent. It figures, yes, but tangentially. Albertine, Brownstein, Thorn and Gordon describe how they learnt to play bass. In each of their cases, it was an exercise in unlearning traditional methodologies and aiming to carve out new sonic spaces. Tutti describes her early fascination with sound and later, when with Throbbing Gristle, how loops and pedals were used in the studio. Thorn notably describes her reluctance to sing in public. But these accounts remain somehow lesser to the narrative of self-discovery and survival. If 'memory can be central to the reproduction or alteration of power relations in society' (Strong, 2011, p. 5), then the memoirs examined here do much to flesh out the lives of the musicians and artists who wrote them, documenting tales of family and friendship that position these women musicians very much in a place where perhaps their pre-performance and extra-performance lives were unexamined but are now documented as integral to their musical identities. What they do is tell us the off-stage stories and so retrospectively settle some subcultural accounts. They disrupt the sanctity of the subcultural boy's club and allow us to see what else was happening behind these musical scenes and within these musical subcultures and they fulfil what Halberstam argues for in her assessment of the historicising of punk:

> Why are these other histories of punk so important? Because without them, punk becomes a rebellion without a cause, a boy's club of heroic art school drop outs and another master narrative within which white guys play all the parts.
>
> (2013, p. 129)

Being seen and looking back: subculture and memoir

Being seen was very much part of the raison d'être of belonging to a subculture, where style and posing in public were integral to youth rebellion. Well it was if you subscribe to Dick Hebdige's seminal 1979 book on subcultures and style. His work, coming out of a sociological tradition which sought to deconstruct surveillance and street culture, positioned punks, mods and rockers as players in a narrative predicated on a feedback loop of surveillance and deviance that was premised on appearance. Style talked: what you wore was what you were. These rebellious youth were 'posing' and 'making a pretty picture of themselves' (Hebdige, 2007, p. 294) in the streets of Britain from the mid-1960s to the late 1970s, and for 'youth', read 'young men'. In 1980, Angela McRobbie wrote a critique of Hebdige called 'Settling Accounts with Subcultures: a Feminist Critique'. In it, she laments his writing out of young women through an emphasis on 'homages to masculinity' (1991, p. 25) claiming that that young women's experiences were being marginalised. She explains it thus: 'in the literary sensibility of urban romanticism that resonated across most youth cultural discourse, girls are allowed little more than the back seat on a draughty motor bike' (McRobbie, 1991, p. 20). She argued that women were not at the centre of subcultural theorists' concerns, that their participation in punk especially was unmarked and that this, given the extent of involvement of young women in performance, production and yes, in posing, was an oversight that she sought to address. To some extent, these memoirs of that time, of punk and post-punk, can be viewed as a retrospective reckoning and settling. They fill in the gaps that McRobbie suggests were absent from the sociological and post-structuralist accounts of the era. Writing specifically as a feminist, McRobbie noted how decried the private and domestic sphere was for both the male subculturalists and their sociologically driven researchers. This was characteristic of an ongoing 'silence' around young women that feminism, in its 1980s' guise, was seeking to speak out about. McRobbie writes of how the 'absence of the self and the invalidating of personal experience in the name of more objective social sciences' (1991, p. 19) only served to silence young women, particularly young working-class women's experiences. Almost 40 years later, these personal experiences are coming to the fore as memoir fiction, and tales of menstruation, sexual failure, ill-health and sexual confusion are wrapped into narratives of subcultural belonging and the pivotal role of music in women's lives. These memoirs speak of the life behind the subcultural 'style', of the emotional, sexual and artistic hinterlands not captured in the academic work of the late 1970s and early 1980s whose central concern was (media) surveillance and (male) display. They allow the reader to hear what those women thought, what they felt. And it is worth remembering that Hebdige's reading of punk subculture was a theoretical reading based on post-structuralist ideas of image and meaning. As writers since have remarked (Bennett, 2006; Bennett and Hodkinson, 2012), he did not seek to incorporate any 'real' punk voices into his reading, although that was not his remit. The memoir, on the other hand, offers the reader that tangled subjectivity.

Between confession and memoir?

The memoir is a subjective account of the self in the past written by the contemporary author, and as such, floats between the autobiographical and the fictitious, indeed, Susannah Radstone (2007), who has looked at the differences between memoir and confession, uses the term 'memoir fiction'. This format is recognised as a type of literary memory work aimed at inserting the self into a specific history. It is, by this token, selective and subjective: a story of the past self that is told in the present. In a book that considers sexual difference and time, Radstone quotes Hart on the crucial differences between memoir and what it is often associated or confused with, confession. For her, and others, the difference is predicated on temporality and ontology: '"Memoir" is personal history that seeks to articulate or repossess the historicity of the self.... "Memoir" places the self relative to time, history, cultural pattern and change. Confession is ontological,... memoir is historical or cultural' (Hart, 1970, p. 491 in Radstone, 2007, p. 17). Confession is reliant on a subject who is willing to change, to be altered by the confessional process. Its roots lie in Christian theological tradition; indeed, in the Catholic Church, it is one of the five important sacraments and is referred to as the Sacrament for Penance and Reconciliation. It is a two-way process wherein wrongdoing (Radstone, 2007, p. 56) is confessed to an audience (the priest) in a specific space (the confession box), with the hope of absolution and re-entry (reconciliation) into the wider religious community and to God. In the Catholic Church, this 'wrongdoing' might be anything that goes against

Catholic teaching and could range from any one deviation from the Ten Commandments. Crucial to the confessional is its confidentiality. It also follows a specific processual trajectory and might be understood as a ritual of apology and acceptance or, as Foucault (1978, p. 194) articulated in 'The History of Sexuality: An Introduction', a ritual for the production of 'truth'. The confessional is used to reposition the confessor on the path to an acquiescence to this 'truth' or prevailing dogma.

Confession is also positioned as a therapeutic healing process and relies on a reading of the individual subject as open to change and transformation. It involves more than one person and is co-temporal, both in its religious manifestation and in its media equivalents. You can talk the evil, hurt or misdemeanour out. Confessional television follows the same trajectory of deviation, confession and rehabilitation, and has its own confessional space (the TV sofa) and confessors (the TV host, live TV audience) (Wilson, 2003). The confessions in these mediated scenarios tend to dwell on sexual misdemeanours and misconduct with the reconciliation being with affronted partners or friends rather than 'the Church'. Viewers from a Judaeo-Christian or Western culture that has the confessional as its core ritual of reconciliation will know what to expect.

Where confession is ritualised acceptance of wrongdoing and rehabilitation in the co-temporal presence of a confessor, be it a priest or TV host and audience, memoir is a life story told retrospectively and selectively that might include a confessional moment. It is also about the temporalised self or 'selves' (Radstone, 2007, p. 193) rather than the damaged self. Radstone notes that there is a separation between the present self that is doing the writing and those that inhabited the past. The memoir is therefore inextricably temporal; it is about reflecting on past times, about subjectivity and time and about staking out some ownership to that particular time. And although there is a clear distinction between the two modes of expression in terms of their ontology, it is clear that confessional narratives can be part of a memoir. At first glance it might appear as if there were something of a tension within the memoir mode as used by women musicians, specifically when it is considered as a continuation of the trope of the confessional singer-songwriter. The eight women were making music in the punk, post-punk and grunge traditions, some of them experimenting outside of the 12 bar blues mode (Albertine, Tutti) and none of them could really be aligned to the singer-songwriter category, which, as Williams and Williams' (2016) book suggests, is a historical and generic contingency. There is a potential pull between seeing these narratives as a retrospective settling, as I set out in relation to the silencing of women's subcultural experiences, and as a corralling of the rebellious creative female musician back into a well-worn narrative of self-disclosure. So to a degree, the tension is around what constitutes 'settling' and in what format. Shumway's analysis of the 'emergence of the singer-songwriter' offers a platform from which to see the confessional mode typified by the singer-songwriter, as constitutive of space from which to speak of topics that were personal, but not apolitical. He argues that it was 1968 when, for a number of contemporary political and cultural reasons, the term 'singer-songwriter' became prevalent and was used to describe Carly

Simon, Carole King and Jackson Browne, among others. He writes how 'These singer-songwriters were not apolitical, but they took a confessional stance in their songs, revealing their interior selves and their private struggles' (2016, p. 11). There are persuasive arguments on how women might be able to fulfil the role of the confessional singer-songwriter in a positive way (Whiteley, 2000, p. 8) and how the 'telling of the tale' (2000, p. 8) is an important enunciative milestone for women. Indeed, Sarah Boak (2016), writing about women singer-songwriters of the 1990s (Amos, PJ Harvey, Björk), notes that the 'autobiographical and deeply personal approach' (2016, p. 261) was a medium through which narratives of 'bodily trauma' (2016, p. 261) could be channelled and heard. There are also counterarguments to suggest that this narrative and confessional role is restrictive since it not only allies women (again) to the embodied self, but it pushes women away from the potentially creative studio and production (see Dibben on Björk, 2013). Writers who have analysed the production and recording techniques of contemporary women singers (Dibben on Björk, 2006; MacDonald on Amos, 2016) and on analysis of their lyrics (Reynolds and Press, 1995; Gardner, 2015) have sought to spotlight the constructive and constitutive techniques that build a 'confessional' singer-songwriter. Closely miked vocals, lo-fi production techniques, 'candid', 'exposed' or 'revealing' lyrics (MacDonald in Williams and Williams, 2016, p. 238) and the use of 'direct address' (Shumway, 2016, p. 16) all work to generate a sense of a 'confessional' performer who is close to her subject matter, concerned with revealing her innermost self to an audience. As Press and Reynolds write, this epithet is more likely to be attached to a female performer, and they see it as part of a discursive and marketing strategy that situates women (again) with the self and the body rather than as a producer say, or a 'sonic wizard' (Gardner, 2015, p. 10). The 'myth' of the confessional singer-songwriter is allied to authenticity and the telling of the real as it is experienced and then communicated, by the self. There are parallels between this mode and the focus on the narrative of the self and of self-disclosure in the memoirs. It is interesting that in their maturity, women whose creative work was about reimagining music (Tutti) and about carving out sonic space (Gordon, Albertine) might be positioning themselves as more identifiable through this writing of their 'memoiric selves', whereby they become intelligible 'as' confessors. Finally, we get to know what was really going on in their lives.

From beyond the post-menopausal gap

Ageing in and of itself does not figure in these memoirs, but there are stories of age-stages, of birth, bereavement, romantic enchantment and sexual angst. And it is important to consider how it is the ageing voice that tells these tales. Disciplines have been traversed; musicians have become writers, and they are safely past the 'menopausal gap'. This change of authorial mode is essential to these voices being heard. This gap affords a space from which to speak; it is literally entitled. Its indeterminacy and menopausal propensity allows older women to write about their past excesses, more such so because of the fact that such excesses were exercised in the past and they now pose no sexual or moral threat. As postmenopausal writers, these musicians become part of a literary tradition that includes older women because, primarily, they are heard and not seen. Their voices are audible and they are being listened to, but there are tensions over how those voices are now packaged. Older voices are being sold via their younger bodies. As these women write and publish their memoirs in their 40s, 50s and beyond, it is their youthful images that continue to market them. There are two potential reasons for this. First, their youth remains the primary visual portal through which they emerge. Their voices are ageing, and whilst they may be performing (Smith, Tutti, Albertine, Thorn, Brownstein) their literary voices are heard, so their ageing bodies are erased at the expense of their youthful bodies continuing to represent them.

The cover of Gordon's 2015 *Girl in a Band* has her holding the camera's gaze, stood it seems, on a subway. She is young in the photo, as is Viv Albertine on the cover of her 2016 memoir *Clothes, Clothes, Clothes, Music, Music, Music, Boys, Boys, Boys*. Sat with her legs planted firmly apart, again holding the viewer's gaze. On the cover of 2013's *Bedsit Disco Queen*, Tracey Thorn is on stage, in the early days of her career, guitar in hand, again looking straight at the viewer. Brownstein, too, is on stage, arm in the air, mouth open, singing into the microphone, looking at no one in particular, but again, she is in her youth. Tutti looks out at us from the cover of her 2017 memoir with *Art, Sex, Music* superimposed over her mouth as if she is duck taped; she, too, is young. Smith's 2010 *Just Kids* has a photograph of her and Robert Mapplethorpe in a photo booth shot, young in New York. The only memoirist to be considered in this chapter, whose image on the cover of one of their memoirs is of her now, is Patti Smith, sat at her favourite café table in New York, pensively looking to one side.

Music and me: my guitar, my body

Clearly when reading a memoir by a musician, you expect to hear about music. But in Patti Smith's *M Train*, it does not appear until page 195, when she recalls hearing some 'discordant reggae' on Venice Beach. Perhaps because the book is less a memoir of her life than a meditation on life, art and her grief over the loss of her husband. Still, it is notable that the woman whose 1975 album *Horses*, who occupies an unassailable position within popular culture as the godmother of punk, has nothing to say about her music in her memoir of 2015. In her earlier 2010 account of her childhood and her years in New York with the photographer Robert Mapplethorpe, *Just Kids* music appears a little earlier on in the narrative. On page 44, she describes her record player, a gift from her brother, on which she and Mapplethorpe:

> listened to my *Madame Butterfly* as sung by Eleanor Steber. *A Love Supreme, Between the Buttons.* Joan Baez and *Blonde on Blonde.* Robert introduced me to his favourites – Vanilla Fudge, Tim Buckley, Tim Hardin – and his *History of Motown* provided the backdrop for our nights of communal joy.
>
> (2010, p. 45)

In both of Smith's memoirs, music is but one strand in a broader artistic canvas that encompasses drawing and poetry. Her 2015 work interweaves memories of her trips around the world (Mexico, Morocco, Japan) with her literary and artistic heroes (Kahlo, Bowles, Akutagawa) and reminiscences from her marriage and recent solo existence. It is not a 'how I got into music' memoir, nor does it tell the backstage tales behind that seminal album and its performances. It is on its own among its peers in this respect. The other six memoirs might be grouped in terms of how they first place music in their narratives in relation to themselves: Albertine and Tutti mention music first in relation to their families, notably their fathers; Gordon and Smith-Start prioritise music (performing and composing) with their marital relationships; Thorn and Brownstein cite their own teen fandom as the musical driver, situated as that relationship was outside of the family and other romantic/sexual relationships; and Hersh discusses music in relation to subcultural fashion.

Albertine remembers listening to *Sing Something Simple* (a light entertainment Radio 2 radio show that ran for 42 years from 1959 to 2001):

> The radio's on, the theme tune of *Sing Something Simple* with the Swingle Sisters seeps into the room, the vocal harmonies – sweet and sickly – pour out into the air and fill the silences. *I still can't stand the sound of those 1950s harmonies – like a drink you got drunk on as a teenager, just the smell of it brings back the nausea.*
>
> (2014, p. 15)

Here her first mention of music is as a memory trigger or prop (Van Dijck, 2007), one that synaesthetically takes her back to a family scenario where her father beats her and her sister with a belt. Paternal punishment is tied up too with Tutti's first recollections of music. She stole into her Uncle Mike's bedroom (who lodged with the family) to play his guitar: 'Mike's guitar was irresistible to me, and when he was at work I'd sneak into his room and play it' (2017, p. 21). This allure was partly due to her uncle's girlfriend, Val, a bleached-blonde 'fun time girl' whom she admired. The secretive playing was discovered and her uncle was given permission, by her father, to 'spank my backside' (2017, p. 21), like Albertine, a cocktail of music and paternal abuse is fixed. But added to this is an admiration for her father's interest in electronics, and with his purchase of a Grundig tape recorder, which fascinated her:

> The recording part was what I loved most. My sister was too shy to do it but I recorded myself a lot. Maybe my dad wanted a tape machine himself and used us as an excuse. I can remember him showing me how to do it and me singing 'Bobby's Girl' into the microphone.
>
> (2017, pp. 21–22)

The relationship between music and marriage starts off two of the memoirs. Kim Gordon describes the last Sonic Youth concert in Itu, Sao Paulo, Brazil. Having been in the band for 30 years, this festival performance is where she begins her account, one that traces her life from her childhood to the present:

> I was the last one to come on, making sure to mark off some distance between Thurston [her husband] and me. I was exhausted and watchful. Steve took his place behind the drum set like a dad behind a desk. The rest of us armed ourselves with our instruments like a battalion, an army that just wanted the bombardment to end.
>
> (2015, p. 2)

Smith-Start, too, describes music in relation to her husband, Mark E. Smith and the song writing process: 'I can't tell you how many times I've been asked about the creative process and how it worked between Mark E. Smith and myself. People seemed fascinated with how we came up with Fall classics as "Cruiser's Creek", "Hit the North" or "LA". In fact, forget the song writing. People just wanted to know how our relationship worked full stop' (2016, p. 11). Here, both Gordon and Smith-Start are articulating how their musicianship is tied up with them being part of something bigger than them, a marriage, a relationship to one other and to a band.

For Thorn and Brownstein, the first accounts of music come early on in their memoirs and they are both driven by fandom. Thorn takes us from a recent moment in *Everything but the Girl*'s history, where she and Ben Watts are considering the offer to support U2 whilst holed up in a plush Australian hotel, to her diary entries of 1976. These entries detail her consumption of late 1970s pop, David Essex's *Rock On* figures. She writes of how her diary talks endlessly about the heat (it was a hot summer) and how, although it was the summer of Punk, this did not impact on her life. But her diaries of June 1977 start to figure The Jam and the Stranglers, a shift to the New Wave that acts to measure her own musical steps against broader cultural shifts. First though, she begins as a listener, as does Carrie Brownstein, whose story, as she declares, 'starts with me as a fan' (2015, p. 5). She continues:

> And to be a fan is to know that loving trumps being loved. All the affection I poured into bands, into films, into actors and musicians, was about me and my friends. Once, in high school, I went to see the B-52s. I pressed myself against the barrier until bruises darkened my ribs, thrilled to watch Kate Pierson drink from a water bottle.
>
> (2015, p. 5)

Hersh's memoir is generated by her detailed diaries of her time with her band Throwing Muses, and so much less a chronological account of how she found her way into music. Akin more to Smith's poetic treatment of grief, memory and art, she instantly spells out where she was at the time in terms of music and subcultural style:

> You can tell painters and musicians apart by their uniforms and expressions. All the musicians except the Goth kids wear torn blue jeans, flannel

> shirts and pajama tops and look perpetually stunned. Painters dress like its 1955, in white T-shirts, khakis and black loafers, all spattered liberally with paint.
>
> (2010, p. 5)

For the eight authors, music first appears in their memoirs inextricably interlaced with others. These others are family (and the abusive or soon to be absent father), romantic relationships and their continuance or breakdown, fandom and their place within a broader popular cultural consumption ecosystem or subcultural landscape. These early observations about the place of music in their lives open up vistas of the domestic and romantic, the affective and the desired fulfilling McRobbie's plea for the private lives of young women to be spotlighted. We are afforded insights into the motivations behind getting involved in music, and these stem from an interplay between family, friends and listening. And more importantly, music is related to their own emotional and creative survival; it is the thing that affords them escape from a life of drudgery (as an office junior for Tutti), a 'rite of passage' (Tutti, 2017, p. 30) that allows them to breathe (Hersh) and through initial fandom (Thorn, Brownstein) offers them glimpses of what life could be like beyond the domestic realm.

Purchase and performance

Less about learning to play, more about playing as a passport to somewhere or someone else, Thorn, Brownstein, Smith-Start and Albertine describe the purchase of their first guitars. Their recollections are less about the process of learning to play their instrument than about how the instrument and being in a band afforded them something else, something desirable. The stories of their first guitars and their attempts at playing are instructive for understanding how they build on what Susan Clary calls 'Feminine Endings' (how music can produce gender), towards what I want to call 'feminine frettings'. These are ways of approaching not only playing the guitar as wholly different to the styles and techniques that the men they knew at the time were doing, but of understanding music not as a technique to be learnt, with its rules, canons and virtuoso geniuses, but as an extension of the expressive self:

> It's August 1979, and I have just bought my first electric guitar. It's a black Les Paul copy which I bought for sixty quid from a bloke in London Fields, via a small ad in the back of Melody Maker. I'm amazed at myself – where have I found the audacity to buy this, well, very masculine icon? And it does feel very masculine – that's one of the things I like about it.
>
> (Thorn, 2013, p. 29)

This is Tracey Thorn's account of her buying her first guitar, one that she hadn't realised she needed to plug in, one for which she didn't know she needed an amp, but one that was essential. She notes that the 'decisive step' (2015, p. 30) behind this purchase was her 'growing conviction that [she] wanted to be in a band [her]self' because it could offer her, 'like many other fundamentally shy and awkward teenagers, …… the kind of local status and prestige[she]dreamed of' (2015, p. 30). Not only this, but she continues: 'I was uncertain about my looks, being a skinny, flat-chested, slightly androgynous girl, and thought I had a better chance of making an impact if I became *someone.* And being in a band surely made you a *someone*' (2015, p. 30). Thorn, who went on to form *The Marine Girls* and then with Ben Watts, *Everything but The Girl*, describes the acquisition of the guitar as both the taking on of a presumed masculinity and of the membership of a band as the affordance of something that would valorise her and take away the discomfort of not fitting in to an ideal template of femininity. For Thorn, this seminal moment indicates her move from fan to player, something akin to Brownstein's account of her first guitar, which is recounted as a rather prosaic affair: 'buying your first guitar in the suburbs does not entail anything that resembles folklore…Rather you go with your mom or dad to a carpeted store that smells of antiseptic'. She leaves the shop 'with a Canadian-made solid state amp and a cherry red Epiphone copy of a Stratocaster. It was the first big purchase I made with my own money. I was fifteen' (2015, pp. 10–11). Brownstein then tells of how she carried on watching and listening to bands, at shows, crushed up against the stage, looking for cues, trying 'to get a glimpse of who I wanted to be' (2015, p. 12).

Smith-Start was working in a department store, dreaming of being a rock star and sleeping in the associated dormitories when she buys her first bass:

> I took the book money I had left over for the month and went down to the second-hand store. As if it was meant to be, just sitting there, waiting for me was an old black electric Carvin bass. It cost $50. I took it back to my dorm room and started messing around. The strings were fat and hard to press down…..I had no idea about where the notes were.
>
> (2016, p. 128)

So she visits the 'best guitarist at school' (male) who tells her that the only way to play is to practise. She goes on to say how the guitar became an extension of her body, despite the pain of blistered fingers.

Albertine dedicates a whole chapter to the 'First Guitar'. Three years before Thorn's purchase, she is walking along Shepherd's Bush High Street with her then boyfriend, Mick Jones, and declares that she is going to buy a guitar, an electric guitar, a statement that she recalls as being ridiculous:

> I'm a twenty-two-year-old girl who's never had a music lesson and never touched a guitar. Everyone I've heard of who plays an electric guitar is male and has paid their dues by starting out on an acoustic, which I can't be bothered to do.
>
> (2015, p. 91)

In the music shop, she is faced with her own inability to play 'I can't even hold down a chord. I'm beginning to feel a fool' (2015, p. 92) but eventually parts with £250 to buy a 'single-cutaway 1969 Les Paul Junior' (2015, p. 93). She can't afford a case for the instrument but carries it through central London and realises that 'Nobody knows [she] can't play it. At this moment in time I look like a guitarist' (2015, p. 94) and as she heads home, she recalls how she felt like herself for the first time in her life. There are hiccups of course. Her flatmates ask her to stop playing, and she finds playing music 'agony' (2015, p. 104). But she perseveres (as we know from history) and discusses the style that she came to typify it its renunciation of a standard musical structure. Keith Levene, a musician friend, helps her out by telling her 'how not to play the guitar' (2015, p. 101) which involves 'no chords, no twelve-bar blues chord progression and no scales' (2015, p. 101). Albertine's method is more about using the guitar as an enunciative tool that is and isn't about music. She asks 'What would I sound like if I was a guitar sound?' and tries to recreate noises and animal sounds. She prefers open string sounds and sets about developing a style that is singular and new. It is also very much in keeping with the DIY and anti-virtuoso approach of punk whose artistic and musical milieu she was part of, whose leading figures she was dating and hanging out with. Albertine then was a guitarist, like Thorn, Brownstein and Start-Smith (albeit bass) and so it is to be expected that we hear their tales of how their careers as guitarists started. But their purchases are also bound up in other relationships, romantic, fan, familial and are written against their specific historical circumstances. They become guitarists in order to be themselves against those broader canvasses of punk, post-punk and grunge and the national and local musical landscapes and scenes they inhabited.

Concentrating on the notion of women as creative agents in the musical activity that made up punk and post-punk, in particular, allows for an acknowledgement that these accounts of their awareness of themselves as guitarists, as members of bands, might just very well be a retrospective 'settling' of accounts. Mavis Bayton in 1997 discussed how it was crucial for women to take up the guitar, to learn it in different ways to how it had been learnt before, to feminise and dephallicise it (1997, p. 49). Well, these memoirs do that same thing. They tell us of a journey into music, yes, but they do more. They bring to the surface the untold stories of how they, as young women, came to be important musical figures in bands that defined the subcultural scenes of punk and post-punk. Bayton's plea for more women to take up the guitar, which is what these memoirs narrate, is based on the desire for a future where 'men would no longer be the yardstick against which women are measured' (1997, p. 48). However, men do figure as romantic and sexual subjects within a number of the memoirs as they seem to be the figures imbricated in a number of the women's initiation into music. What is also marked is how relationships, in particular, are the driving force behind some of the narratives. There is a lot on Tutti's relationship with Genesis P. Orridge (which is tinged with abuse and violence), Gordon's with Thurston Moore (the long marriage that ends in divorce), Albertine's (with Mick Jones, Johnny Rotten, her husband, then divorce), Thorn's (with Ben Watts), Smith-Start's (with Mark E. Smith, Nigel Kennedy especially) and Smith's with her late husband, Fred Sonic Smith. Hersh narrates her pregnancy, but we hear nothing of the man involved.

Tutti's account of her musical beginnings is wrapped up in other narratives of coupledom (with Genesis P. Orridge) and the underground hippy and acid scene in Hull in the early 1970s. She, like Gordon, is as much part of an art scene as she is music, the latter which is part of the former. COUM, the art collective founded by her, P. Orridge and others, worked with music, but was not just a 'band'. She writes: 'COUM's approach to music: anti-harmony, no pre-requisite for anyone to be able to play a given instrument, and the sound the "group" generated was also regarded as a contributory member of the group itself' (2017, p. 78). And, as part of COUM and later Throbbing Gristle, Tutti's emphasis has been on how to perform sound and how sound can be manipulated. She discusses buying effects pedals in Macaris (a guitar shop on London's Charing Cross Road) and knowing what sound she wanted, not tuning her guitar and not doing a rendition of 'Stairway to Heaven' (2017, p. 244). Tutti does not discuss a first purchase or tutelage from male friends; the COUM and Throbbing Gristle were art collectives who experimented and produced sound; and as in the title of her memoir, music is after 'art' and 'sex'.

Where Tutti is part of an underground performance art collective for whom music is a sonic strand, Gordon is (like Smith) on the New York art scene and considers herself less a musician than someone who uses music to be herself and carve out space. Gordon gets given a guitar by a friend, which is recognised by her soon-to-be lover and husband Thurston Moore but as Gordon recalls, growing up she had never sung, and had preferred to 'smoke a little pot, make art and listen to Bob Dylan, Buffalo Springfield, Tim Buckley, the Beatles, Archie Shepp and the Art Ensemble of Chicago' (2015, p. 105). At the beginning of her book she writes that:

> After thirty years of playing in a band, it sounds sort of stupid to say, "I'm not a musician". But for most of my life I've never seen myself as a lowercase rock star. Yes, I'm sensitive to sound, I think I have a good ear, and I love the visceral movement and thrill of being onstage. And even as a visual and conceptual artist, there's a performance aspect to whatever I do.
>
> (2015, p. 11)

Gordon talks a lot about her appearance in relation to her femininity. She refers to her tomboyishness, her reluctance to embrace the 'kinder whore' look of grunge, the awareness of herself as having 'to be a woman' (2015, p. 125). Indeed, she talks about how stage performance enables a kind of nullifying of the self in parallel with an increased awareness of her sexuality: 'When I'm at my most focused onstage, I feel a sense of space with edges around it, a glow of self-confident, joyful sexiness. It feels bodiless, too, all weightless grace with no effort required' (ibid). Indeed, sex and the body, especially the traumatic body and the body in ill-health feature in some of the memoirs.

The memoirs are, for the most part, accounts of youthful sexuality and, as they travel further into the present, they mutate into stories of ill-health or of bodily change. Albertine discusses in unflinching details her experience of crabs, miscarriage, pregnancy and cervical cancer. Gordon and Hersh talk about their pregnancies, in less graphic detail and more in relation to how they work out how to continue being in a band as a mother. Hersh leads us inside the bipolar mind. Tutti takes us to tales of illness: the 'dreaded menopause' (p. 349) and a paralysing condition known as Ramsay Hunt syndrome (p. 427). Albertine and Tutti offer the most visceral accounts of their body's failures. Tutti is an artist whose body has been the location of her performance art work, who worked in the sex industry as a precursor to performance and whose frank attitude to the body and to sexuality was part of, I would argue, a broader frankness characterised by punk. Albertine and Tutti then add in stories that would have either been shameful at the time (STDs [Sexually Transmitted Diseases], sex work, cancer) and weave them into their narratives. These published intimacies, around traumas with which the men in their working and private lives are connected, are part and parcel of this retrospective settling the memoir affords. These events matter. They are inscribed on the bodies of the authors and are remembered for their importance and the losses and scars they engendered. They were, as was music, part of these women's lives.

Just like Alan Moore's (2002) notion of authenticity as potentially ascribed, the gendered make-up of a band is something that is mediated (all girl band, female-fronted band) as the exception to the default all male line up and seems to have required explanation from Gordon and Hersh. There is a comment made by Gordon that is the story behind the title of her memoir; she notes that music journalists, particularly British ones, ask her 'What's it like to be a girl in a band?' (2015, p. 150). Gordon recalls being perplexed about such a question, not ever having given her position as the only female member of Sonic Youth any real thought. Hersh is asked why Throwing Muses' drummer is a male, when the other members are female:

> Tonight one of the sexist journalists is a woman who's angry that Dave is a man. "Why didn't you hire a woman to play drums?" she asks me accusingly.
>
> I'm at a loss. "Because Dave's not a woman," I answer. "I didn't hire him anyway; he doesn't get paid".
>
> "I'm a volunteer!" Dave chirps happily.
>
> She gives him a blank look and then turns back to me. "Surely you would agree that you play female music."
>
> "Sometimes we play female music," I say. "But not any more often than men do".
>
> (Hersh, 2010, p. 198)

Hersh disarticulates being female (sexed) to playing female music (gendered) and so is Butlerian in her understanding of the nature of sex and gender. She still, however, calls her memoir *Rat Girl* and there is, in the first lines of the memoirs, recollections of girlhood that I now want to end the chapter on, tracing out the relationships between the past (girl woman) and the present (mature woman) which is a key factor in the positioning of the memoirs as retrospective settlings and of the configuration of the periods of punk and post-punk as 'youthful' in an ongoing popular literary historicising process.

There is something important in the move from the musical world of expression to the literary. There is a sense of a critical distance, as well as a temporal one, that the memoir achieves, and which allows for any sexual or moral discretions or excesses to become part of a writerly tradition that is, to an extent, removed from the musical arena. Encounters with the written word are different to those with the musical performance or listening, and whilst acknowledging the rather large methodological terrain that I am skipping over here, I want to suggest that this altered mode, along with the temporal gap between the events and their recollection, allows for a more distanciated appreciation, a less embodied encounter, which goes some way to allowing these stories to be aired. There is also too, something perhaps in the invisibility of the ageing woman writer, eclipsed by her younger, youthful self on the page and by the cover photographs of herself as a young woman. This is an erasure of the ageing body, which I have written elsewhere in relation to PJ Harvey and music video (Gardner, 2018a). It is an example of the acceptance of the ageing voice, only when it might be allied to its younger bodily self. It might be that these older voices are viewed as 'women of letters', accepted as that category of older woman author, the 'grande dame' of the literary world. Like Lessing, Forster, Bainbridge, Mantel and Atwood, female authors who, despite working on areas to do with gender and sexuality, are somehow allowed to do so because they are writers: heard but rarely seen. Writing is an appropriate activity for older women, much more appropriate than playing guitar on stage perhaps. Writing memoirs is done in private, out of sight, it has its own mythologies and it has a longer lineage than rock music.

Conclusion: typical girls?

Beginnings are good places to return to. And here are the opening lines of these memoirs:

> When we came out onstage for our last show, the night was all about the boys.
>
> (Gordon, 2015, p. 1)

> I'd always kidded myself that it was punk that got me started.
>
> (Thorn, 2013, p. 3)

> Never did it.
>
> (Albertine, 2014, p. 3)

> I've always felt unclaimed.
>
> (Brownstein, 2015, p. 5)

> When I was young, my mother took me for walks in Humboldt Park, along the edge of the Prairie River.
>
> (Smith, 2010, p. 3)

> It's not so easy writing about nothing.
>
> (Smith, 2015, p. 3)

> I don't do nostalgia gigs.
>
> (Thorn, 2015, p. 1)

> 'Yours was a difficult birth' my mother told me.
>
> (Tutti, 2017, p. 1)

They deal with boys, sex, fitting in, relationships with their mothers; only three of the ten (two by Tracey Thorn) mention music at all and Gordon's remark that the last Sonic Youth show was 'all about the boys' goes some way to flag up how her memoir is, in some respect, a redressing of a gender imbalance where she can, at last, insert her voice into the history of the band. 'When' starts two of the books, placing the narrator and reader somewhere in the past, prone to the fallibility of memory. All of these strategies suggest that the writer is aware of familial, social and musical networks, into which she is trying or failing, to fit. All of them are about the positioning of the self: in time and in musical matrices. And these reflections on how they fitted in, or didn't, constitute a settling of accounts of punk and indie mythologies. The titles and opening lines depict youth and the notion of processual time. 'Girl' is used in four of the ten titles, 'kids', once and 'growing up' once. All of this points to the notion of the older woman looking back on girlhood and adolescence as a stage of ageing, from which they are now disarticulated in some, but not all ways. These ten memoirs are written by women on the cusp of the menopause or beyond it. Safely ensconced behind this 'menopausal gap' their tales of sex, illness, squalor, mental health, of love and loss, are somehow tempered by this distancing. On the one hand, this safety away from youthful sexuality and body allows for an assessment of those experiences from the counterpoint of age; on the other, it underpins the rebelliousness of those eras and scenes and feeds into well-rehearsed narratives that circulate around punk and post-punk. These stories of seediness (Albertine) and the poverty of the creative auteur (Smith) collide with tales of female sexual discovery and trauma (Albertine, Tutti, Smith, Gordon) that add in to these myths. We can now hear these young women speak, as older women. This is allowed, this is OK. There is something around the allowance of older women speaking about the past because those events are gone. But what they do produce are spaces where women of all ages can see their own experiences; they allow for younger women to speak as younger women, for girls to be girls. They do settle subcultural accounts and they do so by achieving the following: they shed light on the systemic sexism of the music industry (as evidenced by Gordon's exasperation at being asked what it was like to be a 'girl in a band'), and they valorise the emotional and affective labour that comes from being a female musicians in a popular music world whose myth making excluded them. These memoirs effectively and affectively redraw the histories of punk and independent music. The histories now are ones that have internal lives, private, intimate, romantic, abusive, creative lives. The girls are back in town, because these ageing women musician/memoirists have written themselves back in.

2 Shirley Collins and Calypso Rose

Grand maternal queens

Queens were the talk of the long hot summer of 2018. We lost the Queen of Soul, Aretha Franklin and we marked the 60th birthday of Madonna, the Queen of Pop. In May, Stephen Moss in *The Guardian* reviewed Joan Baez's farewell tour, referring to her as the 'Queen of Folk' (29/5/18). The term is bandied about popular culture and applied to musicians with longevity and success within their respective genres and this chapter focuses on two such 'queen(e)s' through the nexus of old age and its functional and canonical 'place'. Focusing on the English folk musician Shirley Collins (b.1935) and on the Trinidadian, Calypso Rose (b.1940), it suggests that they have a function as postmenopausal matriarchs. They are 'grandmaternal' figures within their genres, generating a sense of historicity and so valorising their musical canon. Their longevity 'as' older women within a specific familial network cements this functionality.

They both appear on their latest albums, in documentary films, online and in recent music videos 'in place'; that is, they are situated within specific geographical locations that work to underscore their generic positioning. But there is more about 'place' than geography and I extend it to mean lyrical place, canonical place, aged place, and consider the idea of the 'newness' of age, which reissue rhetoric allows. By doing that, a picture emerges of how the two musicians are positioned as grand maternal figures within the various *places* of English folk and Trinidadian and Tobagan Calypso. Collins' work is so indebted to landscape and place and I use Adam Scovell's (2017) critical literary work on 'folk horror', which focuses on landscape as a (usually malevolent) character and the interplay between past and present; how the old impacts on the new.

Collins and Rose might be approached as being within the parameters of 'real old age' (Elliott 2015, p. 78, referring to Bobbio 2001) whereby age is regarded as a recognised measure of lived experience, which, in turn, is validated as testimony or witness. Age bequeaths a sense of authenticity, longevity acts as a generic kite mark. 'Authenticity', especially in Collins' case, is imbricated with discourses of testimony and witness. Brocken writes of how 'Authenticity is used as an index or an indicator of a musical past, as a historical meter in the re-establishment of a living dialogue with a tradition' (2003, p. 89). By extending the notion of the authentic text (the song) across to it being embodied in the living transmitter of that song (the 'tradition bearer', the singer of the song) then the ageing folk singer too is allied, through history, genre and context to 'the authentic' (see too Frith and Horne, 1987; Connell and Gibson, 2003; Knox, 2008).

They are two very different performers, in different national folk traditions and it might seem odd if not wildly foolish to pull them together just because of their age and gender. But then, this book starts with age rather than any other foundational premise, and when you start to note how they are both delivered to contemporary audiences, some interesting similarities occur. Race, class and genre are important factors in their representation and the chapter considers these vectors since their particularities are crucial to how Collins and Rose are positioned. They are both working class, they both operate in musical traditions that are expressive vehicles for the concerns of working people and Calypso in particular is 'central to the articulation of Trinidad cultural politics' (Guilbault, 2007, p. 61). Yes, race separates them. Rose voices the experiences of a Black Caribbean woman and specifically, later on in her career, sings about her familial experiences of an African diaspora. Collins talks of English folk music being sung by those 'on the outskirts of society' (Collins, 2018, p. 171), the:

> poor of England: the farm labourers and their wives, the servants in the house of the wealth, the cottage lace and shirt-makers, the seamen and fishermen, the gypsies, and, most heart-breaking of all, the inmates of Poor Houses and Workhouses.
>
> (ibid)

These are the impoverished and marginalised white of England and folk music has its own, much documented alliances with the English (and American) political Left (Winters and Keegan-Phipps, 2013; Collins, 2018: Gardner, 2018a).

Ageing is, as the introduction proposed, contextual and embodied, it is cultural, contextual and it is lived (Gullette, 2004; Chivers, 2011, p. 11). So the experiences and the representation, the production and reception of Black, differently abled and non-normative women will differ. Ageism will be inflected with any number of local racisms and discriminatory notes. Here I want to tentatively put race as the determining category for enquiry to one side, if indeed that is even possible, and maybe it is only because of my own whiteness, but I want to shift focus to age as it plays out in genre, which, in turn, is related to specific musical histories. And, in doing so, the chapter considers how these two women, working as creative elders in English Folk and Caribbean Calypso, offer up positive models of ageing, as they carve their careers out 'anew'.

Bring out your new

Queen of Calypso and 'Queene' of English Folk (the Shakespearean 'e' refers to Curry and Plester's film title), Calypso Rose and Shirley Collins are lauded musicians, recording and performing in their late 70s and early 80s. Indeed, at the time of writing, Collins is 83 and Rose is 78. They are two of a handful of eminent female performers in 'older age' (Chivers, 2003) such as Shirley Bassey,

Grace Jones, Marianne Faithfull, Petula Clarke, Joan Baez, Françoise Hardy and others who make up a (grand)maternal canon within popular music. This Anglo-American canon goes across genre and includes these women (and there are sure to be more) who are valued both for their ongoing contribution to music and for their participation in the formative histories of those musics.

'Oh, it's so lovely to hear Shirley again', said a man at the end of a panel at the IASPM 2018 biannual conference at the University of Huddersfield on September 4, 2018. This audience member had played with Shirley and was now a member of the music accreditation group JAMES. There was real affection in his voice, an emotion that comes through in all the interviewers, reviews of her and her work, from the film. But I was not being reminded of an earlier Collins. She is not someone I was aware of when younger, nor have I had much exposure to her work. The same goes for Calypso Rose. In this respect, I am part of an audience involved in a rediscovery process, made possible both by Collins and Roses' longevity, but also to all the availability of their back catalogues and current memoir in both literary and film forms. I have become aware that Collins inspires devotion and that Rose is regarded as a form of 'national treasure' (itself an age- and gender-determined category, Dolan, 2012). Pulling them together to consider in one chapter allows for analysis of what their continued work in relation to their pasts says about how age allows them to narrate the songs they do. My entry point to Collins was the 2016 album *Lodestar*, the 2017 film *The Ballad of Shirley Collins* and her 2018 memoir, *All in the Downs*. For Calypso Rose, it was her website, her 2016 album *Far From Home* (2016), the 2016 music video for the title track off the album 'Calypso Queen' and later, the documentary by Pascale Obolo *Calypso Rose, Lioness of the Jungle* (2011). It is these places of performance that form the material for this chapter.

'I thought everyone had forgot about me, except people in jumpers who live in folk clubs', said Collins. This is a snippet of a phone message conversation between Collins and Tibet from an odd piece on academia.edu under Tibet's name. In her book, she refers to her own 'renaissance' and the album, and its related film and book are an example of the newness of the old, or the reappearance of the forgotten.

Collins had not sung for 38 years, Rose had never stopped performing. In this respect, Collins benefits from a 'safety gap', whereby only two stages of her life are public, her youth and her elderliness, the latter affording her (via the film and her memoir, and through other's experiences of her) to reflect on her youth. She has avoided the banality of middle age (Chivers, 2011, p. xvi), a stage whose narrative (in film in particular) holds no real allure. Rose has benefitted from a marketing and promotion drive lead by *Because Music*'s Jean Michel Gibert and renowned producer Manu Chao, which has surfed the wave of reissue culture. They are both benefactors of this reissue culture, whereby it is their age and/or re-emergence that is their novelty. Narratives of the 'returned' or 'rediscovered' underpin both of their current representations to varying degrees.

Both of them were 'rediscovered' or 'redirected' into specific domestic record markets; they were both persuaded and produced by younger male friends.

Speculation could be made over the importance of these relationships and on their impact on the eventual sound of both albums. These younger male producers are clearly 'authorial presences' (Warwick, 2007, p. 149), but I don't want to dwell on them to much beyond noting that the films by Curry and Plester (2017) and Obolo (2011) depict the collaboration and teamwork that went into the albums. David Tibet, David Suff, Ossian Brown and Stephen Thrower were instrumental in securing Collins' 'return'. In her memoir, *All in the Downs* (2018), Collins narrates the process of moving back into recording via these key male figures in her life: David Tibet, of Current 93, and David Suff, of Fledgling Records, both coaxed her back into singing. In Rose's case, it was Manu Chao, an internationally successful artist and producer who had produced the Malian duo, Amadou and Mariam's European breakthrough album, *Dimanche à Bamako*. His role as a mediator of Afro-Caribbean music into, most notably, the French domestic and 'World Music' market was already thus established. An email interview with Jean Michel Gibert, producer of the documentary film *Calypso Rose, Lioness of the Jungle* (dir. Obolo, 2011), revealed the marketing strategies that had accompanied this, which highlighted Rose's 'extraordinary character and life story' and 'her charisma as a performer and as a person'. A review of her album by a self-professed 'island native', Neil Campbell, a musicologist, journalist and blogger, noted that Chao, the 'third world troubadour', was the 'lynchpin for the outward vision of the production and marketing of this new album'; his persona is stamped all over the record. For Campbell, the record is a reproduction of hits from the golden age of Calypso (the early to mid-twentieth centre) with the 'aural milieu of a modern era' and it is worth quoting his views in full on this for how it dovetails with academic work on this idea of repackaging:

> This music is the revival of the cult of nostalgia, not solely of the style of calypso music, but of the veteran artist making new waves in the global music industry almost as an antidote to a storied career. Ageing third World music stars are resurrected late in their careers, are scrubbed, repackaged and discovered by a new audience.
>
> (Campbell, 2016)

Rose's album, as Campbell so astutely notes, is part of a renewal grounded in commodification, that he calls both a 'godsend' and a 'mockery' for calypso, both increasing sales and exposure but also, maybe, diluting the genre and ironing out its progressive potential. This 'new/old' tendency can be counted as part of a broader trend for 'rediscovery' specifically in relation to music documentary and archival culture, whereby the limitless landscape of the internet produces new from old, and erases their temporal differences (Gardner and Moorey, 2016). Collins, unlike the musicians described in that paper (William Onyeabor and Sixto Rodriguez), differs in so far as the *Lodestar* album is neither lost nor did she ever elude recognition, but she had disappeared from performing, had not been a fixture on the UK Folk Scene wherein she had been an acclaimed figure. *Lodestar* is a point on a disrupted narrative; it acts as a counterpoint to Collins' past, her youth, and her youthful, soprano voice. It is sung in a cracked contralto, the voice of a woman in her eighth decade, and comparisons with how she was, how she sounded, are part of the reviews which greeted the album.

Encountering Shirley

It was the English folk song performer and collector, Sam Lee, who first introduced me to Shirley Collins in 2016. He helped kick start her film with a video endorsement (2014) and referred to himself as one of her 'young guard devotees – her toyboy' (Molleson, 2017). I was aware of her appearing at festivals (such as The Green Man in the Brecon Beacons in 2016) to promote *Lodestar.* This was the album that David Suff had spent many years trying to persuade Collins to make after she had stopped singing in 1977. Before that, Collins had been a key figure on the English folk music scene, working with her sister, Dolly and with Ewan McColl. She released six albums from 1959 to 1976 by herself, five with her sister Dolly, who played the organ and died in 1995, and six albums with The Albion Band. Born in Hastings in 1935, she had been exposed to English folk music as a young child and as a partner to Alan Lomax, a co-singer with Ewan McColl, was integral to the second folk resurgence of the late 1960s. She travelled across the southern states of the USA in 1959, with Lomax, on a song collecting expedition. The field recordings of mostly African American singers that resulted from this are acclaimed for shining a spotlight on musicians such as Mississippi Fred Mc Dowell and offering a historical snapshot of vernacular music of the time. Collins was awarded the MBE in 2008, the same year that she became president of the English Folk Dance and Song Society. These institutional and national accolades not only reward her contribution to English folk music but also, with Lomax, make apparent the importance of her input to English and American folk music history. Her own musical output and her association and romance with key figures on the folk scene map across to broader cultural events (such as the McCarthyite years in the late 1950s, and the folk revival of the late 1960s) to configure her presence as historically significant. She is, arguably, one of the surviving cornerstones of English folk music and her story is augmented by a peculiar tragedy. In 1977, she lost her voice to dysphonia, which involves the loss or modulation of the voice precipitated by changes in the vocal chords and larynx. In the film, *The Ballad of Shirley Collins*, Collins reflects on this loss which came shortly after she discovered her husband and the father of her children was having an affair. Forced to share the stage with him at the National Theatre in a production of *The Lark Rises*, she suggests that this loss may have been due to shock at seeing his lover sat in the front row of the evening performance's audience, wearing his jumper, and the film makers do nothing to resolve this ambiguity. What did happen was that Collins did not release another album for nigh on 40 years. The album is therefore so much more than just the release of material from a musician who has not worked for nearly half a century. It is the release of an album by a woman who is a formative part of

Anglo-American music history, is woven into the tapestry of English folk music and is someone whose private life has been punctuated with loss: of her sister, Dolly, of her voice, of her husband.

It would be easy to read some of the tracks on *Lodestar* as imbued with loss, not least because of the difference between Collins' pre-dysphonia and post-dysphonia vocals. On 'Death and the Lady', the arrangements and voice are markedly different from those of the same track when she first released it in 1970 with her sister, Dolly. The sharp, clear soprano is now modulated down to a cracked, low contralto. It is an old voice. There is great work out there on age and vocality (Elliott, 2015) and on the differences across the years that age affords on the voice. Here though I want to think of Collins' (and Rose's) voice as their contemporary (as opposed to late) voice, their 'now' voices and how these ageing vocals and the songs' lyrical contents and histories add into an authenticity that has long grounded the folk music world (Boyes, 2010). I have noted in other work how antiquarian reification surfaces in folk discourses (Gardner and Jennings, 2019), and I want to draw this out to consider how Collins is 'placed' in a specific canon.

Putting Collins in 'place'

In her memoir, Collins uses the idea of a 'chain' within which she is a link that crosses time and places herself within a history of working-class culture. She calls this chain 'mysterious'. She uses Lomax's reference of a communication chain (p. 103) to situate herself as an English folk singer. There is in this acknowledgement, a sense of her place within both a working-class and quasi-mysterious folkloric lineage. She belongs to a people, to a tradition and to a place. She is the real deal; reviews of the album and establishing shots in the film underline her closeness to the land. 'Age has given a new depth to Shirley's voice, a lived-in earthiness', writes Kidman in Folk Radio, 2016; 'At 81, Collins' voice has grit and grain, both old and strangely timeless', observes Louis Pattison in Pitchfork (November, 2016). Her voice has 'weathered considerably' says Alexis Petridis in *The Guardian* (October, 2016).

The language is of the soil and inanimate objects; she both stands outside of time (timeless) and is extracorporeal (weathered, like stones or buildings). She is placed beyond the usual requirements that police the ageing female body. And this is done by two interconnecting mechanisms. First, she operates within a musical scene whose dominant aesthetic has been the 'authentic' and the 'folk' (Boyes, 2010), constructed terms themselves but operationally outside of the image-driven popular culture which has largely driven the mainstream. Second, she manages to exist as a vocal and collecting presence rather than a bodily one by being allied to matter (earth, grit, grain, tapestry). These objects are nearly all related to landscape or nominally (tapestry) the past. They are imbued with authenticity in so far as they are the opposite of the artificial; they are, literally, the clods, furrows and sods of the earth, where in *The Ballad of Shirley Collins* (2018), the film that documents her return to singing and the production of the album in her cottage in Sussex, Collins is shot placed, walking. Worth noting perhaps too that the Goddess of the Harvest, Demeter (Greek) or Ceres (Latin) also controlled the cycle of life and death. And so Collins can be considered suprahuman, referred to as part of the landscape, akin to an ancient, pagan Goddess, divine. She is shot within and against certain Sussex landscapes playing with the relationship between women and land, one which has a long history especially with regard to fertility especially within paganism.

The emphasis on her role within the (pagan) landscape of her home, Sussex, a county in the south of England, and in the canonical landscape of the Anglo-American folk scene is established in the official trailer for the film. We hear her off-screen asking 'Do you want me to start, Alan?', a question from her 1959 self, directed at the actor playing Alan Lomax whilst carrying out the recording sessions. There follows a succession of images that establish a sense of place: the sea, a shoreline, a pebbly beach; white cliffs, then trees, fishing nets and a dual carriageway cutting its way through green fields, leaf-strewn cobbled streets and thatched cottages, bonfires at dusk and an old rust-red caravan set alone among the fields. Then a photograph of Shirley and her sister, Dolly, on either side of a ram – this followed by a still of a Green Man figure or gargoyle. Then we see her again in what ostensibly looks like archive film footage from the US field recordings with Lomax, putting on her headphones. This is revealed in her memoir to be staged, by actors who look remarkably like her and Lomax. Then there is an image of the inside of a large skeleton, a cow's perhaps and then the camera follows the back of Collins' head as she walks through fields and up a hill. Then the edit cuts to the paraphernalia of the recording studio; microphones, headphones and Collins saying 'I'm not focusing yet, my concentration is absolutely gone'. Collins is delivered within the constructed aesthetics of authenticity both by her being placed as in the real, the rural and folkish world, with all its ramifications of 'realness' (Winters and Keegan-Phipps, 2013), and by the tools of the recording studio that emphasise the production and work that has gone in to produce the album, work that is hard, as Collis herself admits.

The language used throughout the reviews of the Collins' album (all written by male journalists) strives again and again to place Collins as somehow beyond the ordinary and as of national import, who has 'a vital place within British musical tradition' (Clarke, 2016). She is 'a true oracle of traditional song' (Deming, 2016), the 'elder stateswoman of folk' (Clarke, 2016).

The Ballad, Lodestar and folk horror

The songs on *Lodestar* are a mix of ancient and modern, and for the most part, they are about violence, brutality, murder and death. They are far from pastoral, more Grimms Fairy Tales than rural idylls. Sung by the cracked, faltering yet authoritative voice of Shirley Collins they manage to shock and bring past trauma into the present day: betrayal, ill luck, immorality and loss. They and the imagery used in *The Ballad of Shirley Collins* might be looked at through a 'folk-horror' aesthetic (Scovell, 2017), wherein landscape and rurality, in particular, stage brutal and supernatural events. Scovell applies the term to a number of

English films and TV series from the late 1970s, whose aesthetic and narrative features he identifies and extends to contemporary film and fiction. He writes:

> Essentially, even more than just being a genre, the term 'Folk Horror' can be seen as a type of social map that tracks the unconscious ley lines between a huge range of different forms of media in the twentieth century and earlier….it connects the past and the present to create a clash of belief systems and people; modernity and the Enlightenment against superstition and faith, the very violence inherent in us as people. It is the evil under the soil….
>
> (2017, p. 181)

The Wicker Man (dir. Hardy, 1973), *Witchfinder General* (dir. Reeves, 1968) and *The Blood on Satan's Claw* (dir. Haggard, 1974) are key Folk Horror films for Scovell, as is the fictional writing of Alan Garner and contemporary film directors such as Ben Wheatley and Eggers. All of them use landscape as a malevolent and living thing. It is this sense of landscape as a character that chimes well with *Lodestar*, as does the eruption of violence in songs 'of olde' which are far from the quaintness of the village green and Cecil Sharpe's Morris dancers. The sense of a Folk Horror aesthetic is palpable throughout Curry and Plester's film, which uses long takes of fields and coastlines to map Collins against. The promotional trailer uses images of wheat fields, cobbled streets, dual carriageways snaking through green, gargoyles, follies, Morris men and men dressed for the Jack in The Green May Day Celebrations in Hastings, Sussex. They are images of white England, rural England, of ritual England. And one of the prime reasons for thinking that Folk Horror as an aesthetic might have something to offer when reading Collins recent work and mediation is this sense of a time slippage. Key to Folk Horror's menace is the interplay between the past and the present, a relationship where each refuses to keep to their allotted temporal place. Collins' present ageing, the age of the songs she sings and her own history all weave together in a manner that disrupts chronology to some extent because Collins is a palimpsest, a body and voice which is aligned to agedness (in the songs) and also to youth (in her remembered voice), inaudible in its ageing present but referred to through archive footage in the film and in many of the accompanying reviews of the album (Petridis, 2016; Pattison, 2016). Collins' 'sounds like' is always compared to her 'sounded like', her 'is' to her 'was'; her current offering can only be consumed as part of a narrative that includes her youth.

The Ballad of Shirley Collins DVD dropped through the letterbox onto my hall floor one morning in March 2018. It came with an audio CD with a selection of English folk songs, and both discs were inserted into a small hardback book with short testimonial pieces written by the director, Tim Plester, the renowned English folk musician, Linda Thompson and Nathan Salsberg (producer, Lomax archives curator, musician). In a small piece entitled 'Larkrise to Lodestar', Plester writes of the memorable moment when he was taken, as a young child, to the National Theatre in London to see *Lark Rise*. This was the production which

Collins was singing in and which changed her life (and is marked turning point for Plester's). He recalls that:

> It was during the run of Lark Rise at The National Theatre, that an act of self- confessed base philandering on the part of Shirley's then husband (and musical director of the show) helped set in motion a chain of emotional events that led to her losing her voice. Or at least to her losing the will and the necessary confidence to use that treasured and fiercely ancestral voice of hers.
>
> (Plester, 2018)

Losing one's voice as a singer in tandem with or as a result of losing one's husband to an affair might be construed as traumatic. And here we return again to the Folk Horror perspective on trauma and the past. Scovell explores how the genre treats the past as 'a paranoid, skewed trauma...especially when bringing past elements to sit with uncomfortable ease within the then-present day...' (2017, p. 14). The Collins' trauma, loss of voice and thereby loss of creative agency, her absence, or the idea that she almost became a ghost, or a shadow of her former singing self, can be folded into the traumas that she sings about on *Lodestar.* Scovell argues that the folk horror aesthetic 'blasts apart the romantic visions of an England gone by (or any other western country harkening back to a fictional past, for that matter) through unflinchingly depicting how violent and brutal the past really was' (2017, p. 184). That Collins should release *Lodestar* at the stage in her life when she could only just begin to sing after 30 years, and that she should sing songs about murder, lost love and horror build into an understanding of her work and the album in particular, as voicing a weird and violent Englishness. It came at a time when, politically, an emboldened form of nationalist nostalgia seemed to be taking over the political rhetoric of Englishness and identity, with the June 2016 Brexit vote and with it, the rise of an English extreme exceptionalism (in the United Kingdom Independence Party, UKIP and the later to be banned Far Right national group, Britain First).

The book's last page displays two images: one of Collins standing on a cliff looking down in profile over the sea, and the other of a figure on a pebble beach against a white cliff facing out to sea, dressed in a long cloak, holding a staff and wearing a crown (the crown as the film established is made up of old animal skulls and foliage). They both stand sentinel. Folk Horror has used the 'Strange British coastline' as a 'place of general violence' (Scovell, 2017, p. 89), that is a place on the edge of England that has served as some kind of 'zone of weirdness' (p. 88) for television plays and films. Petridis too, reviewing the album, uses this word to describe Collins' work 'In the late 60s and early 70s...she made albums than conjured up Old Weird England' (2016).

The beach is an in-between place, prone to erosion and frequent change, as well as the location of the ebb and flow of tides. Writing in 2015 on the liminal places within which PJ Harvey's music videos were shot, I suggested that these kind of 'elsewhere' places echoed Irigaray's ideas on the feminine elsewhere, a place of irrationality and beyond logic, outside of the ordinary. I also suggested the potential of the liminal location to confuse temporality, given that it lies beyond clock time and logic. Some of those suggestions work with how *The Ballad of Shirley Collins* uses the shore line here. It signals an Englishness (by the white cliffs) and is the pagan-like figure a reference to an older sentinel looking out for invaders? Within the films, TV plays and literature of Folk Horror, 'Deep history is constantly on the point of breaking through the surface, often with gruesome, physical consequences' (Scovell, 2017, p. 53). Here, in the film and book, the images narrate that sense of a vibrant and dynamic past. And this comes through even more so in the songs. Alexis Petridis for *The Guardian* writes how:

> for the most part, the songs Collins has chosen for *Lodestar* paint a picture of a brutal, bleak world, where forgiveness is thin on the ground, but violence and death are ever-present. Indeed, *Lodestar's* songs' body count would startle a Norwegian death metal band. By my calculations, there were at least 11 fatalities- including two infanticides- in the space of three songs and nine minutes alone: the old girl keeps knocking them off with the casual amorality of a gangsta rapper.

This part of the review aims at a light heartedness, especially in likening Collins, the 'old girl' to a 'gangsta rapper', the semantics of which are worth looking into but perhaps not at this point. What is of importance in relation to Folk Horror is the notion of a brutal world circumscribed by death and violence and the potential for this world to erupt into the present (perhaps the world of the 'gangsta rapper' is not too far after all). In the cinematic and literary world of Folk Horror, the past is ever present and 'the old ways sit like vivid fissures on the surface of modernity' (2017, p. 28). Many of the songs on *Lodestar* come from the Middle Ages and six of the ten are archived on the Mainly Norfolk folk song site. They might be grouped into songs of dread and/or songs of violence, of fear of violent futures and narratives of violent presents, all archived as past stories but sung now by Collins. This sense of a trans-epocal potential in the songs that their emotion might somehow be playing out now works with the notion of being 'out of time' (2017, p. 10), again, a characteristic motif of Folk Horror.

'Awake, Awake' is a penitential song from 1580 and opens the album with the words 'So repent, repent Sweet England/for dreadful days draw near'. The sense of dread and foreboding appears again with 'Death and the Lady', where she sings 'My name is Death/cannot you see? Lords, dukes and ladies bow down to me', a song which Mainly Norfolk suggests narrates the story of The Black Death. And again, on track 9, 'The Rich Irish Lady', the narrator, a spurned doctor, sings of how he will dance on her grave. These songs are narrated by Death itself, or by those who threaten it. The other songs depict violent acts, some in graphic detail. Track 2, 'The Banks of Green Willow', is a Jonah Ballad, whereby an evil presence, sometimes that of a pregnant woman, is killed to preserve the ship. It was also covered under the title 'Bonnie Annie' by Ewan McColl and Peggy Seeger (1962) and tells of the drowning of a young pregnant woman, who was thrown overboard. The theme of women dying is continued in Track 3, 'Cruel Lincoln', which tells of the revenge of a wronged servant on the lords and ladies he served, and the lyrics tell of blood and gore where 'the lady did fall'. This explicit violence is found again in Track 6, a murder ballad, 'Pretty Polly', which is often associated with Ralph Stanley (The Stanley Brothers' version 1950 has him and his brother, Willie, singing it). Though different in provenance both in geography and time, it, too, tells of the death of a young woman who gets stabbed and buried in a shallow grave. Death rears its head in Track 4 where a 'lady' encounters a 'poor drowned sailor' and in Orlando Gibbons' 'Silver Swan' of 1611, 'death' again approaches 'her' (this time, a swan). Indeed, there is only one track on the entire album where death and violence do not appear. 'Sur le Borde de l'eau', a 1929 Cajun song, sung in French, associated with Alcide 'Blind Uncle' Gaspard (a Louisianan Cajun singer and guitarist) offers some respite from the murderous toll.

The Black Death, drownings, revenge, murder. Some of the songs on *Lodestar* can be viewed as being part of the tradition of the Murder Ballad, tales usually of the violent end of young women at the hands of their lovers. Feminist readings of murder ballads (Kane, 1996; Keathley, 2002) offer routes into rethinking these songs, revealing them as part of a sexist if not misogynist social construct within a '"white" aesthetic' (Keathley, 2002) that denigrates young, sexually active women. What happens, then, when these songs of violence and dread are voiced by Collins, a woman in her ninth decade, a woman who is arguably 'so deeply woven into the fabric of tradition, [that] her own life story could be the dramatic tale of a forgotten threnody' (Pattison, 2016)?

Collins is on record in the film as saying how she wants the songs to be themselves, to come through, that her role is not to interpret or bring herself to them but to act as transmitter (or 'tradition bearer' see Knox, 2008; Gardner and Jennings, 2019). Many of the reviews refer to this (Kidman in Folk Radio calls her 'the humble servant of the disembodied voice of the people'; Pattison says she is the song's 'custodian', (2016) and it is in keeping with the English Folk Music tradition of regarding the song as the primary text and the singer as secondary (Gardner and Jennings, 2019). But despite her intentions and their acceptance of it, Collins' choice and interpretation of these songs has meaning.

The violent acts of the songs on *Lodestar*, its stabbings and blood, its drownings and plague seem to suggest an Englishness whose past not only haunts it but coexists with its present, something the film's aesthetic strategy underpins, with its use of pagan figures and Green Men. This past is largely an agrarian, premodern one (see also Edwards, 2018 on Dolly Parton and Appalachia) and Collins' album suggests that it might coexist in a present that runs parallel to the modern and urban. To be clear, this is not suggesting the time slips of Folk Horror but rather that the acts of the past and the emotions they generate do not only belong in the past. The songs of dread for 'Sweet England', the revenge that the dispossessed take on their 'superiors' and the fear of contagion and hell circulate now, in the England of the early twenty-first century, an England whose future is, cloudy, uncertain.

The Ballad of Shirley Collins begins with expository credits that tell the viewer, over the opening scenes, the story of Shirley and place her as someone royal. The way this story is presented foregrounds the historical weight she carries and the place that she should be afforded. 'The Queene of English Folk...A singer and song-collector...Silent for more than 30 years...Ready to reclaim her voice....The Ballad of Shirley Collins'. The captions cast Collins as some kind of English royalty, ripe to reclaim not only her voice perhaps, but her throne at the head of the English folk scene. It is not by chance, I would argue, that an 'e' is on the end of the word, as this is its sixteenth-century spelling, one that links it to Spenser's 'The Faerie Queene' (1590). The credits also place her as within the tradition of the song-collectors of the earlier folk revivals of Cecil Sharp, then Ewan McColl, affording her a kind of cross-gendered (and further respected) status. This is clearly someone who we should be taking notice of, someone whose importance is linked to nation and artistic lineage. She is placed in a position of unassailability, beyond critique, part of the fabric of Englishness, itself marked out as ageless, across time. This unanimous assertion of Collins' importance to a national tradition is mirrored in a female musician a long way from the coasts of Sussex, whose 2016 album is wildly dissimilar to Collins, but who uses the same title of 'Queen' in her track 'Calypso Queen'. It is worth noting though that on Discogs, both albums are put into the same genre, 'Folk World and Country' with Rose's 'style' being calypso and soca (Collins' style is not mentioned).

Calypso Rose and *Far From Home*

Lodestar's sound world is dark and portentous, its lyrics bleak. *Far From Home*, Rose's 2016 hit album is upbeat; a life affirming, 'glorious summer album' (Denselow, 2016). Its lyrics, belonging as they do to the Calypsonian tradition, are full of social commentary, most notably about women and their relationships to work and to men. In it, Rose sings of her longevity, of African diasporic links and personal histories as well as rerecording old hits such as 'No Madame' in particular, a song first released in the 1970s about the plight of domestic workers. It is firmly placed within a specific national musical tradition, using that to make social comment and positioning herself, Rose, as a musician whose identities are multilayered: female, ageing, Calypsonian, Trinidadian, African.

Again, this was the album that brought her to my attention, a white middle-aged middle-class woman with little access to live Calypso. I saw reviews of it appearing in the media I use and, being interested in age and music, it was (again) the emphasis on her being 76 and *still* working, that grabbed my attention. Jumping in at this, most recent point, there was not much more to go on than a few reviews in UK broadsheet, specialist jazz sites (*The Guardian*, *The Quietus*, The Jazz Cafe) and Trinidadian news sites and blogs (Trinidad and Tobago News, IRadio.tt). Calypso has its dedicated researchers (Dudley, 2004; Guerrón-Montero, 2006; Guilbault, 2007), but it does not enjoy the almost obsessive level of documentation, archiving and historical prominence of Anglo-American folk music. This may have something to do with my locational subjectivity, as a white, middle-aged Western European academic, but it is also about constructing musical prominence.

The official Calypso Rose website http://www.calypso-rose.com positions her as key both to Calypso as a genre and, through this, to Trinidadian and Tobagan cultural identity. It charts her first release in 1955, aged 15, through her many awards and her 'discovery' by Chao and embrace by the French music industry, to her 2018 recording of Nat King Cole's *Calypso Blues*. It presents her creative life on a timeline from her birth as Linda McCartha Sandy Lewis in Tobago in 1940 to the present. This chronological line marks out key moments in her development against other Caribbean music (such as Jamaican ska and her gig with The Wailers) and Atlantic cultural developments (Calypso's role in American film especially), making a claim for her to be recognised as an important (and equal) figure within a national and international landscape. It features the Andrews Sisters' 'plagiarised cover' of 'Rum and Coca Cola' in 1945 to the 1957 film 'Island in the Sun' starring Harry Belafonte, a year when Robert Mitchum released the album *Calypso is like … so* (Capitol), recorded after a visit to Trinidad.

Calypso is referred to in the first instance on the website as 'folkloric music' the roots of which can be found in West African Kaiso music. It is also related, rhythmically, to Jamaican Mento music. It is therefore a music whose lineage is diasporic and whose reach and impact is local to the Caribbean, where Soca is its most recent descendant. It is, like Collins' English folk, a music that is rooted in the oral histories of the vernacular culture. It comes from and speaks to a specific place.

Rose sings not only from this place, but she uses her lyrics to question the place of women within Trinidad, and she has always done so. 'Abatina' is a song about domestic abuse and Rose narrates the familiar tale of a scenario where everyone around the abused is aware of her plight but does nothing to avert the inevitable death at the hands of the abuser. 'Woman Smarter' takes biblical characters and humorously plays with narratives that assert female superiority. 'No Madame' is a song in defence of domestic servants, originally released in 1971, and credited with changing government policy on the pay and treatment of such workers. The title track 'Calypso Queen' is an assertion of her own status, where she, in her late 70s, continues to fend off all potential competition for her title.

The album works as a declaration of independence and it is really only when you watch Obolo's documentary film when she opens up about some of her life experiences that these songs reveal traumatic back stories. On camera, she discloses how she was raped as a young woman by three men. This experience had clearly traumatised her and she says that it meant that she had never slept with anyone, man or woman, since. This harrowing revelation seems somehow similar to Collins' loss of voice. These two moments in both women's lives are moments of trauma. Collin's experience is not conclusive, there is some mystery surrounding her dysphonia, but the tragedy of adultery and abandonment feeds into a specific narrative. Collins survives, like Rose, beyond and despite men and returns, in the end, to music. Rose also suffers a different trauma, a psycho trauma, which she hints at in 'Far From Home' and 'I Am African' where she narrates her desire to foreground her own African-ness. In *Calypso Rose: Lioness of the Jungle* (2011) that preceded the albums' release, she talks about her close relationship with her West African great grandmother and is filmed, by Obolo, taking the trip to Benin to see the slave markets and buildings where people were enslaved and thence shipped to the Caribbean. The trauma of abduction and slavery, of historical, familial and inherited traumas, live alongside the experience bodily traumas that Rose recounts. Slavery scars her, as it does the Black diaspora of Trinidad and Tobago, and Rose works to sing that trauma out. Just as the English land is malevolent and prone to time slips in Scovell's Folk Horror aesthetic, so the history of slavery marks itself out on the Rose's own psyche, another traumatised place.

Placing Rose

The music video for 'Calypso Queen' is also directed by Pascale Obolo, and shares footage from the 2011 Obolo full-length documentary. Rose is filmed at home, in her realm, with her looking down from a balcony, singing and dancing as the Queen. A crown is seen, turning slowly round, to underpin the lyrics. We see her sitting on the beach, floating in the sea, just as Rob Curry and Tim Plester shoot Collins in the fields and seashores of her beloved Sussex. Rose, like Collins, is visually relayed as part of the landscape of Trinidad and Tobago. That this landscape has produced a musical culture whose function within the socio-political realm is so marked is important to note. Trinidad and Tobago gained independence from Britain in 1962 and Jocelyn Guilbault writes that 'For the grand independence celebrations in 1962, a Calypso King competition was organised to mark the beginning of this new era in Trinidad's history' (2005, p. 51). This competition was renamed in 1978 to 'Calypso Monarch' following Calypso Rose's victory (p. 55). Mahabir, writing on gender and Calypso, argues that the genre is a 'linguistic and political musical form' (2001, p. 411) that 'weds lyrical, satirical texts with pounding irrepressible rhythms…their presentation style belie the subtle but momentous transformation they are orchestrating – the reconfiguration of gender and ethnic relations' (2001, p. 409). Using Calypso Rose as the first of a line of prominent female Calypsonians, she argues that their contribution has, specifically over the two decades prior to 2001 when she was writing, enabled individual and collective change through the construction of a new discourse around gender matters. Rose herself, she argues, focused on the 'everyday preoccupations of working-class women' (2001, p. 414).

When she started performing, her sobriquet was 'Crusoe Kid', a name she had given herself to demonstrate her roots in Tobago, Crusoe's Isle. She later accepted the less androgynous 'Calypso Rose' from fellow (male) Calypsonians at the Young Brigade Tent. Rose was subsequently designated by younger female calypsonians the Mother of Calypso. She 'cherishes this title because it acknowledges that younger women look up to her as their mother' (interview January 19, 1994; Mahabir, 2001, p. 416). Mahabir refers to how 'Women calypsonians have helped to forge an incipient social movement for profound social change' (2001, p. 428).

This is taken up in Richie Troughton's (2016) review of her latest work in *The Quietus*, which veers away from her age and concentrates on her history of transgression. This concentrates on her 'breaking down walls' and offers a clear history of Calypso and her role in it as a woman, something which she had to fight to enter, to master and retain. Her mastery, the awards, recognition, longevity and respect are all gathered up into the term 'Queen'.

Queens

> When you are a Queen, a public proclaimed member of musical royalty, almost anything is possible, no song is out of touch, no struggle in the search for a tune that is deemed brace, beautiful of positively full of bounce, is never going to be cast aside and dismissed as out of bounds, for a Queen, especially one who has done so much to bring Calypso to an even greater audience, a woman who broke the domination of the genre and gave it a distinctly female voice.
>
> (Hall, 2018)

'Calypso Queen', the fifth track from the album, is a song of affirmation. In it she sings of her long life and career (her 'reign') and her status at the top of Calypso. She refers to her 'constitution' which can be taken as both her bodily strength and of a more political body. The title and the images refer to Rose as Calypso 'Queen'. Richard Elliott has noted that the noun is a 'power-related title' (Elliott, 2015, p. 104). It suggests royalty, monarchy, stateliness, history and national lineage. Male musicians in Jamaican reggae have used such terms to give themselves status that no white society would, to position themselves as kings and lords within a Black, self-determined realm, wresting back the colonial process of 'naming': King Tubby, Prince Far-I, Earl Sixteen. Similarly, hip-hop's Queen Latifah, grime's Lady Leshurr and Princess Nokia illustrate how this claiming of status occurs across Black popular music practices. Calypso has a history of stage names that assume powerful titles: Attila the Hun, Roaring Lion, Lord Invader, Lord Kitchener, Mighty Sparrow, Sir Lancelot. What is admirable about these male Calypso stars is their wresting of names from the British military (Kitchener) and myth (Lancelot). Calypso Rose acknowledges in the film that the rose is the 'mother of all flowers', and she becomes the Queen and mother of Calypso.

As Hall also notes in his review of her album, 'queenliness' bestows power and perhaps it is one whose proclaimed divinity makes Rose unassailable. Who is going to take her crown off? Like Collins, whose 'Queene-liness' invites her to be compared to Elizabethan English royalty, and so wrap her up in discourses of symbolic nationalism (and myth – does she too have the body of a woman but the heart of a man?). This 'Queene' might be the Virgin Queen, Elizabeth 1 and as Hills suggests of Rose, one who usurps male domination. This version of the queen, different to the consort whose role is to reproduce the future, is one not too far removed from the queer queen. So what then to make of her 2018 performance as Nat King Cole, singing Calypso Blues?

There is also something interesting going on in this performance of which could be seen as a drag king performance, a potential queering of the 'queen'. 'You old queen', 'he's such a queen' are terms we find in drag culture. What then to think again about how they are used across reviews, across film and by the performers themselves (Rose) to position themselves as older women? There has been a lot of work around the desexualisation of ageing, of the masculinising of the older woman, the lower vocal range, the whiskers, the postmenopausal lurch of long road away from femininity as it is proscribed, lived and performed in different ways across culture. Claiming Shirley Collins and Calypso Rose as 'queens' both applauds their creative practice within their chosen fields but also hints at them as no longer being the women they were. Queens don't come young. Young women are princesses.

Ageing well?

> At 76, Trinidad and Tobago's reigning queen of calypso should be on cruise control. Instead, she dazzlingly updates the genre she has dominated for a half a century while restating her sassy, feminist persona. The key to the transformation is a collaborative trio of producer Ivan Duran, Toronto's Drew Gonsalves (plus his band Kobo Town) and the ever mercurial Manu Chao, who between them penned most of what Rose delivers with such relish.
>
> (Spencer, 2016)

The above review is fairly typical of one where age is the milestone against which creativity is determined; where expectations around what should and shouldn't be emerging at '76' abound. Reviews of the album might be divided into two kinds – those that made great play of her age, her role as a Queen and a fighter; one review likens to her to fine wine, in so far as she is 'ageing well' (Fanfair, 2018) and those whose principal concern is less her age, than her renewal and reach, making much of her resurgence into a market beyond the borders of Trinidad and Tobago.

Robin Denselow, a respected World Music critic and fan, introduced his review of the album with this:

> Twelve years ago, that great Malian duo Amadou and Mariam transformed their careers by teaming up with Manu Chao to record for Because Music. Now the label features a new Chao collaboration, with the veteran star McCartha Linda Sandy Lewis better known in Trinidad and Tobago as calypso Rose She's 76, still on impressive form and keen to experiment.
>
> (Denselow, 2016)

Rose's status as a fighter is again marked in another *Guardian* review, this one by Peter Culshaw, entitled 'Calypso Rose: "I'm fighting for everyone, regardless of sex"'. It begins by her claiming 'I'm a party animal, always have been', and Culshaw notes how. 'Even though she is 76' and has suffered a series of heart attacks not to mention' her survival of cancer, she delivers a 'blistering set'. London's The Jazz Café also firmly positions her as a survivor in this opening paragraph of their November 14th publicity release:

> Feisty singer, winding storyteller, feminist pioneer and Caribbean cultural icon, it's more than 40 years since Calypso Rose was first crowned calypso queen – and her new album Far From Home finds her in no mood to give up her throne.

It goes on: 'Petulant, energetic, vehement, jovial, gregarious… there aren't enough words to describe her live performances, which she generously dispenses her joie de vivre with the voice of a young girl'. It might be noted at this point that the misalliance between Rose's age and her vocal age points to what Susan Sontag refers to as youth's metaphorical potential. Writing in 1984 on the different standards expected of men and women when ageing, she argues that 'youth is a metaphor for energy, restless mobility, appetite: for a state of wanting' (Sontag, 1984, p. 100). Youth is set as a binary opposite to 'old' that Calypso Rose's presence and music confounds. She is both old and new, she is 76 with the voice of a 'young girl'. How then might we place her in within a chronologically linear discourse that separates those two ages; how might she be appropriate?

Appropriate ageing is a term that has been used by feminist scholars of ageing and popular culture (Whelehan, 2013; Whelehan and Gwynne, 2014) and is concerned with women's appearance within the realm of film, television and popular culture in relation to postmodernity and youth. A not dissimilar term, 'successful ageing' has been discussed in ageing studies by Barbara Marshall, Stephen Katz and others (Baltes and Carstensen, 1996; Chapman, 2005; Rozanova, 2010) to describe the ageing, contributing sexually active 'zoomer' (a term coined by Moses Znaimer in 1998 and subsequently used as the title for a Canadian lifestyle magazine aimed at people in their 60s and above). This idea arises as contrapuntal to narratives of age as decline (Dolan, 2017, p. 4) which has established a 'rhetoric of the old as the culturally residual, the decrepit, the distorted' (Russo, 1999, p. 27). Appropriate ageing is different to this. Whereas 'success' lies in the ability of the aged subject to actively contribute as a neo-liberal individual, and not be reliant on the state for their health or welfare, maintaining a youthful ability to defer decline and decrepitude, 'appropriacy' is more about 'fit' than it is about 'being fit' although the two can overlap. Appropriate ageing is about conduct as well as appearance, both of which should be suited to a chronological age. It is about performing ones age 'correctly' and in line with dominant attitudes on what is acceptable. It is also about time. To age appropriately is to follow the dominant life course patterns of climbs, peaks and declines. Everything has its place within this agreed timeline. But Mary Russo, in her piece 'Ageing and the Scandal of Anachronism' (1999), suggests that one might act against ones age by 'not conforming to normative ideas of age-appropriate behaviour' (Chivers, 2011, p. 41). This relies on what might be, at any date and in any place, 'normative', but Chivers notes that Russo's model relies on a 'randomness', a refusal to be constrained by linear chronology in relation to how one might, indeed, act. Collins and Rose have a specific function within their musical traditions, which is to be the grandmaternal queen. Their musical lives are important to these musical traditions, of which they are now canonised. They are ageing appropriately in so far as they fit into the narratives of English folk and Trinidadian Calypso but they do so on their own terms, as artists and musicians. Moreover, they are now able, like the memoirists in the previous chapter, to voice their traumas. They can tell the stories of their abandonment, their betrayal and their rape, and across very different geographic and generic places, they can age noisily.

Conclusion

Comparing two very different women united only by their longevity in their respective musical traditions does offer points of connection. Thinking with age is a useful spotlight with which to work out what might be going on with the re-emergence and reissue, the re-selling of Collins and Rose. These centre on how, as elders in their field, they enjoy a functional role. I might be upsetting John Berger here to note that for some ageing female musicians, who are way past the menopausal gap, action may very well be as important as appearance. Shirley Collins and Calypso Rose lie outside of the mainstream 'pop' realm, and are not subject to an appropriate ageing based solely on appearance and the approximation of youth despite their youth being recalled. Interviewed making *Far From Home* in a Parisian studio in Obolo's film, Rose says 'At 70, I keep on creating and energizing like a new battery' and at home in her New York house she says to camera 'nothing could stop me in the 50s, 60s, 70s and nothing can stop me now'.

Collins and Rose are not in decline, on the contrary. Their creative outputs do not fit the chronological expectation of such decline. Rather, their renewed and continued presence as ageing female musicians indicates that they fulfil a canonical and a typological function, which are linked. Their canonical function is to act as a marker of longevity within a national and diasporic cultural landscape or place, as part of a 'continuum' (Wade, 2000; Guilbault, 2005; AllMusic, 2016). Their typological function is related to their canonical, in as much as they are placed within the canon 'as' grandmothers and Queens, placed within narratives of continuum. They are not subject to an appropriate ageing based solely on appearance and the approximation of youth (despite their youth being recalled by their reviewers). Aided by their producers and 'young vanguards' (Lee, in 2014), they are Queens urged on by younger courtiers. They are placed within the narratives of their own lives and of those that narrate them in film, online and in review as grandmaternal matriarchs.

3 'Tilted'

The queer ages and sideways spaces of Janelle Monáe, Christine and the Queens and Anohni

In the 2018 'emotion picture' for *Dirty Computer*, Janelle Monáe declares that she has always lived her life 'left of centre', which is 'right where' she belongs. The album, and much of her back catalogue, both musically and audio visually, is neo-Afrofuturist and queer. Hers is a Black, queer voice at the centre of pop. At the same time, Héloïse Letissier's alter ego 'Christine' (in 2015) and later 'Chris' (2018) inserts a gender fluidity into the pop mainstream with her band 'Christine and the Queens'. The third musician of this female trio that offer tilted pop is Anohni, formerly known as Antony Hegarty of Anthony and The Johnsons. She uses the production techniques of pop's sonic vocabulary to release *Hopelessness* (2016), a protest record. These three musicians all use performance spaces in a way that upsets bodily borders and time. And they all use time queerly.

This chapter looks at how theories of queerness and time might be explored to apply to their music video work to uncover queer futurities (in Monáe's work), future nostalgias (in Letissier's) and trans-ageing (in Anohni's). The chapter is therefore not about the chronological aspects of ageing, more the ways in which heteronormativity has organised temporal flow and how queer/gender fluid artists subvert it through locating themselves elsewhere, in the past, the future and outside of themselves.

The motive for looking at these three through this type of lens resonates with a line from a 2012 Nick Cave and The Bad Seeds' song called 'Jubilee Street'. Here, the protagonist recalls his visits to a 'girl' who has to 'make ends meet'. He discovers that his name is in her little black book. He is a marked man. He describes this feeling by saying 'I was out of time and place, over the hill, out of my mind'. He is dislocated, aged, irrational. His sense of where he belongs, chronologically and geographically, has been disrupted. I want to take those lyrics out of context because for me, they resonate with the performances in music video and film that form part of the output of these three female musicians working in the early twenty-first century. There are similarities in how they occupy performance spaces and what, in turn, this has to say about their versions of 'femininity'. This might not, at first glance, seem to be related to 'age', and, indeed, it is not about them looking back on youth, as the rock memoirists were doing, nor is it about their functional places as aged subjects within a lineage, as were Shirley Collins and Calypso Rose. This chapter shifts the idea of age as a remembered and represented stage of embodied life, to considering it from queer theories that question the heteronormative parameters and propulsions that are bound up in such stages. All three performers are queer and/or transgender; 'Christine' (Héloïse Letissier) made an impact on the Anglo-American pop/dance market with her album *Chaleur Humaine* in 2015 before striking out the 'tine' to become 'Chris' for her second. This 'swaggering masculine alter-ego delivers Letissier's punchy statement of intent, wrapping themes from gender fluidity to female agency in heady electronic pop' (Petridis, 2018a). Janelle Monáe is, in her own words, a 'young, Black queer woman' (Leighton-Dore, 2018) releasing funk, neo-soul, swing pop and R'n'B (www.Discogs.com). Anohni is a transgender musician who started her career as Anthony Hegarty and releases 'chamber' pop. It is not their sexuality it and of itself that impels me to want to draw them together and comment on their work, but it is the spaces they occupy in their music video performances especially where something interesting is going on. And I want to suggest that this 'something' is important as, when taken together, they are staking out different arenas from which to speak as queer and non-binary subjects, within the mainstream pop realm.

I have written elsewhere of how music video might be described as ontologically queer (Gardner, 2018b). 'Is it a short film? Is it an ad? Is it progressive? Is it representational? Is it art? From the late 1980s up to the present day, music video has been arguably 'queer'. It shares a reluctance to be any 'one' thing …; it is a trans-medium' (Gardner, 2018, p. 155) and writers in the field have long vouchsafed for its ambiguity (Kaplan, 1987; Goodwin, 1992; Cubitt, 1993, 2002; Vernallis, 2004). It is therefore a medium well suited to 'tilted' performances, like the ones from Monáe, Letissier and Anohni, as it offers an experimental space. Where a music video is set is important (Vernallis, 2004, 2013). Indeed, in all these three cases, where they are set is crucial to understanding what critiques are being made. And these critiques are around the acceptable, binary, well-behaved body. Before I go any further in this it might be worth reflecting on what is at stake here, why does this matter? What matters here, in these performers' work, is the sense of a positive space beyond the binary where new forms of ageing are being presented that decouple the self from ageing presents and propel them into imagined presents, pasts and futures. Vanessa Fabbre (2014) noted that 'Concepts of time are ubiquitous in studies of aging'. Of course, they are. No account of ageing cannot consider the temporal context within which that ageing happens, and as I set out in the introduction, ageing is staged, recalled, represented and experience in a multiplicity of ways. What I want to consider here is how time as time displaced, time gone, time past is important for these three musicians. They are not old. But they use older women (Anohni), refer to older spaces (Letissier) and future spaces (Monáe) to perform their work. This mode allows them to be somehow separate to the present; it enables them to make work that is comment on their place, as queer women and non-binary individuals. They offer a temporal displacement and perform in the queer alterity of their chosen, liminal (Anohni), nostalgic (Letissier) and utopian (Monáe) spaces.

Tilted: staging the self-outside of heteronormative time

In 2005, Jack Halberstam proposed the idea of 'Queer temporality', where he argues for the concept of a 'queer time' that lies beyond the logics of heteronormative and capitalist temporal certitude and trajectory. I use this to look at Christine and the Queens' 'Girlfriend' and Anohni's 'Marrow', and add it to work on Afrofuturism and Black Queer Futurity (Munoz, 2009; English and Kim, 2013; Elia, 2014) to unpack Janelle Monáe's 'emotion picture' for *Dirty Computer*. In this respect I am also mobilising Linn Sandberg's (2008) work on 'thinking old age in relation to queer theory' and applying it to these three musicians. Sandberg refers to Halberstam's positioning of queerness in relation to temporality in order to open up spaces for discussion over old age. She pulls in Halberstam's comments that 'part of what has made queerness compelling as a form of self-description in the past decade or so has to do with the way it has the potential to open up new life narratives and alternative relations to time and space' (2005, p. 2). The narratives of a heteronormative life course are thus positioned as just one route through life, one that can be rejected. Halberstam unpacks this narrative to argue that it is premised on two temporal modes, each of which can be resisted. These temporal modes are the 'time of reproduction' and the 'time of inheritance (Halberstam, 2005, p. 2). The first is linked obviously to reproduction or 'repro-time' which is positioned within a heteronormative culture as natural and desirable. The second is about 'generational time', where the heteronormative family is connected to a nation's historical past (and also its future via familial legacy). Not participating in either of these 'times' enables queer temporalities to be imagined. And Sandberg sees in this move, what she calls a 'critical challenge to normalcy' (2008, p. 117), the possibility of re-imaging age.

Halberstam's articulation of 'queer' encapsulates not only non-normative sexualities but also extra-normative life courses and activities that lie beyond or deny the normative, in particular how they refuse to obey clock time in a way that the Protestant Work Ethic in particular has delivered it. He argues that clubbers perform a 'queerness' in their refusal to obey established capitalist rules of time and paid activity, and how homeless people actively 'queer' urban spaces with their presence. Activities that lie outside the rules of capitalist, heteronormative narratives, that subvert the time and space of heteronormative capitalism, are 'queer'. He also refers to 'junkie-time', whereby time is ordered by the pattern of addiction. The term becomes not merely a statement of sexual orientation but an avowal of maverick anti-normative intent. It obscures and obfuscates the lines which have come to delineate place/space and time; it queries what is day/night, what is street/home, what is work/pleasure.

This utopian potential appears in Jose Munoz's (2009) writing on queer futurity where he argues that queer aspiration needs to be directed away from the present (time and space) towards a more utopian future, what Jodie Taylor calls a 'striving towards queer(er) horizons' (2012, p. 213). She suggests that translocal gay scenes can offer an 'augury of queer worlds' (2012, p. 209), given their distinction from the present, straight world. Monáe, Letissier and Anohni fashion these queer worlds in their refusal to set them in the present time or in their present bodies. These presents for them are dissonant in that they do not 'fit' them ideologically and they mobilise musical excursions back in time (to Michael Jackson, to Prince) and out of their bodies (Anohni) to construct a music whose ingredients and performances straddle temporalities.

Another writer on the subject of queerness and temporality is Elizabeth Freeman (2010) working on the connections between temporal and sexual dissonance. She uses the term '*chrononormativity*' which is an organisational matrix geared towards ensuring individual productivity which produces in turn a sense of collectivity 'through particular orchestrations of time' (2010, p. 3). She refers to Dana Luciano and her use of the phrase '*chronobiopolitics*, or "the sexual arrangement of the time of life" of entire populations' (Luciano, 2007 in Freeman, 2010, p. 3). This work underlines the sense that time and its organisation are not only culturally constructed and therefore contingent, but that it is bound up with sexuality, given that much heteronormativity travels on Halberstam's two axes, reproduction and inheritance. These three performances take place in spaces of refusal and potential which is a rearticulation of liminal spaces beyond Halberstam's two time modes.

Dandied pop stars

Christine and the Queens' debut album sold nearly one million copies worldwide, with 160,000 copies in the UK (Music Business Worldwide, January 22, 2017) and in 2018 she went on a sell-out tour of the UK and Europe. Janelle Monáe's latest got to the top of the US R'n'B charts and earned her two Grammy nominations. Anohni is perhaps less 'pop', emerging from and continuing to perform in a milieu that has performance art and drag as its centre. She did, though, want the album *Hopelessness* to have a 'plastic' feel to it (Gardner, 2018) and its production aesthetic is 'pop'. All of them might be considered to be experimenting with borders, generic (Monáe), bodily (Anohni) and musical (Letissier). Monáe and Letissier perform the gender fluid dandy at times. They are all 'pop' stars who manage to bring narratives of 'border work' into the pop mainstream, where this means experimentation with gender, aesthetic and musical boundaries.

Letissier and Anohni have both had encounters and working relationships with drag queens (see *Turning* (2006) dir. Atlas) and reviews of all of them, at some point mention their gender, or their ambiguity towards expressing their gender uniformly and consistently. Two of them, Letissier and Monáe, have presented themselves in music video, on stage and in promotional material *as* dandies, Monáe as Little Richard (in 'Tightrope' (2010) and Letissier as the matador (in 'La marcheuse', 2018).

Hawkins' work is the only one to address the figure of the (male) dandy in popular music with the focus on English musicians (among them Jagger, Morrissey, The Pet Shop Boys, Robert Smith). His (and others') work on the dandy acknowledges the importance of Beau Brummel, Baudelaire and Oscar Wilde in his understanding of the history, aesthetics and political potential of the dandy. He argues that the dandy is a 'border' figure (2011, p. 44), who can cross the 'borders of say, class, racial and gender identities' (p. 44). The male dandy 'reinforce[s] a long tradition of performative display that can be read as institutionally transgressive' (2016, p. 9). Some of this theatricalised (Hawkins and Niblock, 2011, p. 48) transgression might be attributed to the dandy not only suggesting an androgyny but putting on clothes that are from another time. Prince, for example, dressed in clothes that recalled eighteenth-century France in 1980s' America (Womack, 2013, p. 170).

His list of key female dandies includes 'Patti Smith, Siouxsie Sioux, Annie Lennox, Madonna, Kylie Minogue, Björk, Gwen Stefani, Beyoncé and many others' (2016, p. 6). Close in position and role to divas, they display the qualities of 'irony, camp and vulnerability' (2016, p. 6). The diva is a figure of power and tragedy, determination and vulnerability (O'Neill, 2007; Bradshaw, 2008; Gardner, 2015), one whose proximity to death (of herself, of her lovers, her dreams) makes her more of a tragic and heroic figure than the dandy. She is also a figure whose existence is accepted within specific musical and theatrical spaces; her excesses are expected and accepted, be she male or female. In contrast, the female dandy is transgressive, specifically of gendered roles and of temporal norms, and she has transgression written onto her body via its stylings. There is little work on female dandies (Lusty, 2007; Gill, 2011). and there is nothing about how being a female dandy in pop might be something worth looking at through the prism of ageing, when that prism is modulated by prescriptions of hetero-chronometry. Lusty's work offers a way in to thinking about this as she sees the female dandy appearing 'at points of transition' (2007, p. 106). The dandy is an unsettling figure (2007, p. 106) not only because of their rebellion against norms of heteronormative masculinity and bourgeois acceptability, but in the very mutability of their body; transforming it into a work of art (p. 107). This mutability is key as it presupposes a fractured subject. Writing on female dandies, surrealism and photography (in particular, the work of Cahun) she notes the sense of fissure, both of the subject and of temporality, that 'the subject's transformation, its difference from the other and its difference from itself over time' (2007, p. 115). The dandy represents a self that is in a continual state of becoming a work in progress and 'work of art' (Waldrep, 2016, p. 66). Her argument is similar to Robertson's on feminist camp, in that the dandy is only possible within certain historical contexts.

Camp is an aesthetic whose heritage has been linked to queerness (Meyer, 1994, Cleto, 1999; Dickinson, 2001; Taylor, 2012) and feminist camp (Robertson, 1996) has foregrounded how important 'time' is to it. Exaggerated and ironic, it has the potential to be part of political praxis, mobilised as a tool that 'juxtaposes seriousness and paradox to reveal the unnatural state of something that is often perceived as real or essential, such as gender or sexual desire' (Taylor, 2012, p. 73). But rather than seeing camp as an ahistorical aesthetic, Robertson proposes that the artifice and excess that heralds camp is used by women at specific moments of anti-feminist backlash or 'high-camp epochs' (1996, p. 18). Robertson's shift in understanding camp positions it as something that women can do when history allows them too. She argues that the camp 'effect' happens when practices, objects and ways of behaviour that were previously acceptable and 'natural' are no longer so. This enables us to have 'an ironic, laughing distanciation' (Robertson, 1996, p. 5) with past cultural products. Camp becomes a tool in the hands of women wishing to comment on alienation through reconceptualising past models of identity and desire, but it is only possible as a feminist praxis when it is not part of the 'now'. Robertson's argument rests on the idea that women might be able to critique, laugh at and maybe subvert what they might be (as women) after a suitable time lapse. Being in time means being too close. So feminist camp is only possible as a review of 'what was'. What though, if we consider 'what is?', what role might there be for dandies or campness in future spaces and third places?

Monáe and Afrofuturism

Monáe has released four studio albums, *The Audition*, 2003; *The Arch Android*, 2010; *The Electric Lady*, 2013; and *Dirty Computer*, 2018. From *Arch Android* to *Dirty Computer*, she mobilises key tropes from the Afrofuturist aesthetic, specifically future technologies (androids, computers), and the album covers are fully commensurate with an Afrofuturist aesthetic. On *Arch Android*, Monáe is on the cover, set against a background of stars (or space), wearing full body armour with a headdress that resembles the city in Fritz Lang's *Metropolis* (1927). On *Electric Lady*, she is in monochrome, her hair in a pompadour, a twenty-first-century incarnation of Little Richard riffing on the tile of a 1968 Jimi Hendrix album, inhabiting and reworking the Black (and queer) heroes of American pop and rock. *Dirty Computer*'s cover sees her in chain-mail macramé veil, eyes closed, with a yellow halo. Fulfilling the popular music industry's requirement to present the self via album, Monáe does so with wit and elipticism, and within the aesthetics of Afrofuturism.

Janelle Monáe figures in Womack's list of Afrofuturist musicians, along with Clinton, Sun Ra, Perry, Outkast, Grace Jones, Erykah Badu, etc. 'even Coltrane and Miles Davies' (2013, p. 56). She has worked with two of these (Big Boi from Outkast on 'Tightrope' (2010) and Badu on 'Q.U.E.E.N' (2013)). Womack calls her a 'modern-day musical paradox' (2013, p. 74). She refers to her 'coiffed 1950s pompadour and snug tuxedo', her 'frenetic dance' that is reminiscent of James Brown, her 'masculine façade [which is] a shout-out to Grace Jones' and her vocals that 'evoke memories of jazz greats' (2013:74). Monáe is an amalgam of the greats of African American music; she is them all, men and women, alive and dead. English and Kim situate her as a neo-Afrofuturist, and see her operating in a direct line from Ra, Clinton and Perry with her nods to 'outer space and other times' (2013, p. 219). On the opening track to *Dirty Computer*, she duets with Brian Wilson bringing White American pop history to her own Afrofuturist world. She looks like Little Richard and Jones, and on her latest album, she sounds like Prince (especially on 'Make Me Feel' with the guitar chords' work and vocals that are reminiscent of 1990's 'Kiss').

From her first EP, *Metropolis*, through *Arc Android* and *Dirty Computer*, she has offered a narrative through an android alter ego, known as Cindi Merriweather. The android is a figure whose gender fluidity offers a model that is beyond a clear-cut binary, and as English and Kim note, 'From the start of her recording career, Monáe has foregrounded the contingency of the human, particularly of the black female body, through a narrative about an imagined android alter ego' (English and Kim, 2013, p. 218). In her latest album, and in particular in its accompanying 'emotion picture', this narrative is explored in an explicitly queer way, with Monáe singing odes to female genitalia (on 'Pynk'), performing a newly publicly acknowledged queerness.

Womack argues that Afrofuturism offers Black women creative freedom because 'black women's imagination, image and voice are not framed by the pop expectations and sensibilities of the day' (2013, p. 101). Monáe is afforded a different space within which to operate, one set apart from the dominant white pop world. Afrofuturism offers a 'free space for women' (Womack, 2013, p. 100) wherein they can 'define blackness, womanhood, or any other identifier in whatever form their imagination allows' (2013, pp. 100–101). And Monáe 'explodes any notion that Afrofuturism is no more' (English and Kim, 2013, p. 217), reinvigorating it for the twenty-first century, what Anderson and Jones call 'Afrofuturism 2.0' (2016). Monáe is an Afrofuturist. Like Sun Ra, George Clinton (with Funkadelic) and the dub reggae artist, Lee Scratch Perry whom Womack compares her to, she uses the aesthetic, critical and political space opened up by Afrofuturism to experiment with race, gender and sexuality.

The term was first applied in 1993 by Mark Dery in a piece called 'Black to the Future' (Elia, 2014, p. 83) and then developed by Mark Sinker and Kodwo Eshun (Womack, 2013, pp. 16–17). Its roots went back decades, but the 1990s were when specific components and concepts were gathered together and labelled as 'Afrofuturism', with its aesthetics drawing from sci-fi and African history: futures and pasts. Its key proponents in literature are Octavia Butler and in film *The Brother from Another Planet* (dir. Sayles, 1984).

Afrofuturism is both an 'artistic aesthetic and a framework for critical theory' (Womack, 2013, p. 9). It is also a 'political agenda' (Elia, 2014, p. 84) that 'empower[s]images of black power through futuristic imagery and control of technology' (McLeod, 2003, p. 340). This is because 'The history of black people is a history of alienation, almost as if they came from another planet and science fiction represents a privileged vehicle to express this idea' (Elia, 2014, p. 92). Within the USA, it might be argued that African Americans have to create their own future given that they have no past. And this future is a messed up, glorious mash up of all possible futures and pasts combined. It is an 'African American cultural production and political theory that imagine[s] less constrained black subjectivity in the future and that produce[s] a profound critique of current social, racial and economic orders' (English and Kim, 2013, p. 217).

> Afrofuturism combines elements of science fiction, historical fiction, speculative fiction, fantasy, Afrocentricity, and magic realism with non-Western beliefs. In some cases, it's a total reenvisioning of the past and speculation about the future rife with cultural critiques.
>
> (Womack, 2013, p. 9)

It is a 'program for recovering the histories of counter-futures created in a century hostile to Afro-diasporic projection' (Elia, 2014, p. 84 citing Eshun, 2003, p. 301). It is able to offer rewritten histories, spotlighting lineages of resistance for those alienated both from power and their own histories (and futures): resistance that has been launched via 'improvisation, adaptability and imagination' (Womack, 2013, p. 37). And as Womack argues, 'the imagination is a tool of resistance. Creating stories with people of colour in the future defies the norm. With the power of technology and emerging freedoms, black artists have more control over their image than ever before' (2013, p. 24). It offers a space for 'other voices' (Nelson, 2002, p. 9; Halberstam, 2013, p. 132) for the imagining of alternative pasts and potential futures and comments on alienation and Black history (specifically that of African Americans), allowing artists to 'present new and innovative perspectives' (Anderson and Jones, 2014, p. 92). It is also a vehicle which 'also allow[s] room for alternate, more pluralistic definitions – the space alien as a transcendent form of Other capable of challenging simplistic binaries of male/female, black/white or rich/poor' (McLeod, 2003, p. 339). And this challenge is exactly what Janelle Monáe does in her work. Rose discusses how Afrofuturism has often posited the Black subject as an alien or robot slave, which is a response to African American histories where Black subjects 'were labour for capitalism' (McLeod, 2003, p. 342), The space ship is, too, a metaphor for the slave ships of the Black Atlantic, which within the Afrofuturist discourse becomes the enabler and 'Mothership' (P-funk) rather than the de-racinating transport carrying the stateless and the enslaved. As Elia writes, 'Being outsiders, slaves – and, more generally, people of African descent – aliens and robots are all closely related in this kind of aesthetic, each becoming a metaphor for the other' (2014, p. 85).

In music, Afrofuturism accommodates performances and aesthetics that confuse time, juxtaposing the past (notably Egyptian motifs) with the future (space travel, cyborgs). Sun Ra, Perry, Clinton and Parliament are famous for their use of these visual aesthetics and Parliament's privileging of 'The Mother Ship' which they emerged from in live shows illustrated the idea of them making a narrative of having come from elsewhere. *Dirty Computer* follows in these footsteps. This is also mirrored in Monáe's production techniques, which on the *Metropolis* EP were described in *Hip-Hop DX* magazine as 'having a production style that takes its clues from something made in the past as well as the future' (Anderson and Jones, 2016, p. 97). This ability to collapse time sonically mirrors the idea that Afrofuturist aesthetics is able to imagine and produce an alternate temporal model that is disarticulated from a white, colonial chronometry. 'If you can create a new vision of the future, you can create a new vision of the past', says D. Denege Akpem (in Womack, 2013, p. 154). Afrofuturism has been about uncoupling experience from a colonial history, imaginary and trajectory and imagining something else beyond it, beside it and behind it. Gipson argues for the compellingness of Monáe's work in its ability to 'highlight the past, present, and the future within the African American diaspora' (2016, p. 93) and talks about how 'Monáe can travel through time and space recapturing and reclaiming what was taken' (p. 94).

What I want to hone in on, and which I think has something to add to this chapter's broader concern with spaces and time, is the idea of 'Wondaland'. This is the name of her own imprint, of which she is the CEO (and she is also signed to Atlantic Records). The title is also a track on *The ArchAndroid* (2010), recorded at Wondaland Studios in Atlanta. English and Kim suggest that 'Wondaland may represent an imagined future' (2013, p. 226), an Afrocentric, queer one, where, like Lewis Carrol's Alice, she can escape to. The alien worlds of Wondalands and Afro futures are positive, enabling; they offer control and agency.

Janelle Monáe's 'emotion picture' and future queer utopias

The narrative film, or 'emotion picture' as she calls it, that accompanies *Dirty Computer* is on the official Janelle Monáe website next to gifs from the music videos for 'Make Me Feel', 'Djano Jane', 'Pynk' and 'I Like That'. In it, Monáe plays Jane 57821, a 'dirty computer' who needs to be cleaned. Cleansing involves deleting her memory, and the memories, the music videos for the albums, are played out in turn throughout the film. It becomes clear that Jane 57821 is queer, and her queer Black life is being wiped to make her 'clean' so that she can become a 'torch', an individual whose job it is to nurse the 'unclean' back to cleanliness. This process is about making the abject Black female 'straight', to restore order and thus avoid a queer Black female future. The purifying process is done with white steam, or gas, which itself references the Holocaust and the Nazi notions of a 'pure' race. Once purified, the now newly named 'torch' (or a Mary) becomes 'the robot [who] represents the prototype of the modern slave, displaced and oppressed by the colonialist white' (Elia, 2014, p. 96).

Monáe is first seen lying supine on what looks like an operating table in a hospital-like space. The voice-over tells us how you were 'dirty' if you 'looked different', if you refused to live the way they dictated', 'if you showed any form of opposition at all'. Overlooking that space and in charge of wiping her memories are two white men. Their job is to 'trash and bag' all of Jane's queer life, a life that is 'left of centre' (Monáe, 2018). Jane is being tended too through the cleansing process by Mary Apple 53, who in her left of centre life was her lover, whose memories have already been (almost) erased and with whom Monáe and their male companion escape at the end of the film, back towards their queer life. The two white men in charge of erasing her past, one more sympathetic perhaps to her life than the other, for whom she is dispensable, are able to view and delete all her past memories expect for one: the vagina monologue. The video for 'Django Jane' shows Monáe speaking from a mirror held over her vagina; it is humorous but her point is serious; no one listens to women in a phallocracy. What we need, she sings, is a 'pussy riot' reference to the Russian punk activists and bands whose performances in churches (and on the pitch of the 2018 World Cup in Russia) resulted in imprisonment. So Monáe's film, its featured music videos and her lyrics are pointedly political; she exhorts us to take a bite of an apple, an explicit reference to Eve and the Garden of Eden, another space outside of time.

The videos for the album's tracks are stitched into the narrative of the film 'as' memories. The language of these videos is reminiscent of David La Chappelle's photography; they use high colour, are hyperreal, glossy. The first memory to be wiped is shown the video for the track 'You Got the Juice'. It references Lady Gaga and Beyoncé in 'Telephone' (dir. Åkerlund, 2010) which in turn alludes to *Thelma and Louise* (dir. Scott. 1991) and 'B-movies, Tarantino's *Kill Bill* and *Natural Born Killers*' (Vernallis, 2013, p. 16). Monáe is in a car (with no wheels, it is hovering along the highway) with her girlfriend, when they hear police sirens. They are pulled over and ID'ed by the flying robot cops that descend. Once monitored and OKed, they carry on, before stopping to open their boot, from where more of their female friends emerge. The reference to police harassment of Black people in America is clear. Monáe inserts what sounds like (but isn't) the voice of Martin Luther King referring to the American Declaration of Independence which states that 'All men and women are created equal' and that all should have equal access to 'life, liberty and the pursuit of happiness'. The videos also comment on sexual objectification; in the track 'Screwed', Monáe wears a T-shirt that reads 'subject not object', and on 'Make Me Feel', she has her playing guitar dressed in a chain-mail bikini with chain-mail veil in a dance routine that subverts Robert Palmer's 1986 'Addicted to Love' video (and by extension, Robin Thicke's 'Blurred Lines', 2013).

The action for all the videos within the film takes place in liminal spaces, highways, motels, deserts, graffitied subways and rooftops. The only internal space used as a setting is a club in 'Make Me Feel'. In 2004, Carol Vernallis suggested that a music video's setting could be used as a kind of generic shorthand, with indie bands in small grimy spaces, hip-hop using the 'street'. Her key argument is that 'settings are segregated, and the ways of inhabiting them seem strictly codified' (2004, p. 73). This argument can still be applied in relation to music video aesthetics, whereby certain spaces are more likely to be occupied by musicians working in specific genres than others (Vernallis, 2004, pp. 73–74), but Monáe works across genres, inhabiting a range of spaces, including dystopian urban landscapes, colour saturated deserts and high gloss motels. These are places both on the edge of life in their liminality (being outside the domestic and the public sphere, wherein daily life and politics, business takes place), but simultaneously they are central to an American cultural, filmic and aesthetic imagination. Monáe appropriates these spaces of the cultural imaginary to inscribe her life of Black queerness, a life that has been lived (and so is erasable as a memory) and a life that is a potential future (which she goes out to reclaim at the end of the film). Even though she seems to have been 'cleansed', and has mutated from Jane 57821 to Mary Apple 54, and is now tasked with turning others, she reveals that she and her lover have resisted and are able to go out and claim their queerness.

The science-fiction scenario allows Monáe, like other Afrofuturists before her, to use the future as a space for critiquing the present. The film could be thought of as a narrative about gay conversion, whereby black queer women are returned to heteronormativity by white superiors and white operatives. The raced element of this is hard to deny, where it is young white men who erase young black women's sexual identities and queer lives. And so, with its positive ending, it is a film about how 'Black queer lives matter'.

Chris(tine) and the Queens' future nostalgia

'Chris' is the 2018 alter ego of Héloïse Letissier. Before 'Chris', 'he' was 'Christine'. Both of them have been accompanied by 'The Queens', a troupe of dancers and backing musicians. Letissier, from Nantes in west France, sings in French and English, and her songs are dance and chanson inflected pop songs. Her personal biography, repeatedly referred to in profiles and reviews, recalls her time as a theatre school dropout living in Paris, then moving to London and being taken in by drag queens at Soho's (now defunct) Madame JoJos and given lessons in life, performance and make-up (Cragg, 2016). Her life and her performances suggest the open endedness of identity as a construction and process: a becoming. Her first album *Chaleur Humaine* was 2016's biggest selling debut album in the UK, bringing her to an Anglo-American audience getting to Number 2 in the Official UK charts. Her second, *Chris*, got to Number 3. Both albums use music videos to experiment with space: spaces of the body and spaces where the body becomes itself. The album has been reviewed and commented on as being nostalgic, as versed within the pop aesthetics of the 1980s. Letissier uses these musical and locational spaces to project a future nostalgia, one where s/he can ask questions about who s/he might be and why not knowing, or not fitting in, is perfectly fine. The spaces the music videos are set are 'somewhere elses', but unlike reading these as liminal, I suggest they are both mundane and iconic, and so have the potential to be both aspirational and identifiable and Alexis Petridis, a music journalist, reflects on the nostalgia of *Chris*: 'Like "Girlfriend", the rest of *Chris* harks back to the early 80s – tellingly, a period when the charts were populated by the queer, transgressive and ostensibly marginal' (Petridis, 2018b). These acts were part of the British New Romantic movement and post-punk/ electronica (Duran Duran, Visage, Spandau Ballet, Flock of Seagulls, EMD). But Letissier's work also mines the Jacksons', Janet and Michael, in its live stage performances especially and in its music videos. Many of the comments on YouTube under 'Girlfriend' note how it 'reminds' them of the 1980s, of Michael Jackson.

> Every time I hear this on the radio I thought it was an 80's track, wouldn't be out of place on GTA Vice City
>
> Darth Dainese 4 months ago
>
> i kinda get michael jackson vibes from this
>
> Ellis 3 months ago
>
> This for me is hands down the most authentic late 80s/early 90s sounding thing i have heard produced NOW. Its like ive gone back in time…amazing!
> thebatman1019

> This is like if Michael Jackson and Enya had a baby in 1980s America
> JG16riffin 4 months ago
>
> Fabulous nostalgia in such a new track - it has the vibe of New York City in the middle of August with a touch of Madonna & Michael Jackson...
> Seagreentangerine 3 months ago (edited)
>
> Domage pour l'accent anglais qui est vraiment pas top on dirait mm pas de l'anglais limite ... apres musique au top vraiment, un ptit son a la MJ des annees 80.
> 4 months ago (shame about the English accent....sounds of MJ in the 80s)
> (all accessed 5/10/18)

Letissier is involved in some part here in 'aural time travel', a term noted by McLeod (2003) in a piece on space and alien motifs in Pop and Rock Music. He uses the phrase to illustrate the use of sampling and multitracking in 'African-American musical genres' (2003, p. 345). Samples of speeches (from Martin Luther King) or tracks (from James Brown) figure prominently and work to establish an alternative African American history, what he calls 'a collective notion of African-American historical memory' (2003, p. 345). What Letissier is doing here is not so much interweaving voices from the past into a restructured present, but reworking musical textures and sonic motifs from 1980s pop to rethink the queer potential of those artists and those times and then refocus those potentials back into a further away past, that of the building to the USA and of a certain type of masculinity. Letissier's use of musical textures and music video aesthetics from the 1980s is not though about a reminding or a trigger back to a historically accurate past, but to demonstrate 'how queer attachment and fantasy operate temporally in relation to the past' (Luciano, 2011, p. 129). It is less about remembering the 1980s or 'generat[ing] nostalgia for this period but to provoke remembrance of what it meant to desire something different, in order to reactivate the moment of difference itself' (Luciano, 2011, p. 125). In the music videos for 'Girlfriend', '5 Dollars' and 'La Marcheuse' ('The Walker'), 'Chris' is visually (and sonically) 'placed' within *somewheres* that are redolent of historical, literary and cinematic pasts.

The title track from *Chris* is 'Girlfriend'. The video opens with a shot of the back of a pair of white sneakers hanging, legs are dangling from something. The legs' owner is sitting on some kind of swing or moving bench that seems to overlook New York City at dusk. The sky is orange. As the 'swing' lowers, the viewer sees the title of the video scrawled on the back of the seat and the back of what must be Letissier, with a white dove on her right shoulder. There is no music, but there is sound. We hear doves cooing – surely a reference to Prince's 'When Doves Cry'. A cooing that accompanies the opening few seconds is the sound of wind. Music kicks in when the dove flies away. We are in a space high above the city that recalls the iconic photographs of the workers who built New York's skyscrapers, having their lunches on the crossbeams. Instead of workers, Letissier populates this space with gender fluid dancers who again, as in 'Christine' (2014), dance with her to the track. The archetypal masculine worker, the body of men who built America, are replaced by Letissier's dance troupe of queens, with her singing about her 'girlfriend':

> Letissier is taking the role of Christine, the genderqueer character she adopts to showcase her delicately bruised electronic pop songs about non-conformity, fluid identities and sexual awakening (the Queens, named after a group of London drag artists, are her imaginary support system).
>
> (Cragg, 2016)

'5 Dollars' is the only real video to have a narrative to it, as opposed to staging a dance performance. In it, we see Chris getting dressed. S/he starts with a work-out; the camera focused on the muscles of her back as she does push ups on her carpet floor. We follow the process of her dressing ritual; in the shower, naked with scratch marks on her back, in her leather brace bra, big black knickers and dog collar, she flicks through a pared down wardrobe of leather/bondage gear, suits, shirts and brogues. The setting has all the trappings of the twenty-first-century yuppie flat, say of Christian Bale in *American Psycho*, as well as the bland adverts for expensive built in wardrobes. We literally see Chris putting on her/his suit, leaving the flat resplendent in tweed three-piece, tie and black leather gloves, carrying a leather briefcase, ready for 'work' after the 'work' of becoming male has been done.

The video for 'La Marcheuse' ('The Walker') is also, like '5 Dollars', a development from the staged dances of the first album towards more of a narrative that amplifies the music (Goodwin, 1992). This time Letissier, as Chris, is dressed as a bullfighter. S/he appears dressed in a starched white shirt with an elaborate high decorated collar, reminiscent of sixteenth-century ruffs or seventeenth-century collars. High-waisted black trousers, and with one gold earring, s/he puts on a matador's jacket. It is pale pink with a white lace trim. She is performing Chris performing the matador, possibly the dandiest of dandies, the beautified (yet deadly and macho) male. The video then shows Chris walking through a ruined, seemingly abandoned village. It could be in Spain or the South of France from the architecture and landscape. Her/his walk through the main street of the town, with five villagers secretly watching her from within their houses, recalls the films of Sergio Leone, when the lone gunfighter arrives. Into the street a bull appears. The video suggests perhaps some violence – this is what we expect from such characters, settings, such ingredients. And Chris has a raw scar down his/her left cheek, perhaps from a previous fight. But the bull starts to walk with Chris; they leave the village and towards the sunset as she strokes it. In this video is a 'walker'; that is, s/he is a flanêur/se. As a dual gendered being, s/he is in charge of 'the street'.

Much has been written on the male flanêur as privileged modern masculinity, untethered to the Protestant Work Ethic, free to roam and, according to Dreyer, free to consume. Dreyer (2012) notes that when women assume the role, they are moved into a position of power within a consumer economy wherein they have been subjugated (and subject to the male consumer gaze). And here we return to Halberstam's (2005) articulation of queerness, where those who do not use spaces as they were intended, nor perform their gender right (Butler, 1990, 1993) are rendered queer.

All of Letissier's music video performances are set in spaces that are somehow liminal. They are empty stage spaces, generically representative of theatrical and dance space, places that are temporally contingent and host to the 'make believe'. Empty streets, ruined landscapes, places where people once were but no longer are. They are on the edge of society. The only video set within the ostensibly domestic space of the bedroom is '5 Dollars' wherein Letissier performs the construction of masculinity, thereby querying the bedroom (and the bed) as the preserve of femininity. (Vernallis once claimed that women would be always positioned at some point in or near a bed in a music video, with the sexualised potential of that positioning clear, 2004, p. 82.)

Her previous album *Chaleur Humaine*'s (2014) videos are set in colour-saturated empty performance spaces, reminiscent of theatre and dance rehearsal rooms and stages. Emptier than the second album's music video settings, they hint at the possibilities of invention. Maybe in part, a nod to her background in theatre studies (in Lyon and Paris), they are suggestive of her beginning to write her own script; the empty spaces are slates she can write on, and she uses her body as a space for invention too. They are also out of time. There are no temporal markers, nothing other than the body (or bodies) in space.

The music video for the hugely successful single 'Christine' (YouTube views 14,529,883, 3/10/18) showcases Letissier dancing with four male dancers on top of a platform in an empty space. They are first seen in silhouette against a vivid, dark blue. The camera shoots from underneath the platform, honing in on her feet as they dance and the whole video's aesthetic could be described as minimalist, where architectural form (of her body, her dancers' bodies and the shapes they cast against the blue space) is prized. Its setting suggested artiness, seriousness. It looked like it could be an installation in a high-end art gallery, but its pop sound, hooks, production all geared it to a dance track. The emphasis in that music video was on Letissier's body as it danced, the movements it made. It focused on the female body in process. It was about the female body in dialogue – with the male dancers around her, and with her internal dialogue about being 'tilted', a phrase which the setting emphasised further by having the platform they were performing on at an angle.

Carol Vernallis' classic work on the aesthetics and components of music video argued that the form differed from film in its use of settings in the following way:

> The functions of music-video setting differ from those of classic Hollywood film. The locations that appear most often in music video tend to be generic depictions, suggesting a concept of place, or representing a kind of place, rather than providing a detailed description of a specific setting – a beach, train station, concert hall, bridge, toilet, apartment, bar or street corner.
>
> (Vernallis, 2004, pp. 74–75)

The generic space of Letissier's 'Christine' and 'Paradis Perdu' (11,647 YouTube views, 4/10/18), where she is alone against a blank stage, sat on a chair in a dusty pale pink suit, are spaces of invention. They suggest the stages of contemporary dance, of 'high art' theatre. This is echoed too in 'No Harm is Done' (YouTube views 2,758,528, 3/10/18), where she walks, again in a dark blue space, this time through neon white tubes. Dressed in beige vest and high-waisted beige trousers the emphasis is again on her body, but on its sinews and movement. There are close ups of her and clearly, she is the focus, as the video is part of the commodity that is 'Christine (and the Queens)'.

Letissier also works with the space of the body, manipulating it, dressing it, building it up; using it as a canvas. The first album showcased her as a suit wearing chic French chanteuse. She wore black suits, white buttoned up shirts. When not in black, she was in muted single colours, pink oversized suits in 'Paradis Perdus' (2015) and beige vests and trousers ('No Harm is Done'). They are simple, pared back, androgynously classy. On the second album, the video for the title track 'Girlfriend' sees her wearing a cut off white vest, loose trousers and white sneakers. Her hair has been shorn into a close crop. The look, as does the music, channels the 1980s' pop of Michael Jackson, Prince and early Madonna (the white crop top from *Desperately Seeking Susan* (Seidelman, 1985). Importantly, the vocal range is the same as on *Chaleur Humaine*; Letissier has only changed her look and her videos' performance spaces. The videos give her 'space to experiment with image' (Lewis, 1993, p. 109) as Lisa Lewis argues it did when it first appeared in the early 1980s.

The videos act as a space where Letissier can showcase not how to perform gender, but how to reveal it as a construct and a myth. They provide a forum wherein she can deconstruct the 'accoutrements of femininity' (Mulvey, 1991, p. 141) and masculinity. That she does this within a medium that is dance, pop oriented, no matter how 'eccentric' (2018) it might be illustrates how her work, along with Monáe's and Anohni's, makes sense now, in the second decade of the twenty-first century. She (as Christine) and he (as Chris) are finding a third space within which to operate outside of a gender binary. Like Monáe, this third space may include bisexuality, like Anohni, it definitely acknowledges gender fluidity and her work, as Letissier, puts into popular culture work that looks at gender as a continuum rather than a category.

A French pop star has travelled across the Atlantic and is reworking the myths of Americana, in playfully dancing across its historical building sites and remaking its 1980s music (it is indebted musically to Michael Jackson with its licks and to Prince with its guitar riffs) from an avowedly 'gender queer' alter ego. The practice of being 'someone else' on stage (and across the many sites of the pop star's persona, video, performance, interview, etc.) goes back to Bowie (Ziggy Stardust), Nina Hagen, Klaus Nomi, Gary Numan, Sun Ra and Clinton (Dr Funkenstein). Not to be conflated with stage names, the alter ego becomes the pop star whilst its originator takes back stage. Letissier (as Christine and Chris) and Monáe (as Cindi Meriweather then as Jane 57821) both use their alter egos to explore non-binary spaces and places across popular music's history where queerness and transgression were being explored.

Anohni and the nowhere places

Anohni doesn't use an alter ego in her performances but she does use other bodies in ways that might be interpreted in very opposite ways. She is a transgender musician whose recent 2016 and 2017 musical work and artistic collaborations emphasise intersectionality and feminism's relationship with ecology. Anohni is the chosen name of the musician formerly known as Anthony Hegarty. Born in the UK in 1971 and raised in The States, she studied at New York University and established the avant-garde drag theatre group known as 'The Blacklips Performance Cult' (1992–1995) that performed plays in small clubs such as The Crow Bar and The Pyramid Club, a gay bar in Manhattan. She produced four albums with her band The Johnsons, started in 1998, winning critical acclaim for the 2005 album *I Am a Bird Now*, which won The Mercury Award the same year. In 2014, she publicly referred to herself in the feminine in an interview with *Flavorwire* (Halperin, 2014), and since then, she has performed as Anohni.

All except one of the videos for her 2016 album *Hopelessness* feature Black, ageing, non-normative women mouthing her lyrics, in what is a ventriloquist strategy of displacement, whereby the sound of the voice coming out of the body is not the body's. There are two potential bodies here: O'Grady's visible one, and Anohni's 'vocalic' one. The term 'vocalic body' (Connor, 2000, p. 35) describes the 'body that is produced by the voice when it is heard' (Jarman-Ivens, 2011, p. 7). That is, sound invites the listener to imagine the body from whence it comes. The imagined 'vocalic' body is thus reliant on individual memory, cultural norms and tradition. When Anohni appears within/through the lips of other women in her videos, she upsets a singular subjectivity through this process and foregrounds not only a fractured self (Waldrep, 2015, p. 113) but a compound self. This is underpinned further by the displacement or dissociation of her voice from her body, that it is somehow out of sync (Connor, 2000), and so, somehow 'out of time'.

Underpinning this sense of dischronicity is the fact that the performances are set in what I'd like to call 'nowhere' places. The videos for Hopelessness set their 'narrators' in the interrogation room and tunnel of 'Drone bomb me' or the black, blank space of 'Marrow' (and 'Crisis', 'Obama' and 'I don't love you anymore'). These are all liminal locations, on the thresholds between certainty. Either refusing to 'be' any one place (the blank backdrop of 'Marrow'), secret spaces (the interrogation room/chair) that are redolent of questioning, of torture and of tunnels, these are conduits to other places whose psychoanalytical and mythical reverberations run deep. Anohni's projected bodies are displaced people in displaced places; they are bodies in-between.

In the video 'Marrow' (2016), an elderly woman takes centre stage. She is set alone, against a blank, black space. Only her head and shoulders are in view. She wears silver earrings, a silver necklace, and has her lips painted red. She is a Black woman. And she smiles as she lip-syncs. 'Marrow' is a harrowing song of despair told from the point of view of Mother Earth. Anohni uses the language of cancer treatment to narrate Earth's tale, a story of repeated abuse, rape and plunder. O'Grady smiles at us as she lip-syncs the lyrics, the willing conduit of

Anohni's trans-gendered vocalic body. She is there as an elderly, proud, naked, Black female artist, red lipped, bejewelled, with the song sung from a white trans-gendered musician emanating from her. We have a composite subject comprised of two people for whom marginality, within a dominant heterosexual, racial and aged matrix, may materially determine their position as outsiders.

Underneath the video on YouTube, it says 'Featuring Lorraine O'Grady'. The term is different to 'starring' (see, for example, Cate Blanchett on Massive Attack's 2016 music video 'The spoils') but both are drawn from cinema culture and imply the importance of that person's participation in the project. The comments underneath the video show appreciate for both her and Anohni. She is credited, named, acknowledged and it is through this that I found out about her past. Emerging onto the New York art scene in the early 1980, her work encompasses performance pieces, photography, film and writing which have deconstructed the visual and ideological constructs around race, sexuality, power and desire. Using her own body and the bodies of others, she has questioned ownership and agency specifically with respect to relationships that are scored with historical weights and expectations. In 'Where Margins Become Centers', at The Carpenter Center of Visual Arts, she plays with ideas of racial re-location and the colonial/raced gaze. So, for her to be centre stage in an Anohni music video means something, because she brings to the performance her own history as a Black American woman who has questioned and rearticulated certain norms of representation.

Both artists confuse boundaries of gender (Anohni) and medium (O'Grady) by their refusal to observe imposed limits; they create between them a music video performance that shatters the illusion of any one secure, singular subjectivity. They offer up a performing body that is made of differing components, Black, white, ageing, female, trans. They query the predominance of one fixed speaking normative subject and offer instead the potential of a multi-aged and multi-vocalic body. This is in line with a postmodern reading of the decentred subject, or indeed its disappearance (McLeod, 2003, p. 352, referring to Jameson, 1984). There is a positive way of reading this collapse of two into one, and that is through the idea of 'idealistic non-differentiation' (McLeod, 2003, p. 350), a term used to describe the disappearance of the self-experienced by ravers on Ecstasy who encounter the idea of 'communitas' at a rave, where the self dissolves into the whole.

The video performance by Anohni's vocalic body and O'Grady's filmed body invites appraisal through the concept of 'trans-ageing'. This is the idea, developed by Deborah Moglen in 2008, that ageing is not experienced as linear. She calls for two models of thinking about ageing, the vertical and the horizontal. The vertical model is driven by repression whereas the horizontal is constituted by dissociation. This in turn takes two forms, the incorporative or the introjective function. The incorporative model is defensive, maintaining 'ghostly spectres of youth as consuming objects of loss and desire' (2008, p. 297). The introjective model, by contrast, 'initiates a dynamic and creative process in which multiple self-states of past and present are available for recognition and enactment' (2008, p. 297). This embraces the 'endlessly overlapping states of being and stages of life' (2008, p. 306). It starts to see the potential for a non-linear model of ageing, one disarticulated from a rigid chronology and characterised, instead, by relations, moments, experience and memory.

This slippage in the subject in relation to time and its experience is mirrored in the slippage around singular subjectivity and the ownership of voice that Anohni was aiming to achieve in the music video. In an interview with Edward J. Nixon (1/6/17), a colleague who mixed the *Hopelessness* album, this strategy was explicit. Nixon notes that in conversations with Anohni whilst working on the album, they discussed, for 'Marrow', 'What Mother Earth would sound like?' and that by removing her body from her voice and using the ventriloquist tactic of focusing on O'Grady she hoped to relay the possibility that she was 'speaking for all of us'. Contrary to this utopian vision of the potential of a singing splintered, multi-aged and biracial subject is the more reductive and materialist position and a question might arise as to whether she is allowing the other to speak (Waldrep, 2015, p. 134), or does she reaffirm raced power dynamics?

The liminal, nowhere places that seem to offer a productive and positive space outside of hetero-chronology might also be read in wholly different way. In Anohni's music videos Black, ageing and differently abled women are presented against black, blank canvases and reading these spaces through Jordan Peel's 'sunken places', from his 2017 film *Get Out* yields an entirely opposite possibility, one which is a racistly enabled paralysis. In the film, the protagonist is invited into a seemingly liberal white family home, made welcome, hypnotised and sent spinning out of consciousness to await lobotimisation and to have an elderly white neighbour's brain inserted in his young Black body. The film depicts the protagonist post-hypnosis as falling through a black space; there is nothing there, nothing to orientate him, nothing he can do; he is paralysed. He has been disarmed, made slave, appropriated. In a tweet, Peele explained this place 'The Sunken Place means we're marginalized. No matter how hard we scream, the system silences us' (Peele, March 2017). We could read O'Grady (and the other female bodies across her music videos) as puppets, controlled and silenced by a white puppeteer. It is always instructive to return to Stuart Hall's writing on popular culture and his 1993 work on essentialism and race suggests that 'There are always positions to be won in popular culture' (Hall, 1993, p. 108). I am a white, middle-aged academic, one of Richard Dyer's 'unmarked' in terms of race. My views on whether or not these blank spaces are or are not positive are largely irrelevant, they are indeed, 'academic', given that my body is not 'raced' and subject to discrimination in the ways that Peele notes. And the conversations around real, material, murderousness attitudes around race (particularly in the USA) temper and inform conversations around these 'sunken places' or 'nowhere places'. Conversations around power, access to representation and enunciation within popular culture and in these videos reveal schisms between different lived experiences, where different histories and embodied memories are brought to them. Maybe I saw age in them first as age is what I was looking for. And maybe I ignored race because I, as a privileged white person, could do so. This was a mistake. Having acknowledged this, the question of whether Anohni 'allows the

Other to speak' (Waldrep, 2015, p. 134) has emerged as a result of where the video has landed: in a popular cultural environment where the politics of the real has collided with an artist's perhaps naïve intentions of voicing the self. In an interview with *The Creative Independent* (October, 2016), Anohni discusses her work, her art (installation pieces in Bielefeld, Germany) and her reluctance to always put her body in the frame. She says 'I don't have to fulfil this expectation that my body is always fully exposed and front and center' (2016) and lists all the areas (which appear in her songs on the album) that she laments:

> I think of things like the subjugation of women, drone warfare, neoliberal capitalism, Christian and Islamic fundamentalism, racism, police brutality, mass incarceration, massive wealth disparity, corporate sovereignty, the weapons industry, the fossil fuel industry, the chemical and pharmaceutical industries, population explosion, factory farming, and the destruction of wilderness as opportunist infections.

Arguments will be made for whether her decision to put Black and elderly bodies centre stage in a blank space is progressive or not, and this speaks into the idea that Paul Railton and Diane Watson described in their 2011 work on the politics of representation in music video, where they argued that music video's meaning is very often ambiguous and 'messy'.

Despite this, I would like to argue that there is a degree of similarity between these three female musicians in their attempts to carve out queer spaces: spaces where difference might emerge and linearity (and progress) might be queried. Monáe seeks to mobilise science-fiction spaces as positive and enabling, as other Afrofuturists have done to 'provid[e] an empowering voice to many marginalised identities' (McLeod, 2003, p. 338). Letissier uses these nostalgic and chronologically external spaces as places for creative examination of gender and sexuality, and Anohni uses an amalgamated self, from the bodies of elderly, Black women with the voice of her transgender, non-binary vocalic body to release an anti-war, pro-environmentalist album.

Conclusion

Monáe's, Letissier's and Anohni's music video performances all draw on the idea of a 'somewhere else'. It's not 'over the rainbow' but it is close. Be it Monáe's Afrofuturist future mode, Letissier's use of future nostalgia or Anohni's problematic use of nowhere places and deflection of the self, all three musicians locate their work in places of potential. They are making music that as McLeod, writing so persuasively of aliens and space/place in 2003 argued, maps out a 'politics of potential, of who we might become' (McLeod, 2003, p. 339). And they work in the broad arena of 'pop'. They insert queer voices, bodies and desires into a mainstream popular discourse and they are being seen and heard by large audiences.

All three musicians are involved in 'de-centring' (Waldrep, 2015, p. 165), whereby they divert attention from their own body via alter egos (Monáe and

Letissier) and other bodies (Anohni). These alter egos and replacements for themselves perform in spaces outside of the recognisable 'now': in times outside of a contemporary space. These are de-centred spaces that exist on the margins of both the real (as in time) and the heteronormative imaginary. They are the imagined futures of Black, queer voices, the safe spaces of a queer archive of pop histories and the black future voids of disembodiment. They are queered spaces wherein queer, gender; fluid, transgendered voices and ageing bodies are emblematic of a 'queer time' (Halberstam, 2005, p. 4). Writing in 2005, Puar argues that 'Queer times require even queerer modalities of thought, analysis, creativity and expression' (2005, p. 12) and the video performances and musical presence of Janelle Monáe, Heloise Letissier and Anohni are part of these queer modalities. And as they perform in their chosen future, past and nowhere spaces, they map out a way of being that is living across times and bodies. And as living is ageing, so they age queerly.

4 Ageing with alt-rock and folk

> 56-year-old twin sisters just recorded the best punk track of the year. Now THAT'S punk!
>
> (Raasch, 2018. www.youtube.com/watch?v=5i76b0OrdIQ)

The Breeders are past their youth. They are in the late 50s. But the musical milieu they work in, an 'alternative rock' that is indebted to punk, is coded 'as' young. The Rheingans Sisters and The Askew Sisters are young female musicians working in an 'old' style of music that reifies antiquity: British folk. This chapter looks at these three bands' current output and performances across music video, websites and blogs to argue they depict a collision, or a *time-crunch*; an encounter between an embodied, represented age and a genre-age, which results in a generic ageing.

Imagine two lines: one is the linear route from youth to age that has been queried by writers who queer it (Halberstam, 2005; Freeman, 2010), see it as too unaware of multi-modal fluidities of memory and the subconscious (Moglen, 2008) and which were looked at in the previous chapter. The other one, running in parallel, is a 'genre-age' line. It has a specific historical point of origin (so UK punk will start at 1976, grunge will start in 1991, folk is 'timeless' but its resurgences have specific points of origin) and will continue in a recognisable linear fashion. The 'point of origin' is important and how it has been delivered into popular culture is reliant on this point as it is on key players, events and historical moments of its life story. My contention here is that musicians can be considered as operating on two different points on those two lines where the 'genre-age' line is flexible, bendy; it can envelope the 'life line' at any point and circumvent it. When it does this, the individual musician or artist becomes generically aged. Genre-age is made up of two core components: points of origin and metatextual aesthetics.

This is a phenomenon not restricted to women, but it has implications especially for the interplay between female expression and for female representation. Indeed, a key question that will be addressed is to ask if the suturing of generic youth onto the ageing Breeders' bodies somehow accompanies an ongoing absence of age within these ageing female bodies by ensuring they remain a 'continuing site of gender and sexuality?' (Woodward, 2006). Or, alternatively, that the 'genre-age' works to de-emphasise, or downplay The Rheingans Sisters and The Askew Sisters' embodied and youthful age in a way that focuses more on their musicianship (ageless) and place within a recognised British folk lineage. In both cases, the 'real' bodies are displaced, always somewhere else; they have a 'generic age' which is their positioning within the historical narratives and aesthetic of the genre within which they are identified.

To do this, the chapter explores arguments on ageing in popular music (Melina, 2008; Bennett, 2013) and agelessness (Katz, 2018) to suggest that historical memories of genre as distinctively *aged* 'narratives' are present within the materially ageing and materially youthful bodies of these musicians (Hubble and Tew, 2013). The stories of punk, 'alternative rock' and 'folk' are stitched into the current performances of these musicians as cultural memory. The musicians chosen are sisters and I do this to suggest that their bodies are inscribed not only by (generic) cultural memory but that this is compounded by cultural myths around sisterhood that position it as an 'outside' or 'elsewhere' space.

The chapter is an exploration of the flexibility of age. It is about how age is written into particular generic bodies, both as bodies of work and real bodies, performing and playing music, bodies that 'still' engender desire in their fans. It is also about timelessness, a concept that emerges in some of the writing on the Breeders comeback album *All Nerve* (2013) and in the music of The Rheingans Sisters and The Askew Sisters. I think through that idea of timelessness in relation to the 'classic' status of two genres whose own time codes, despite the role of young people within it (folk) and its ongoing longevity and meaning to older people (alt-rock and punk), remain set very specifically, and stubbornly, to old (folk) and young (alt-rock and punk).

Staging age

When this chapter was first proposed, its focus was on youth. I considered starting from the premise that the 'band' is historically, discursively and popularly constructed as male: a band of brothers. What seemed to be happening was that more young women's bands were being promoted, reviewed and making a play for recognition. The premise was that bands such as Haim, Hinds, Goat Girl, Cherry Glazer, Honeyblood, Savages and Warpaint were ushering into Anglophone popular music culture, particular notions of female desire. The emphasis was to be on female sexuality and independent desire, exploring constructions of innocence and sisterly community within 'the band' to ask what scope it offers for new representations of 'sisterhood' and how tied to the notion of 'girlhood' and desire these expressions are.

This was underscored by noticing how many bands whose members are all, or majority, women are referred to in the music press and online radio as 'female-fronted' (*Rolling Stone*, 2008; Braidwood, 2018; Cooper, 2018; Radiox, 2018). This feeling was woefully misplaced. I was victim of what Marion Leonard noted Kim Deal of The Pixies had complained of in the 1990s. Women have always been part of popular music history. This may seem obvious, but as Leonard points out, journalists have a habit of repeatedly writing about women in popular music and rock as a resurgence or 'exposé' (2007, p. 34), which makes 'this history of women within popular music – or more specifically – rock music, appear stilted and discontinuous' (2007, p. 34). I had fallen prey to that narrative. Leonard quotes a personal communication with Kim Deal, September 5, 1995, who laments how:

> Since the Pixies started I've been doing interviews since about 1986….This is the question I hate: "What about the resurgence of women in rock now?" I get asked that about every six months, or not even every six months, about every three months I get asked about the resurgence of women in rock.
>
> (Leonard, 2007, p. 35)

Deal's quote forced me to reconsider my approach, and to think not only about youth as an age stage within a life course, but to consider youth/age as age stages that could be performed on older/younger bodies through the process of generic ageing. I am not talking about girlhood, as that area is ably covered by other researchers (Warwick, 2007; Warwick and Adrian, 2016) and I am not interested here in expressions of 'girl'ness, nor even of Riotgrrl-ness, as that would be to double up on work already written and this is not about girl 'groups' as defined by Warwick but 'the band' (similar to O'Brien's 2016 work). So rather than dwell on the liminality of the teenage years as the word 'girl' invites (Warwick, 2007), the shifting of the focus to how different manifestations of youthfulness, as opposed to 'girl'ness (that include 'cuteness'), are staged within ageing bodies and antiquities of lineage is hosted within performances by younger women.

'Staging age' is about age as performance (Woodward, 2006; Melina, 2008), of a chronological masquerade. This means that like gender, it can muster any number of 'accoutrements' of (young) femininity to perform that age stage. Vocal techniques (Warwick, 2007), vocalic bodies (Connor, 2000), self-presentation in performance and discursive positioning all combine to project youthfulness onto bodies no longer 'young'. These performances of age all take place within generic mise-en-scenes; that is, 'alternative rock' and 'folk' music are historically situated and discursively policed. Performing age is achieved within specific generically constituted matrices that are embedded within cultural memory.

Generic ageing (embodied genre-age)

Before going any further, I want to clarify what I mean by 'generic ageing'. The key argument here is that age is pegged to specific moments of generic phenomena and that these accompany the band and its members as they age. This is not restricted to women, nor is it for bands only, it also works with solo artists, but the focus on the 'band' brings into the discussion some interesting issues around ageing and female 'voice'. For example, Paul Weller is a British musician who has been working in the music industry for over 40 years. Starting out with The

Jam in 1972, he is still recording and performing. But he is the 'Angry Young Man'; however, old he gets, his ageing present is haunted by a youthful past that, in turn, is imbricated with periods in British youth culture of progressive politics and rebellion. At 53, his ageing is inflected both by his own past and by the broader cultural movements that he is contextually bound up in, specifically two English subcultures, mod and punk. He functions as a reminder of past progressive politics; on YouTube, The Jam are described as 'mod revivalist/ punk', clearly heralding a band whose music looks back to the 1960s but is also versed in the pared down confrontational rhetoric of punk and its anti-racist and anti-sexist politics. Through these ongoing alliances, whereby Weller acts as a 'memory product' (Van Dijck, 2007, p. 7.), he, as a successful ager, manages to retain this sense of youthfulness, which is exemplified by his industry presence as an ongoing creative force and his refutation of nostalgia, despite claims of the problematically nostalgia-drenched nature of his earlier music with The Jam (Reynolds in Zuberi, 2001, p. 66). Weller's age is determined not only by his bodily age but by the genres and histories he is aligned to.

Genre-age

> "Punk is not an easy thing to define," says Andy Linehan, curator of popular music at the British Library. "As with any type of music, people will say, 'That's punk', 'No, *that*'s punk'. Some say punk died in a specific year, others say punk lives." For the exhibition he's staging, to mark the 40th anniversary of the movement, Linehan has decided to limit his focus to the explosive period between 1976 and 78 when punk first gatecrashed the public consciousness. "We're looking at the initial burst," he says, "and the impact it had – punk's legacy."
>
> (Fox, 2016)

Linehan is spot on. It is very difficult to define punk, and indeed the same goes for 'folk'. And the opening sentences of this chapter used the word 'milieu' to describe the environment which the Breeders work in. There is a difference; milieu is similar to Bourdieu's 'habitus' and encompasses the multiple layers within which the music is produced, disseminated and lived; genre seems tighter, more taxonomised by musical type. I am using 'genre' here as a musical marker that is inflected by time and experience. There are obviously very many subgenres of both punk and folk and so for the argument here I am closing those off in order to prioritise ageing and to think through more broadly, what is at stake when considering how age appears within these genres as it is performed by the older and younger women within them. 'Genre' lies at the centre of numerous musicological debates (Fabbri, 1980; Bannister, Gamble, Hansen and Kennedy at 2018 IASPM conference, Holt, 2007) and generates entire panels at academic conferences.

Trying to 'nail' it down is fraught, as distinctions related to emotion, streaming start to add into musicological ideas about it (Ratliff, 2016). As the introduction established, this book is not written from a musicological perspective but from a Cultural Studies one and so this chapter is underpinned by Franco Fabbri's 1980 notion of genre. He calls it 'a set of musical events…whose course is governed by a definite set of socially accepted rules' (1980, p. 52). Acknowledging that there are a number of taxonomical avenues into understanding 'genre' (Aucoutrier and Pachet, 2003), not least that they are part of a broader nexus of locale and belonging (Lena, 2012), my way into marking out genre is in the visual and sonic stories they tell, and which tell them. They are historically positioned and aesthetically and sonically 'coded' into recognisable, but contentious formats. This means that genres are aged. They have a 'time stamp' (Charles, 2019). They can be identified as starting somewhere, some place and their achievements and key stories are subject to memorialisation and institutional legitimisation. They are referred to with temporal adjectives to determine when they were, like this sentence from Kitty Empire's 2017 review of the band playing live in London in 2017, 'Deal is known, superficially, for having the grunge era's best pop ear'.

The Breeders are alternately punk, grunge, alt-rock or indie-pop depending on who you read that has written about them. On I-Tunes, Discogs and Wikipedia they are 'alternative', and so for the purposes of contingency and alliance with key market taste co-ordinators and archives in the industry, this is the genre that they will be considered within. 'Alt- rock' can trace its (musical and ideological) ancestry back to punk. Reviews of their most recent 2018 album refer to them as 'punk' (Bhatiya, 2018; Vaziri, 2018), 'alt-rock' (Empire, 2017; Jenkins, 2018), 'indie' (Mackay, 2015) and 'alt-pop' (Johnston, 2018). These three different ways into situating the Breeders conjure up related sonic signatures, key figures and bands as well as specific places. Alt-rock emerges in America in the late 1980s and builds on the anti-establishment ideology of punk and indie music, where indie is 'a genre with a strong investment in difference' (Bannister, 2006, p. 58), which has played a 'counter cultural role' (Bannister, 2006, p. 78), providing 'space for women to perform and produce' (Schilt, 2004; Leonard, 2007; Reddington, 2007). It is typified by The Pixies and Dinosaur Junior. Because it is reliant on punk's DIY and anarchist aesthetic, the 'spirit of punk' that journalists refer to haunts it; Punk is in alt-rock's DNA. And punk, as Linehan at the British Library explains, is choosing his own way of defining punk to celebrate its anniversary, by limiting it chronologically to a specific two years of intense production. A musical scene whose musical aesthetic is now memorialised by national institutions (as well as recalled in women musicians' memoirs) is one that is considered, among other things, as an important cultural event. It is thus affixed to a point of origin.

Punk did not merely last two years as is well documented. Its adherents, musicians and fans continue to listen to and 'be' punk (Bennett, 2006). Rebellion festival happens every August in the north of the UK (line up 2019); punk has travelled, making sense as it encounters sociopolitical and cultural traditions that are germane to its ideologies and aesthetics (Indonesia, Thailand, Los Angeles China). As Worley, going partly against Hebdige, notes, it 'may be understood as an ethos and an attitude rather than a music or sartorial style' (2011, p. 70). As a lifestyle it is both of a time and temporally adaptable. As a genre, it is coded as young even as it ages. This is because of its original rebelliousness against the music which predated it (Rotten's famous 'I hate Floyd' T-shirt). It had a youthful disregard for virtuosity and authority which was played out in the media as a moral panic narrative, with youth's major role being the new 'folk-devil' (Cohen, 1972). It didn't respect, or need, age. It was starting from a Ground Zero.

Folk, in contrast, is firmly grounded. It is a genre whose elders and archives are crucial to its sense of self. It has many different points of origin: be it through Cecil Sharp's early twentieth century collecting, Ewan McColl's 1960s' intervention or the recent 'resurgence' (Winters and Keegan Phipps, 2013; Gardner and Jennings, 2019). It is a genre whose own archives are fixated on points of origin and interpretation and in determining some kind of 'ancestry'. In a paper on American folk music and race, Roy argues for the idea of 'aesthetic identity' working to act as social boundaries whereby certain music becomes racially 'coded' (2002, p. 463). Not wanting to step into a whole different debate, it is his idea of coding especially that can be transferred across to British folk music and 'alternative rock' as it is delivered via different discursive mechanisms such as album covers, websites and reviews that surround the music itself, to claim that it is 'coded as' old. The oldness that is circulating around The Rheingans Sisters and The Askew Sisters is such as to make writers claim them as 'timeless' (a term used for other folk music too, Dishman, 2015; on Sam Lee's recent work, see Gardner and Jennings, 2019), because despite their provenance being so particular (rural Derbyshire for The Rheingans Sisters), they can't be 'placed' within any one chronological point. Oldness here, and so 'age' becomes less a point on a linear chronology but more a textural aesthetic: one that is encoded into the instruments themselves, the violins, banjos, dulcimers, pipes, tambourin à cordes, flabuta, that are either old, handed down or whose own histories go back to the Middle Ages.

Age is also apparent in the idea of the interpretation of a repertoire, where another folk sibling duo, The Askew Sisters' 2014 album *In the Air or the Earth*, contains many folk standards, whose origins, covers and lyrics are hosted on the 'Mainly Norfolk' website, an archive of British folk music. 'Maid on the Shore' (sung by Peggy Seeger in 1959 and Martin McCarthy in 1966), 'The Wife of Usher's Well (covered by Peggy Seeger, 1957 and Bellowhead, 2002), 'The Unquiet Grave' (covered by Shirley Collins in 1959 and again in 1967), 'Young Girl Cut Down' (again, covered by Shirley Collins, 1970) and 'I Wish That The Wars Were All Over' (covered by Eliza McCarthy and the Ratcatchers in 2007) are all part of an established Anglo-American folk repertoire to which they are contributing as part of a continuum which is always being added to.

Folk has antiquarian reification at its very heart, in its own archiving procedures, in its honour of lineage and in the grain of others' voices whose songs now reside in the present. Age has long been valued within British folk music because it is conflated with tradition and canon. In her ethnographic study of music making in Milton Keynes, Ruth Finnegan notes how local folk musicians 'regarded the test for whether a song (even a new song) really was "folk" as being whether it passed into the "oral tradition": "if it's valid after twenty years then it's folk"' (2007, p. 67). This endorsement that age bestows is also apparent in the reference throughout folk music and its internal and representative discourse, to 'roots', such as 'regional, rural roots' (Frith 1996, p. 84; Finnegan, 2007, p. 67). References to folklore 'as something that is implanted deep in the soil and soul of the people' (ibid., p. 66), also fix folk music as emerging from a time possibly beyond recorded history. Folk becomes aligned to fairy tale or myth, and thus also potentially conflated with the fantastical and the fictional, which are the very opposite of the 'real' or 'authentic' which also defines it. And I want to draw a line from this notion of folk myth to myths around sisters, siblings, as there is in this alliance a congruence of narratives that place both folk and sisterhood, as somehow beyond, or past; genres and units that have a mythological force.

Addressing absences

> There's something about the chemistry between musical siblings, possibly even a research study in there somewhere.
>
> (Ainscoe, 2018)

At a biannual IASPM conference in Huddersfield in 2018, some delegates found themselves around a table playing a game when they should have been in panels; I was one of them. The game was called 'name a band with siblings in it' and it threw up The Jackson Five, Hanson, The Everly Brothers and UB40. These were all bands of brothers. They did come up with The Carpeneters, then Sister Sledge, The Pointer Sisters and The Andrew Sisters, but few others. These delegates, men and women, were all music academics, some with an encyclopaedic knowledge of music, able to reel off band member names with aplomb. Why then were they (and I include myself in that) slower off the mark to name sisters in bands?

This is anecdotal, yes, but there is something worth commenting on in it. Absence is important to notice because, as Sara Ahmed has written in *Living a Feminist Life*, 'if a world can be what we learn not to notice, noticing becomes a form of political labor' (2017, p. 32). Coupled to Richard Dyer's benchmark work on 'Whiteness' where the unmarked white is powerfully absent and the Other is always marked and spelt out, this chapter is about noticing the unmarked, arguing not only, as others have done, that 'the band' is historically, discursively and popularly constructed as male and white, but that it carries with it certain marks of agelessness. I want to illustrate that with a second anecdote.

Another light-hearted game followed a month later, this time on Twitter on October 10, 2018, I asked followers to name 'sisters in bands'. I didn't specify genre or time frame and this is the list that was generated:

> Haim, The Unthanks, The McGarrigle Sisters, The Breeders, All Saints, the Orielles, The Nolans, Tegan and Sara, Wilson Phillips, Heart, Dixie Chicks, The Staples Singers, Boswells, The Roches, The Reynolds Girls, Mel and Kim, The Corrs, B'witched, Eternal, Destiny's Child, The Ronettes, The Partridge Family, Throwing Muses, The Shaggs, Five Star, First Aid Kit, The Mandrell Sisters.

Yes, it was a kind of 'pop quiz', but it highlights two ideas: one conceptual and one material that I want to address. First, this is a historically 'mixed bag' and I will develop this idea of a chronological 'mix' as I go through the chapter. It goes back to the 1960s and to African American 'girl groups' (The Ronettes); it covers pop from the 1980s (Mel and Kim), the 1990s (The Corrs, All Saints) and the 2000s (Destiny's Child). It has the cult/obscure (The Shaggs), the kitsch (The Partridge Family), the rock (The Breeders), the AOR (Haim, Heart), the indie (The Orielles) and the folk (First Aid Kit, The Unthanks, The McGarrigle Sisters). This list came from music journalists, popular music academics and administrative staff from my networks. People brought their own experiences and knowledge to the list. And asking for a list of 'sisters in bands' obscures the genre and time of those bands, since the primary identifier was 'sisters'.

A lot of academic work is about noticing a 'gap' and working to fill it: about adding to the debate. Looking in on something with a different lens, with the focus on siblings, 'sisters' offers a really interesting space within which to manoeuvre. It means that looking at bands of sisters takes me away from the 'female-fronted band' or 'women in rock' (which includes solo artists) tag and establishes a pan-generic connection from 'girl bands' to 'girl groups' where a group, as Warwick explains:

> comprises several distinct elements: an emphasis on the concerns and interests of teenage girls in its lyrics…; material prepared for the most part by professional songwriters; origins in the recording studio and dependent upon professional session musicians; an instrumental sound often dominated by orchestral instruments….and above all, the audible adolescent voices of girls interacting in dialogues between lead and backing vocalists.
>
> (Warwick, 2007, p. ix)

Warwick's (2007) work on girl groups of the 1960s is a compelling and exhaustive history of the field, and her co-edited collecting on 'voicing girlhood' (Warwick and Adrian, 2016) has already mapped out the area of girl studies in relation to popular music, beyond girl groups. My intention here is not to reiterate this work but rather to build on some of its findings in relation to age (especially Appolloni's chapter on ageing and ingénues, 2016) and innocence. I want to wrest the attention towards the idea of ageing, where age is neither a singular nor chronologically linear matter. That is, age is not fixed to one body, but attributed to what that body means in its role as one part in a generic and historical nexus. As I have already said, I am not arguing that this only happens with sisters, or for women. But by focusing in on bands with sisters or bands of sisters (and twins) offers a specific field of enquiry enabling the exploration of ideas of the mythology and literature of sisterhood that are added into the discussion in order to augment ideas around timelessness and spaces of ageing.

I am also using Luce Irigaray's (1985) notion of the 'elsewhere'. 'Elsewhere' is the term she uses to mark out a non-phallocentric space. Her work has been used by feminist popular music scholars to understand the presentational techniques deployed by musicians such as Annie Lennox (Reynolds and Press, 1995; Whiteley, 2000). Which largely drew on her idea of mimesis, a strategy of destabilising representational codes and to 'reframe how women might be placed within culture' (Gardner, 2015, p. 26). As a strategy it relies on excess, in over-doing so that the natural becomes strange. This 'strange' space then becomes a place of production external to a universalising phallocentric economy. When writing about PJ Harvey, I suggested that 'elsewhere' might be added to mimesis and used to understand places that were also 'removed from the present' (2016, p. 119); that disarticulated or distant spaces which might enable women to speak Irigaray's elsewhere is a space for the female irrational that is outside of a phallocentric economy. It lies beyond the ordinary, the logical, the rational. It is where women have been consigned as irrational, a space that Irigaray validates; 'where women write, think, paint and create' (Gardner, 2015, p. 119). I suggested here that the notion of 'elsewhere' could be extended to be a place removed from the present or from the self. It then becomes a productive place (Diamond, 1997) where women can reflect, negotiate and speak from. I have used this in previous work, notably to mark out PJ Harvey's music video performances as being staged in elsewhere-like spaces (underwater, beaches, motorways, motel rooms) and what they might mean. I used this idea in previous chapters to talk about the enunciative potential of future/nowhere spaces. Running with this idea again, I use the term to understand (familial) sisterhood as an elsewhere place.

Another 'elsewhere place' is the band itself. It lies somewhere beyond the domestic and private sphere yet it is not fully within the public. For young punk women, 'being in a band was a political act' (Bayton, 1997, p. 68). It meant some kind of incursion into male terrain. When Robert Walser, writing about heavy metal, noted how 'notions of gender circulate in the texts, sounds, images and practices of genre discourse' (1993, p. 109 cited in O'Meara, 2003, p. 302), he did not mention how the 'band' itself is coded as 'male' and a young maleness at that. As Warwick (2007) argues, girls were in 'girl groups' in the 1960s, not bands. They were in duos, they were backing singers, they were lead singers. Women were always 'with' the band as opposed to 'in' the band. It is also persuasive to read 'the band' itself as marked by time, in so far as it emerges as coterminous with 'rock' in the mid- to late 1960s. Whilst the band, like genres, is historically positioned, it is clearly, obviously, both a real thing, tangible, marketed, lived, represented, encountered and of its time. It is also trans-temporal, and linked to genre histories and points of location. How might sisters be members of such units?

Sisters are 'elsewhere' (doing it for themselves)

If we play with the idea of 'sisterhood' a little, we get the sense of its feminist history of solidarity and community. It has come to mean a perceived commonality of female experience. If we move across to the idea of 'sisters', we maintain that sense of a shared history and a commonality of experience, but we add into it the potential for family strife, secrets, dysfunctionality and of a specifically female only unit. I am not suggesting that sisters might be represented as ageing differently to non-sisters, but that focusing in on sisters allows for the idea of a potential elsewhere to be added to the idea of embodied and genre-age. In 2001, Chris Rojek suggested that the rock star has access to a moral and sexual elsewhere (Gardner, 2015, p. 127) set apart from the everyday, and although this was focused on a particular type of male rock star, it does offer another tangent to the sense of sisters operating in a space that is configured as its own moral universe.

> I dreamt last night of the three weird sisters.
> To you they have show'd some truth
>
> (Banquo (21–22) *Macbeth*)

In English literature and Anglo-American cinema, sisters have been used as a vehicle to examine female solidarity, desire and dysfunction. These stories go back to Greek myth (The Three Fates, Three Muses, Three Graces) and Shakespeare, whose 'weird sisters' became witches as the historical and political context developed. Shamas (2007) charts how the initial adjective 'weyward', in the first folio of Macbeth, became 'wyrd' and how this then turned into 'weird'. Her account refers to the cover of the first imprint of the play, where the three sisters are well dressed, young, with elaborate and ornate headgear. The print change from wayward to wyrd heralded the myth of 'Wyrd' a Saxon triple goddess (Shamas, 2007, p. 3); one of many female Trinitarian archetypes and the weirdness of these foretellers of doom have since been represented as voodoo priestesses (by Orson Welles in 1948), as an old hag (Kurosawa, 1957), as 'ugly mortal witches, sexy siren temptresses' (Shamas, 2007, p. 1). She argues that the Macbeth sisters, and the way in which their mutation from three 'sisters' to evil incarnate witches are crucial in contemporary representations of women: 'Our cultural understanding and definition of women, as evidenced in classical dramatic English literature, was forever transformed by this representation of three female witch sisters as part of the "collective shadow" of western culture' (2007, p. 5). Shamas' observations dovetail with classic feminist readings of the Madonna/Whore narratives (Warner, 1994).

Writing about sisters in Victorian literature, May (2001) observes that they come to signify chasteness and are key to a successful Victorian domicile. When ideas about the private and public sphere were changing as a result of new ways of working due to the Industrial Revolution, new versions of femininity were needed. The mother could police the domestic space and be considered virtuous but she too was stained by sex, by the very requirements of her role. It was the sister who lay beyond desire and was thus sacrosanct, or as May puts it, 'the sister is a sanctum sanctorum of moral virtue' (2001, p. 18). Literature has used the place of sisterhood as a key enunciative space within which to consider contemporary issues of the time (Hirai, 1998; May, 2001), but at the heart of this space is the sense of distance from a phallocracy that allows for critique, for humour and for Macbeth, damnation.

These myths and historical narratives of the sister inform cinema: sisters as evil or 'wyrd', *Whatever Happened to Baby Jane* (1962, Aldrich), *The Virgin Suicides* (1999, Coppola); sisterhood as a supportive 'sanctorum', *Hannah and Her Sisters* (1986, Allen), *Ginger Snaps* (2000, Fawcett), *Soul Food* (1997, Tilman), *Sense and Sensibility* (1995, Ang). This is clearly not an exhaustive analysis of the role of the 'sister' within Anglo-American literary and film culture nor do I want it to be. It is meant to flag up some of the myths circulating around the notion of the sister that might be apparent in the representational methods used to deliver musicians, who just so happen to be sisters, to their audiences and, in so doing, add in another dimension with reference to how they age. We might add 'sister' as a third trajectory upon which these bands might travel through time. That is, a trajectory of myths of sisterhood that stretches back to Greek myth and still holds sway within Anglo-American popular culture today. In short, sisterhood is a transhistorical unit that has been mobilised by writers and film-makers to suggest both female/familial solidarity and female exceptionalism.

Antiquarian youngsters

> The sisters hail from rural Derbyshire, where they were steeped in folk music, not least by that of their mother, herself a talented musician. They learned to play the violin on instruments handmade by their luthier father (Helmut Rheingans, who still provides their violins and banjos to this day), and this has led to a closeness of the relationship between instrument and player that lends Bright Field an extra layer of personal history and familiarity.
>
> (Blake, 2018)

There are a number of 'sister' bands on the contemporary British folk music scene. One of these is The Rheingans Sisters, whom Blake, writing in *Folk Radio* (March 21, 2018), describes as 'hailing from rural Derbyshire'. The piece works to place these two sisters not only in a specific geographical location but in a family lineage that is not merely historical and familiar but historically weighted. 'Hail' is not a word in current parlance in the UK. They are the recipients of a particular type of heritage, inheriting instruments and musical knowledge from their parents. This is not a new phenomenon within the British folk scene, which is characterised by a reification of provenance and lineage. Part of this discourse is a veneration for age, both within performance and as understood *as* tradition. 'Age' within the folk music traditions of the British Isles (in this case) is allied to authenticity (Connell and Gibson, 2003, p. 43). This term has generated and continues to engender, numerous debates (Moore 2002; Knox, 2008) but for understanding how it fits with age and folk music, Brocken's contribution is clear. He writes that 'Authenticity is used as an index or an indicator of a musical past, as a historical meter in the re-establishment of a living dialogue with a tradition' (2003, p. 89). By extending the notion of the authentic text (the song) across to it being embodied in the living transmitter of that song (the 'tradition bearer', the singer of the song) then the folk singer too is allied, through history, genre and context to 'the authentic' (Knox, 2008; Connell and Gibson, 2003; Frith and Horne, 1987). For The Rheingans Sisters, authenticity is generated by the music they produce (as they work within a recognised generic tradition), in the familial networks within which they operate (with the family being an 'authentic' 'anti-commercial' (Roy, 2002) unit separate from 'the industry'). Obviously, family groups have operated across genre (The Jacksons, The Partridge Family, The Bee Gees) and management by a family member over another (Paul Weller and his father), but the fact that the 'family' is reified as the creative unit from within which these musicians emerge does have some coded sense of them being within a unit that is not predicated on commerce.

The sisters are from the countryside. The album features a field. Their work belongs to the strand of British folk music that has pastoral rather than protest leanings. Theirs is not the folk of, say, Richard Dawson, Dick Gaughan, or even Ewan McColl and (some of) Shirley Collins, where it is the voices of the forgotten working classes, of violence and oppression that we hear. Neither is it the whimsical pastoral of the William Morris type (Gardner, 2018a), lauded as a respite from the urban. However, this pastoral 'place' is safely outside the contemporary *time* of the city (Gardner, 2017) and carries some of the pastoral's temporal traces, as this review suggests:

> 'Bright field' crackles with pastoral energy as wooden instruments and human voices connect to the landscape. From Kathleen Neeley's evocative woodcut imagery on the sleeve, to the woodland photos inside, the power of nature revealed in *Green Unstopping* and the masterpiece that is *This Forest* a sense of the power of the natural runs through.
>
> (Higgens, 2018)

Landscape looms large in The Rheingans Sisters' album, just as it does for Shirley Collins. It is not merely the subject of lyrics, upon which human loves and lost are acted out, but it is the place from which those musicians come and to which they seem bound. Six of the ten tracks on the album are about nature and their place within it: 'Bright Field', 'This Forest', 'Honeybee', 'Green Unstopping', 'Edge of the Field' and 'Three Springs'. 'This Forest' in particular might be suggestive of a British folk concern for songs of place, where that place itself (fields, moors, rivers, forests, mountains) is subject to a different time flow than the people that happen to walk over it for their span. Circadian rhythms are evoked in their songs, as is an awareness of the lives that were lost on it through war, with pipes being played at the end of the track. In his book *The Late Voice* (2015), Richard Elliott observes how folk music is typified by its preoccupation with time, where 'songs are often about the seasons as well as being traditionally used to reflect the coming or passing of times of the year' (2015, p. 22). Looking at examples of this concern with time and its passing, he suggests that folk tradition is, broadly speaking, an expression of being in the temporal world, with death emerging as a dominant theme (Elliott, 2015, p. 102).

The visual world within which the Rheingans Sisters are marketed is similar to that of their contemporaries, The Unthanks, The Askew Sisters and, to a lesser extent, The Staves, who straddle the folk/pop market. The Rheingans Sisters appear on the mast heading of their website sat against a dry-stone wall, dressed casually. Album covers for *Already Home* (2015) depict them in what appears to be a luthier's studio, possibly their fathers. *Glad, Gold Hearts* (2013) seems them sat holding their instruments in long grass and *Bright Field* (2018) uses woodcut to illustrate the fields and forests of the album. They are very much placed as women in rural working and musical environments. This is the same for The Askew Sisters, whose website image features them dressed in black sleeveless dresses upon what looks like a black hill (or a slag heap) against a cloudy sky and leafless tree, their long hair blowing in the wind. The album cover for *Through Lonesome Wood* (2010) is a black-and-white wood and they are playing their violins against a blurry green background for *All in a Garden Green* (2007). So far, so folk. The Askew Sisters' website (http://www.askewsisters.co.uk/pages/site/biog-duo.htm) describes them as follows:

> Emily and Hazel Askew have become known as two of the foremost performers and interpreters of English folk music. Their live performances brim with the depth and connection not only of two sisters, but also of two musicians who have been immersed in folk music all their lives.
>
> http://www.askewsisters.co.uk

The musical world that might be said to connect all of these bands is one conversant with the tropes of British folk music: its instrumentation, lyrical bent and concern with love, death and mortality played out upon a largely rural stage. The Rheingans Sisters are also versed in European traditions of folk music (Scandinavian and Occitan (Southern French) especially) and the one traditional song on their album is a French song ('Le Segoner').

These young women working in folk have a particular generic function. They act as the interpreters carrying on an age-old tradition, to be the latest incarnation of the songs, to be the 'tradition bearers' (Bohlman, 1988; Gardner and Jennings, 2019). They are rejuvenating figures, proving that the genre itself is a 'timeless' genre that gets handed down across generations, slightly modified as it goes. They articulate the 'maids' voices, the laments of the young women across British folk history whose songs depict love, loss and grief. They sit within a genre whose connection to the rural, be it real or ideal, situates folk again as an 'aged' genre. The rural is a place from which the young run away from/to the city. The rural is a place left behind by waves of industrial expansion and capitalisation. The rural is 'the backwater' The rural may have its own musical scenes (Driver and Bennett, 2014), but what resounds thus far within popular music history and its documentation is largely the sounds of cities: Manchester, Liverpool, Detroit, Chicago. Where they are not cities (Ibiza), they are a local that is an escape from them rather than being a place where the everyday is lived. The 2020 meeting of the IASPM in London is dedicated to 'The London Sound'. Running parallel to these dominant discourses of city-specific soundscapes and scenes is British folk. It has marketed its young musicians as coming from specifically somewhere (Gardner and Jennings, 2019).

But the rural is still a place to retire to. It is a place in England where the young cannot afford to live. All of this adds up to the swirl of agedness that coalesces around folk music despite its history being one of its resurgence being spearheaded by young people (Winters and Keegan-Phipps, 2013; Gardner and Jennings, 2019).

It is not a genre grounded in youth and desire, despite its core narratives consisting of lost love and courtship. It is a genre whose stories are told with an eye on time running out, on death creeping in and on winter freezing love and the land over. It is a genre that is coded as old, as I have already argued, and the young women musicians working in it now work to regenerate it as a vernacular, living medium for its contemporary age. Folk is a genre whose existence runs in a parallel stream to that of alternative rock and 'pop', but I would suggest that its emphasis on musicality, musical interpretation and lineage has pushed appearance into a less dominant place for the women who work in it, and older women have worked and continue to work in it as performers, such as Shirley Collins, Vashty Bunyan and Linda Thompson.

The Breeders. Alternative agers?

Kim and Kelly Deal occupy an exalted position in Anglo-American rock history, some of which is down to serendipity. They are allied to the grunge scene through being in a similar place and time as the key players on that and its associated musical scenes. Kim played bass with Pixies whose lauded 1988 album *Surfer Rosa* Steve Albini produced. Albini produced Nirvana's 1993 *In Utero* and The Breeder's first studio album *Pod* (1990). These alliances matter as they imprint sonic and temporal resonances onto the band. The Breeders' original line-up was Kelly Deal and Tanya Donnelly (who went on to play with Throwing Muses) and the twins began recording and performing together in 1989. It is important to stress how important a role in this position might be attributable to Albini, whose production techniques imprint bands with an 'Albini sound' which is shared across Pixies, The Breeders and Nirvana. Novara and Henry (2009) define The Pixie's 'alt-rock' sound as 'obscuring hooky pop tunes under layers of noise while creatively subverting standard pop structures' (p. 821).

This 'sound' is apparent on *All Nerve*, a 34-minute album consisting of 11 songs. These Breeders' songs are not 'about' anything, but they are sonic canvasses that hint at traumas, anxiety, horror, loneliness. 'Wait in the Car' exhorts the listener to do exactly that because Kim 'has business'. She has 'stuff' to do, but that phrase conjures up contract killers, Mafioso, secret 'stuff'. When do women say that in contemporary popular cultural texts? This is where The Breeders are 'still punk' in their 'dissent' (Roy, 2007) from convention. A song about a woman about to be murdered by a serial killer 'Walking with a Killer' is inspired by an event in Kim's past where 'rape victim' was yelled at her as she nipped out to go to a store (2012) gives a voice to the voiceless. 'Spacewoman' imagines the loneliness of the titular protagonist and the band act out space travellers reeling from a crashed landing in the music video, directed by Richard Ayoade (director of feature films *Submarine* 2010 and *The Double*, 2013).

The video is set in a forest with Kim or Kelly walking down a slope carrying an acoustic guitar. She is dressed in what looks like a cross between a bee-keeper's outfit and a space suit. She walks along a dirt track past a fire. It is unclear what is burning, but we can see disused pipes and rubbish. The camera pans past Jim McPherson, the band's drummer. He is wounded, crawling along the floor beating a drum, his cymbal and bass drum on his sides. The camera pans in and we see that it is Kim who then walks up into the forest past her bass player, Josephine Wiggs, who has crash landed in her parachute and is hanging from the branches of a tree. She, too, is accompanied by her instrument. Kim starts to run up the hill towards the light beyond the forest to join her twin sister. They stand, facing the empty landscape, both with their guitars, facing a large burning circle in the sky. They throw their guitars through the circle into what seems to be the sea: through a portal to another place. Ayoade's directorial aesthetic augments that of The Breeders by painting a surreal, strong picture of the sisters as survivors, literally of a space ship crashed to earth. Like Bowie in Nic Roeg's *The Man Who Fell to Earth* (1976), the band are depicted as from yet another 'elsewhere', this time from space; another way of portraying them as 'timeless' by representing them as aliens, space women (from the past? From the future?). The twins occupy one more 'elsewhere' place too. As twins, their relationship goes back to pre-birth, to the amniotic elsewhere of the womb, and their alliance and how they are viewed is with a curiosity that 'constructs twinship as significant and extraordinary' (Dillon, 2018, p. 133).

Still…

> 'I'd still do Kim'
>
> https://www.youtube.com/watch?v=Cvas5q0R000

The 'still do Kim' comment appears under a YouTube video of The Breeders performing on 'L'Album de la Semaine' broadcast on Canal +, a French TV station, on March 3, 2018. The 'still' part of this claim indicates the incredulity at a 56-year-old being desirable. Other comments on YouTube and other sites (notably RoadBike Review) by those commenting on the Breeders' album circulate around a joy at their re-emergence, an incredulity over how 'timeless' their sound is and how it transports listeners back to their youth. 'I still have a mad crush on Kim Deal' notes a comment on RoadBike Review. There is then, in this, some shared generic age with folk. Timelessness, here, is to do with being chronologically unfixed. Steve Albini says that Kim 'has an internal sense of timeless beauty that fits in the continuum from Edith Piaf to Patsy Cline and Dolly Parton'. Here she is placed in a parallel chronology, one premised on a 'timeless' aesthetic. Neil Gaiman, author of *Neverwhere* (1996) and *Coraline* (2002) among others, writes an essay on The Breeders to accompany the release of their *All Nerve*, 2013 album:

> People change over the years, and we hope that the we that is us never changes. Yesterday we were kids, and tomorrow we'll be old, and we think we're the same people we were, despite all evidence to the contrary. .....But

> sometimes we play music that lets us be us then and us now and us still to come, and it's all worth it, every minute, every aching second, every gaping now.....And then *All Nerve* arrives and it's as if no time at all has passed. Music slices us in time, and I get to remember what it means to be excited by music all over again. For a start, *All Nerve* sounds like a Breeders album: it's not retro, it's not 90's, it just is what it is: smart rock music with a Breeders sound and an oblique Breeders point of view.
>
> (Gaiman, 2018)

Gaiman's lyricism is compelling and persuasive, but it is not entirely convincing. It might be that we are 'taken back' to a place where we once were 'as if no time has passed'. There is a considerable bank of work on this process of recollection and travelling back in time, not least Van Dijck's important intervention for understanding memory triggers. What I want to look at here specifically is that idea of 'as if no time has passed' since this is the hallmark of the 'timeless' (and the classic). It has almost a judgemental or qualitative tinge to it; that music (or other cultural artefacts) that cannot be assigned a specific 'time' are somehow worthier that those whose 'sonic footprint time stamp' (Charles, 2019) is clear. Timelessness is allied to 'the Classic'. It masks a hegemonic dominance. The 'classic album' is not 'timeless'. It has been agreed upon 'as' a classic 'as' a piece of work that is classic across times and it benefits from a discursive structure that positions it as such. Albums such as 'Sergeant Pepper' benefit from critical acknowledgement, anniversary events, memorial documentaries, reissues and remastering. 'Timeless' for popular music merely means important music that the critical 'we' have decided is important.

The argument here is that The Breeders' 'sound' is from a specific time and place. It has a sonic geography (Boland, 2010) in that it has the aura of sounds from Seattle around the early 1990s. It has a chronological sonic stamp: a temporally fixed sonic signature if you will. And this sonic signature, if it remains consistent over the course of a career, is then considered 'timeless'. This is echoed in journalist discourse about the 'comeback album' which 'can arrive with a suite of expectations attached many of which tend to boil down to one question: Will the artist revive their signature sound, the one most likely to trigger a dopamine rush of recapture youth in the listener?' (Johnston, 2018). Sounds do come from somewhere and some place. They might be a mix of old and new (The Rheingans Sisters using a tambour and are digitally produced), and they might be exploring similar sounds as they age to when they were younger, but they are not 'timeless', which implies an ability to buck ageing and be unattributable to any one chronologically fixed point. Bucking ageing is achieved too by somehow remaining the same. Longevity in the music business is not only what Laura Snapes, *The Guardian* newspaper's deputy music editor writing about Robyn's 2018 release, suggests is essential to the maintenance of a career: 'Longevity – especially for women – often depends on a willingness to protect an enduring brand, as Spears is doing with her extensive Las Vegas residency, or to disappear into the background to write for younger artists' (2018). It is also the ability to produce work that keeps to that sonic signature. Nevertheless, the idea that The Breeders somehow sit outside of time appears in reviews, this one from *The San Francisco Chronicle*:

> The album reconfirms that the group exists in its own galaxy, one where no time passes and its punk spirit remains impenetrable. Not only could the songs here fit seamlessly into any of the band's previous albums, the signature surf guitars and otherworldly vocals on "Nervous Mary" and "Dawn: Making an Effort" have lost none of their cathartic powers.
>
> (Vaziri, 2018)

The reviewer applauds how they have not aged. 'It's over in 2 minutes, but it sounds like the work of a young band, and like the old band we know, which is all one can really ask for' (Bhatiya, 2018). So, this is what this fan wants, a band in aspic, frozen, a band whose voices sound young, a band whose ageing is not heard. The vocalic body (Connor, 2000) remains young for the reviewer; it remains as it was and erases the potential of the current ageing body from which it emanates. The pleasant surprise at not hearing a bodily decline is echoed in this YouTube comment: 'I though[t] rock bands were supposed to degrade over time, but this is amazing! What gives?' (Zack Stewart: https://www.youtube.com/watch?v=5i76b0OrdIQ&frags=pl%2Cwn).

It appears as though sounding like you were is preferable to the sounds of ageing being scored into your vocal. This sense of keeping hold of the youthful vocalic body at the expense of recognising the present ageing one is compounded by the editorial use of young photographs when publishing copy about recent releases. An example of this is how Sade released a single to soundtrack Steve McQueen's 2018 film *Widows*, but the accompanying photograph was of her decades ago. When older age is made audible and visible, as it is with Shirley Collins and Marianne Faithfull, the reviews are all about age marking itself vocally. Other reviews are pleased at the idea that the band has 'endured' and that they 'still' wear similar clothes to when they were initially performing:

> The Breeders are a unique breed: a female-fronted band that has endured over time. They're tough and vulnerable, but don't fall back on being cutesy. In concert, performing songs like "Hag," they still rock cargo pants, stringy hair, and make-up-free faces. And in 2017, the more women who are unapologetically rattling the cage in bodies and lives they fully, proudly inhabit, the better.
>
> (Kraus, 2017)

> A strange review appears in *The New Yorker* which comments that: These days, what feels most remarkable about the Breeders is extra-musical: the band is anchored by three women in their fifties, none of whom, incidentally, chose to breed. They haven't ceded their pulpit to a younger generation or disappeared into a domestic routine.
>
> (Petrusich, 2018)

The idea that a female musician in her 50s might choose not to have children, nor to stop making music, nor for that music to become irrelevant, nor to retire seems to imply that it is odd. That carrying on with your profession is, for a woman, worthy of comment. If the review was written like this, the gender-related ageism is apparent:

> These days, what feels most remarkable about the (insert male band, all in late 50s – say The Beastie Boys) is extra-musical; the band is anchored by three men in their 50s, none of whom, incidentally, chose to breed. They haven't ceded their pulpit to a younger generation or disappeared into a domestic routine.

Yes, the reviewer is playing with the band name 'The Breeders' but by changing the gender so simply, the expectations of women over 50 within the music industry as musicians are exposed, something that Kim Deal refers to in a *Guardian* interview in 2018 (Ellen, 2018).

Conclusion

The Breeders 'real' chronological age is remarked upon and clearly labelled. They are 56. Middle-aged. However, their bodies perform, their instruments play and their voices sing within a genre, alt-rock, which is in turn indebted to and linked with other genres (punk, grunge, indie) that remain couched within mythologies of youthfulness and rebellion and are considered 'timeless'. Similarly, The Rheingans Sisters and Askew Sisters work within a folk tradition and aesthetic that depicts them as part of an old tradition, a lineage whose antiquity is reified. They sing ancient songs and play old instruments. They are young, but their youth is forced up against this antiquity and results in the same dual *time-crunch* as we have with The Breeders. Age here, as suggested at the start of the chapter, is flexible. The ageing and youthful bodies sing and play within generic formats that have their own histories and mythologies, their own points of origin and their lifespans. Far from being timeless, these female musicians are aged within the narratives and histories, stories and spaces of genres that themselves are aged.

5 Rude Girls

Ageing, race and place

'It feels like we've gone back in time', said my daughter on a trip to the Coventry Music Museum in mid-November 2018. We were sat in the Two Tone café drinking milky tea. The walls are painted with Two Tone's black-and-white chequers motif and the menu runs from full English breakfast to jerk sausage, rice and peas. The museum is set in the red brick residential streets just outside the city centre and was set up in 2013 by Pete Chambers. Along with a memorabilia shop and the café, it forms a living heritage unit which is supported financially by grants and aided by 13 volunteers. One of the volunteers is Ruth, who within two minutes of our arrival, has us decked out in Two Tone 'stingy-brims', ska sunglasses, taken our photo and uploaded it to the Facebook site. Ruth's daughter is lead singer of The Primitives and their Top of The Pops performance is being beamed on one of the screens in their collection. With pieces from fans, musicians and collectors, the compact museum tells the story of Coventry's music and its famous musical stars, from The Middle Ages, through vaudeville to the 1980s. Delia Derbyshire, King, Punjabi MC and Two Tone, with exhibits on The Specials, Neville Staples and Pauline Black and The Selecter.

The Coventry Music Museum is a memory hub. It hosts the clothes and artefacts of Pauline Black and Two Tone: 45s, posters, flyers, posters; it has all the paraphernalia expected of a museum built by and for fans. It is, as Sara Cohen and Les Roberts note, part of the Two Tone trail, and 'integral to the success of its performative role in terms of culture-led urban regeneration policies, local history and identity-building, or the development of a local and regional heritage industry' (2015, p. 224), an industry that is highly contested and increasingly multilayered (Bennett, 2018, p. 476). Black figures in that performative memory-making process, and is indelibly connected to the place (Coventry) and the time (Two Tone of the 1980s). Two Tone is part of that local Coventry heritage, and going to the museum and the café afford an affective present experience informed by memories of popular music. The café clientele was made up of a number of people whose clothes (Harringtons, Doc Martins, Pork Pie Hats (Stingy-Brims)) marked them out as ska fans and whose accents hinted that they were local, or at the least, from The Midlands. This was a place of musical, subcultural and geographic belonging. And most of the people working and visiting on that Saturday were middle-aged.

Figure 5.1 Author photo of Coventry Music Museum (taken 17/11/18).

There are other avenues for going back to those places and times, for 're-living' Two Tone. In December 2018, The Selecter played on a 1980s' line-up in their 'hometown'. As the *Coventry Telegraph* wrote,

> In December, the Coventry based 2-tone ska band join the likes of Tony Hadley, Bonnie Tyler and Chesney Hawkes in performing a mix of Christmas classics and their own smash hits. The hometown band were one of the latest additions to the lineup…..Lead singer Pauline Black said: "2-Tone music originated in Coventry almost 40 years ago, so it is a real honour for The Selecter to be representing this pioneering multicultural movement at BBC's The Biggest Weekend in May in our hometown, particularly in the aftermath of Coventry's successful City Of Culture 2021 bid last year."

Writing in her memoir *Black by Design* (2012), Black notes herself that in the 1990s, she was aware of 'The unnerving fact that 76 percent of our current audience were chubby white blokes' (2012, p. 315). Unnerving perhaps because it made her aware of time passing, as she also says of her 1996 tour, 'Sure, the old stalwart skins and Mods were there, but they were now paunchier and greyer and tended to parade photos of their teenage kids in front of you, a constant reminder of how much time had passed' (2012, p. 309).

This UK format is similar to a French 'commercial force' (2012, p. 242), called Âge Tendre, where stars of the 1980s' French pop and chanson world tour all over France. In 'Step Back', the 1980s is rendered through the recognised stars of that decade who perform the nostalgic memory bridges of the songs of their youth. Chris Tinker has argued that this type of event is circumscribed by a nostalgia that offers a 'fantasy return to youth', which is preferred over the present (2012, p. 247). Black's own memoir is not forgiving of this 'fantasy return', noting that 'The older a band gets, the deeper the nostalgia that surrounds them. People stop believing that you might have anything new to say and are content just to explore the shallow pools of their memories' (2011, p. 393). In those 'shallow pools' Black exists as a sassy Rude Girl, placed within a specific time, place and look, and the museum, the concerts and her status as a 'Rude Girl' combine to allow her both the space to vocalise dissent around race and politics and fold her back into a specific place (Coventry) and time (Two Tone) where she is forever 'placed'.

Rude Girls, Gaga Girls

Apparently, Neville has his breakfast every Saturday in the Two Tone café and we had just missed him. According to Pete, the museum is the Number One visitor attraction in Coventry and the most visited museum in the Midlands. A local music journalist by trade, Pete had run a market stall for 30 years selling music-related paraphernalia and the museum for him is a 'dream'. Visitors are of all ages and Pauline Black 'drops in' whenever she is in town. Indeed, Black's sheepskin coat is on display, part of what Roberts calls the 'contagious magic' of popular music memorabilia (2015, p. 4). Pete reckons that she and the band Selecter 'define the Two Tone movement' and cites Black's vocals, her presence as 'a great front woman in a man's world…spitting out acerbic lyrics written by Neil Davies, H on drums, Desmond on keys…' as their defining characteristics.

Black, on vocals, has been with the band since 1979. Her 'look' is distinctive, and in her memoir, she narrates how she pulled it together over time (2011, p. 136, 144). It is indebted to the Rude Boy aesthetic, commensurate with Jamaican Reggae from the 1960s and 1970s and Black is a Great British Rude Girl. The Rude Girl is a female incarnation of the Rude Boy. She is a ska fan and so wears the 1960s-inspired sharp-lined suits, the button-down shirts, braces, white socks and Doc Martins like her male Rude Boys. The figure also suggests someone who might run close to or below the law, typified by Jimmy Cliff's character in *The Harder They Come*. This character, clever but disadvantaged, smart and sexy, sharp and suited, dressed (literally for Cliffe) to kill, is the template for the Two Tone Rude boys and girls of late 1970s and early 1980s Britain. Black came to the style via a process of elimination and serendipity, not wanting to wear dresses and not having much money (Borelli-Persson, 2018).

Using that figure of the Rude Girl, I trace out how some Black British female musicians' musical lives are placed in specific 'lokalszeit's (Schütze, 1922) or to 'sonic footprint time stamps' (Charles, 2019) and how that 'placement' polices them. It is not about the experience of ageing or its representation. Rather it is concerned with life courses being mapped into specific locales and considering the broader political implications of those. Rather than the performance of ageing in young and old Black British female musicians, it is about the performativity of their generic, coded positioning. In particular, it looks at the Rude Girl's ability to vocalise personal and national politics and suggests that it is the Rude Girl's androgyny, which in part allows Black to age successfully (Baltes and Carstensen, 1996; Katz, 2013). It then shifts across to two young Black British women working in grime, hip-hop and neo-soul, specifically Lady Leshurr's 'Queen's Speech' work and Lava La Rue's 'Tetra' (2018) video, to argue that they continue in a 'Rude Girl' tradition, which is an enunciative as well as an aesthetic position and tradition.

The Rude Girl subverts the norms of feminine fashioning and of speaking; her voice is 'rude', noisy, political. It is almost 'gaga'. Halberstam uses this term to describe a process 'that involves a wild form of singing that becomes an ecstatic loss of control and that links queer, punk and anarchist forms of feminism to be fugitives of blackness' (2013, p. 9). Referring to Fred Moten's (2013) work that advocates escape, a state of being that 'refuses the refuge of home', Halberstam files Pauline Black alongside Lady Gaga, Grace Jones and Rhoda Dakar as women whose vocal presence and embodied Blackness have collided within popular music terrains to engender a discomfort that is the mark of queer feminisms indebted to punk (and she notes, to Two Tone). She argues that:

> Rhoda Dakar of The Bodysnatchers and Pauline Black of The Selecter were much more than female lead singers: they were part of England's colonial dreaming, which comes back to haunt the metropole as traces of an otherwise unthinkable union of feminism, anti-colonial struggle, anti-racism and queerness'.
>
> (2013, p. 129)

These women, Halberstam claims, create alter egos (and this is very much in evidence from Pauline Black's own memoir where she writes how 'In The Selecter I had created an alter-ego, a feisty, angry, opinionated young woman') (2012, p. 245). This feistiness and anger are the hallmarks of The Rude Girl, who was visible in Two Tone.

Two Tone

Two Tone was a musical movement whose title comes from the mohair suits that change colour with the light, worn by ska fans in the 1960s. It began in 1979 in Coventry, a city in the UK's Midlands, which had been bombed heavily in the Second World War and was suffering from disinvestment and unemployment in the 1970s. Part revival, chronologically post-punk, it didn't last long but it had musical and, as is evidenced by the Coventry Music Museum, geographical and personal importance. In 1979, political, economic and social conditions for working-class youth in Britain were dire. The 'no future' of the punks was not their preserve only. As Hebdige writes in his book on Caribbean music, Two Tone emerged at a time when prospects for young people were limited and the Empire was contracting; 'As the sun sets on the British Commonwealth, Two Tone braided musical strands from England, America and the Caribbean colonies and turned the wake into a carnival' (1987, p. 110).

Dick Hebdige's account of the arrival of Two Tone onto the British musical landscape points to its fusion of anti-racist politics, entrepreneurial chutzpah (specifically in the shape of Jerry Dammers of The Specials) and its ownership of the image; aesthetics and how Two Tone was seen, as well as heard, was integral to its initial success and its enduring appeal. It was, in the words of 'market speak', a strong 'brand'. Coming out of the DIY aesthetic pioneered by punk, it was a 'new music' that both Black and white working-class young people could gravitate towards and which offered a new, hybrid cultural identity (1987, p. 109). This hybridity was born out of what Hebidge argues was the 'unique way' (1987:111) that Black and white kids grew up together in Coventry (and Birmingham):

> The rock and reggae communities have never been as segregated there as in London. In pubs in the predominantly black area of Birmingham's Balsall Heath and Handsworth, it's not unusual to see black and white musician of all ages jamming together. Birmingham must be one of the only places left in Britain where it's still possible for a white man to get into a shebeen without wearing a blue uniform and kicking the door down'.
>
> (1987, pp. 111–112)

This view of the conditions from which Two Tone arose certainly accentuates the emphasis on locale as opposed to race, and the sense that Two Tone offered a new multicultural vision for British youth is echoed in Black's memoir where she recalls how in their first photo shoot, The Selecter really did seem to be the 'the embodiment of the Two Tone ideal: blacks, whites, men and women, working class with a social conscience' (2012, p. 191). This conscience was realised in what Hebdige describes as the more 'modest' political objectives of Two Tone compared to Punk which preceded it. Where punk was an aggressive assault on the political, musical and social status quo, Two Tone's 'targets were more clearly defined: unemployment, the police, and authoritarian government' (1987, p. 110). The soundscape of Two Tone, heard in the music of The Selecter, The Specials and The Beat, especially, represented the landscapes from which it came: areas of the Midlands that were depressed by unemployment and disinvestment, attitudes to poor employment prospects, pleas to government to 'stand down'. In her memoir, Black is very clear on how her own identity, as an adopted and 'mixed race' child brought up in working-class Essex, shaped her music and her politics (and continues to do so). She spoke from a 'somewhere' and Two Tone's Rude Girl persona afforded the expression of such a placed politics. The notion of a 'somewhere' from which a subject speaks is an important one to turn to now, as it goes some way to explain the investment in this subject that I have.

I am white and thereby unmarked (Dyer 1997). I am middle-aged and now, middle class. I speak with what might be called a 'posh' accent, gained from getting a scholarship to a 'posh' all-girls school in 1979. Living on a new-build estate on the outskirts of a small village in Somerset, I was also a Two Tone fan in 1981. I had a 45rpm copy of 'Too Much Too Young' by The Specials AKA and listened to it obsessively after purchase, never realising that Terry Hall's final exhortation to 'try wearing a cap' was a reference to contraception, rather than being a recommendation for headgear. Two Tone had a similar ethos to punk in so far as it 'retained both an implicit and explicit political agenda at a time of economic dislocation and heightened social tensions' (Worley, 2011, p. 70), and as Dick Hebdige notes (1987), it wore its politics with wit and humour. Halberstam also argues that the 'undifferentiated spaces of punk rebellion from the 1970s, where ska and reggae and hardcore punk sit comfortably alongside each other, drawing on multiple histories and reinventing new spaces of overlap and conversation' (2013, p. 128) are an optimistic lineage within which to locate female musicians who 'go gaga', like Black (and, I will argue, like Leshurr and Rose).

Successful (ageing) Rude Girl

The last line of Pauline Black's memoir is 'This woman is not for resigning' (2012, p. 406). It wraps up the final chapter, 'A Raisin in the Sun: Women Don't Resign', which opens with an epigram from Louis Armstrong saying 'Musicians don't retire; they stop when there's no more music in them' (2012, p. 383). The Selecter released *Made in Britain* in 2011, in part a response to the riots of that year across cities in the UK, and then *Strip Theory* (2013), *Subculture* (2015) and *Daylight* (2017). Black still has music in her and something to say, notably, about the British Black experience. She acknowledges the issue of ageing within her industry, where middle-aged women (she marks this out as 45–55, as menopause takes effect) are 'faced with… unwelcome scrutiny' (2012, p. 390) that requires them to absent themselves from the visual arena and turn instead to creative pursuits outside of performance.

It could be argued that Black is, in some respects, a 'successful ager'. This figure is one who continues to contribute to a neo-liberal society (Marshall and Katz, 2002; Katz, 2013; Marshall, 2014). They work, they remain sexually active, they are not dependent on anything, family or welfare state. They are the ultimately successful capitalist subject as they plough into older age 'successfully', where that equates to doing the same things as they did when younger. Black's alter ego, her Rude Girl persona, has not changed since she honed it at the start of The Selecter's career; she is an 'enduring brand' as Laura Snapes says (2018). This brand is celebrated in fashion bibles like UK Vogue, which traces out her trajectory from Rude Girl to fashion muse in the following:

> Pauline Black, the "defiantly chic" frontwoman of the Selecter, a politicized two-tone ska revival band formed in the late '70 that is still making people

> dance, is no stranger to fashion. She famously played with androgyny by adapting the tailored, mod-ish Rude Boy style to her own stylish purposes while performing music that was a pointed response to Thatcherism in '80s Britain.
>
> (Borelli-Persson, 2018)

The discourse here is one of survival and resistance; 'still' and 'defiant' infer a continuation of activity that is unexpected, in both longevity and content, for both her and her audiences. Successful ageing is here recorded via continued exposure. Black is also ageing appropriately, in so far as she has positioned herself as a woman whose androgyny affords her a masculinised ageing trajectory too. Her suits may now be Prada (to skim the older body), but her Rude Girl look somehow sets her apart and allows her to age 'as' a man and 'as' a Rude Girl. So, Black grows older within a discursive regime that is part of a 'culture of timelessness and the marketing of agelessness' (Katz and Marshall, 2006, p. 91). Katz and Marshall are writing about cosmetics advertising and cultural gerontology in general, but their ideas on 'timelessness' here can be considered within the archetype of the 'Rude Girl'. This look, however premised on Caribbean diasporic fashion and Skinhead culture, remains a 'look', which can be referred to 'as' timeless in the same way as the 'classic' album can (which was discussed in the previous chapter). For timeless, perhaps instead we need to consider the term 'not ageing in the way we expect older white women to'.

Pauline Black is a Rude Girl and her body is a conduit or portal to other places and times that she cannot escape. The Rude Girls linked to place, to Coventry and to a time, the early 1980s of Two Tone. Black is 'fixed'. By this, she is connected to a place and that place is Coventry, Two Tone. And from Two Tone we go back to ska, from ska to Mod, from Mod to Windrush, and that generation's contributions to British music and experience of British racism. This is all wrapped up and into her ageing body. She is a heritage site. Her body recalls place and time, and it, and her band, is at the centre of the 40th anniversary events being celebrated in 2019 by the Coventry Music Museum. She carries with her all these histories, burdened by them.

Placing Black within this context is important; she cannot be understood without it. Her body is part of the continued narrative of Coventry and Two Tone, and her 'music plays an important role in the narrativisation of place' (Cohen, 2007, p. 2). Her 'place' within history and that history within a place is what determines how her ageing body and presence is configured and represented. That place is Coventry and Coventry is Two Tone. 'Bodies are the means by which scenes must be continuously re-produced' (Driver and Bennett, 2014, p. 100) and Black's body fulfils this role. She is the 'authenticated' voice of that place and time, and has a 'temporal identity that fix[es her] in time' (Forman, 2014 cited in Little, 2018, p. 36). 'Place' for Forman in his work on hip-hop is 'defined by its closeness and proximity to individuals and groups and by its localized character' (Forman, 2002, p. 25), and this sense of proximity and familiarity is rendered too in Black's bodily 'place'. It is a geographical location that is both real (and realised) (Forman, 2002, p. 35), something that Pete Chambers uses to determine his sense of self as a 'proud Coventry boy'.

The 'place' of Coventry within the body of Pauline Black is an 'interface' (Grosz, 1998), a construct that reaches beyond itself (Massey, 1994) back in time to encompass Black British and Two Tone histories. And one of the potential consequences of this is a certain stereotyping and minimising of potential (both in terms of influence and possibilities). In 1992, Paul Gilroy wrote about place, and Murray Forman's 2002 book on hip-hop and place recalls it, writing how: 'Gilroy's concern is, importantly, that the fragmentation into localized and particular patterns of identification reduces the expansive possibilities and enabling potentials of a mobilized cultural politics of race' (2002, p. 62). This critique goes some way to suggest how Black's history and current persona of Rude Girl of Two Tone give her no room for manoeuvre. It delimits her. It disallows her space (whilst putting her in place).

Underpasses and urbanity

The Rude Girl archetype emerges from ska and thence to Two Tone, but it doesn't stop there. It allows for an attitude that is visible in the work of two young British musicians, Lady Leshurr and Lava La Rue. Age (young age) appears on them through the prism of the 'Rude Girl' and so they appear within a history of Black British artists whose lyrical contribution is in line with Pauline Black's, notably in relation to personal politics and gender. In the music videos for the singles 'The Queens Speech', 'Black Panther' (Leshurr) and 'Letra' (LaRue), the women are placed within urban settings that are both a take-over (Lewis, 1993) of a male (and a public civil) space and a potential restriction within it. They both 'go gaga' (Halberstam) in ways that extend that space, to it being the language of young Black British women and the pop culture references which they (especially Lady Leshurr) refer to: the snap chat generation. Their lyrical preoccupations around personal hygiene, gender and Black identity speak from a specific place, a locale which both affords and restricts. This cityscape is represented in music video by the underpass, the underground car park, the tunnel and the street. It is 'urban', a term which when applied to music, as Andrews argues (2018), infers Blackness, this despite the histories of (white) punk particularly as mythically welded to the city (despite much of it emerging from small towns and suburbs, see Huq, 2013).

The Queen's Speech

Every Christmas since 1957, the British Queen has broadcast her Christmas Speech. In it, she talks to the nation, covering the highs and lows of the year. It is an informal speech, written from her perspective, distinct from the 'Queen's Speech' that accompanies the annual state opening of the UK parliament where she reads out a prepared speech on the incumbent government's bills for the coming year. The first speech is the Queen as 'grandmother' of the nation, and the second is as its constitutional head.

Online there is another set of media clips related to the 'Queen's Speech', and they are seven videos released between February 1, 2015 and October 17, 2017 by a British grime and hip-hop artist called Lady Leshurr. Leshurr is a freestyle grime and hip-hop performer; her songs are three- to five-minute meditations, exhortations and humorous accounts of her life as young British woman. Freestyle is a form that prioritises lyrical dexterity and improvisation, a hip-hop version of the Jamaican sound clash and MC culture, where two artists, or two sound systems, would compete to outdo each other either in track of in delivery. Braggadocio is part of this format, and Leshurr adds a very localised, national angle to it.

As in Calypso (Chapter 2), Leshurr's stage name assumes a monarchical grandeur. She was born Meshelle O'Garro in Solihull in 1988, on the outskirts of Birmingham, the UK's official 'second' city. As a young Black woman growing up here, the chances of her ever 'being' a 'Lady' are slim, unless she wrests the title for herself. The English aristocracy is white, the only people of colour 'admitted' to its tiers are those whose titles have been bestowed upon them by the Queen herself for services rendered (usually though politics, education, public service, etc.) and these are nonhereditary. Lady Leshurr claims her own place in a different aristocracy by naming herself, and her Queens Speech videos are further examples of her 'take-over'.

'Take-over' is a term referred to by Lisa Lewis (1993, p. 109) where she notes that music video and MTV in the early and mid-1980s offered women a chance to symbolically 'take-over' male space. A 'take-over' was made possibly either through the idea of 'access' (i.e. going to places previously or dominantly coded 'as' male) or 'discovery' (foregrounding 'feminine' experience). The idea is predicated on spatial codings that are themselves reliant on an essentialism but she and Vernallis later (in 2004:83) note that women 'quirkily' appearing in the street and mechanics shops (Björk in 'Oh so quiet', 2005) exemplify this kind of 'take-over'. Lady Leshurr continues in a tradition of women 'taking over' the street in all seven episodes of 'The Queen's Speech' over the two-year period, 2015–2017.

In Forman's reading of American hip-hop, the 'street' has been both a real place, represented as such in lyrics, and a 'mythical' construct (2002, p. 84). It has 'been a consistent site for emergent hip-hop practices' (2002, p. 83) as it is able to accommodate 'forms of expression that occur in outdoor or unsanctioned public spaces' (2002, p. 83). The 'street' is both the public sphere and beyond it. It is ultimately within state control but it is indistinct; thoroughfares, roads and motorways are ways through places, on to somewhere else. They are also representative of a night-time economy within which women have historically been coded as 'street walkers', prostitutes. Feminist movements from the late 1970s across America and Britain have worked to 'take back the night' to ensure women could walk safely through their towns and cities. Lady Leshurr occupies streets at night, motorways and underground tunnels, putting her youthful self in places marked out as danger zones, or as not fit for people (motorways, streets in LA).

In Episode 1, she is in an underground car park; in Episodes 2 and 3, she is outside in the dark. In Episode 4, she is in a particular place, West Parkside SE10, a housing estate in Greenwich, South East London. In Episode 5, she has travelled. This time she walks along a palm tree lined avenue in bright sunshine; it must be the USA, California or Florida maybe. Episode 6 sees her walking down Woolwich Tunnel, and the final episode sees her on dual carriageway, first on a camel, then walking.

Settings, as Carol Vernallis argues in her 2004 work on music video, are crucial to placing the piece within a generic context and the street, tunnel and underground car park visually render the inner city which represents some of the urban environments experienced by young British people living in London, Birmingham and elsewhere. These places are also loaded with symbolic weight, drawn from cinematic and media imaginaries, almost a cliché: the underground car park as crime setting, as shoot-out territory; the tunnel as ghostly; the motorway as escape. Leshurr turns the dark histories of these places around by putting herself in them as a comic book character, using humour to diffuse the locations. In Episode 5, she wears a red-and-white Santa hat; in Episode 6, a Superwoman outfit; and in Episode 7, she is dressed like the game heroine, Lara Croft. All episodes use animated cartoon like script to underpin key lyrical moments ('Mad Ting' in Episode 3, 'Brush Your Teeth' in Episode 4, and 'Crizzpy' in Episode 5, to refer to crispy bacon).

Grime's history is tied to locality, with narratives and myths woven about its provenance from East London, with arguments coming from South London groups who dispute this (Charles, 2019). It is an amalgam of dancehall, reggae, drum and bass and not a subgenre of hip-hop (de Lacy, 2015), characterised by lyrics sung in local, London accents about the specificities of the London Black youth experience (for extensive methodological and critical work on UK grime, see Monique Charles, 2019). Its rather tired (if not unexpected) media representation within broadsheet and tabloid media is as an 'edgy' form (Beauman, 2006; Jackson, 2017) often allied to a criminality, with which it is problematically and sloppily often conflated (see Berry, 1994 in Forman, 2002, p. 48). The estates and non-gentrified areas of London are grime's ghettos and Black youth are, in the same way as Forman details about American hip-hop, wrapped up into dominant narratives weaving criminality, economic and educational stagnation and moral and social breakdown. But grime, as Charles (2019) argues, is where young Black subjects have agency, are able to 'take the mic' and be the centre of their world, command respect. In a society where structural racism remains endemic, this ability to speak your own story is crucial.

Lady Leshurr uses her platform to inject the form with a humour. Focusing on the minutiae of life, on hygiene ('brush your teeth' in Episode 4), relationships and rave etiquette ('not to take your heels off at a dance please as your feet smell' also in Episode 4), her narratives foreground the complexities and delights of her Black British experience. Singing in a mix of UK British Birmingham, slipping into Jamaican patois occasionally (Mad 'ting'; 'dem man') hers is a peculiarly British sound. She doesn't swear, she exhorts young women to learn to cook rather than twerk (lamenting how they eat pot noodle or beans on toast) and her concerns are more with an almost pre-sexualised form of romantic relationship intercut with female rivalry. Her heroines are Superwoman, Lara Croft, Santa Claus and The Queen (she wears a T-shirt in Episode 2 with 'Defend the Queen' on it, under an image of the Queen similar to that portrayed by The Sex Pistols in 1977). She is shot in all videos from below, in keeping with a film aesthetic that has come to dominate the portrayal of hip-hop and grime performers on video. The performer declaims down to the audience via the camera: the direct address as if from the stage. And Leshurr performs a Rude Girl aesthetic. She wears a black leather biker jacket (Episode 1), army fatigues (Episode 2). When she is in shorts (Episodes 3, 4, 5, and 7), the camera is on her face not on her thighs. She plays tough, with her street wear' style, recalling all the symbolism of the biker jacket, baseball cap and camo and in all of the tracks, her focus is not on sex or sexuality, but on the minutiae of human relationships. Her politics is the personal. Hers is the discourse of the college common room. Her music, coming as it does from a musical culture used to talking to and of itself, is not 'political' in the same way as Black's Two Tone is. She does not sing about the street as a place of danger for (specifically) young Black men, nor of state miscarriages of justice (Grenfell) or lack of opportunity. Her 'rudeness' is targeted more at how she takes over the mic in the neglected, danger zones of Britain, and invests them with dispatches from the 'Mean Girls' lives of her and her friends. Men figure less in her narratives than women, either as rivals or objects of humorous derision.

Leshurr performs youth as it negotiates friendship and romance. There is nothing here on desire or sexuality, nothing on the body other than the need to maintain personal hygiene. It is childlike, comic. And yet there she is, walking alone in a Superwoman outfit through an empty tunnel on Halloween (Episode 6), in a lonely underground car park, on the streets at night. And she is there because these places should be available to her and her humour, to dressing up and going out, to a night-time economy. Leshurr acts as a Rude Girl in her work, performing a comic and de-sexualised persona, and claiming the city as her space (her potential). But she is also delimited by those parameters and consigned to the urban. The one video where she emerges from these dark liminal places of Britain is in Episode 5, set in a sunny USA. An English girl in LA? But still here, she is on the road, travelling, Santa hat on, displaced.

Black and Leshurr, Rude Girls both, are aged against places that are generically sanctioned. Their performances on music video (Leshurr) and within the popular music heritage industry (Black) of the Coventry Music Museum construct their status as integrally place related. Those places are cemented within a British popular cultural imagination *as* Two Tone and the early 1980s and *as* contemporary 'urban' Britain. There is a tension here, and it is one flagged up by Kehinde Andrews in his critique of the term 'urban' to describe Black British music (*The Guardian*, August 14, 2018). 'Urban' is shorthand for 'Black' music, delimiting it as well as ignoring punk's spatial history, for as Hebdige saw 'Two Tone grew out of punk, and there were links between the two movements, Punk and Two Tone both cultivated the romance of the street (an important mythical site in the geography of rock, at least since West Side Story)' (1987, p. 111).

Murray Forman is writing on American hip-hop specifically, but his ideas on the 'hood' as a mythically and racially bounded place come to the fore when considering how Rude Girls are placed visually within cityscapes and memorialised within locally produced heritage practices like The Coventry Music Museum. He writes how: 'The central elements of race, class, and cultural identification are recast and revised within a coherent if not entirely consistent spatial discourse, one that relies on the spatial construct of "the hood"' (Forman, 2002, p. xix). The 'hood' is depicted not in terms of a 'block' (which is the American version of neighbourhood) but in recognised (London, SE10) and generic (underground car park, tunnel, street) settings. This confirms Leshurr 'as' a grime artist, sealing her 'authenticity' as coming from the streets. Forman notes convincingly that 'race is spatialized and space is racialized' through the 'complex dynamics of discourse and practice' (Forman, 2002, p. 10). The 'coming from' and 'appearing in' the streets generically fixes Leshurr through visual discourse; her lyrics fix her 'as' young, Black and British; as she moves from her Solihull accent to Jamaican patois, we hear the sounds of the granddaughters of the Windrush generation.

There are a number of other British female musicians, young, Black, People of Colour working in musical styles drawing from grime, hip-hop, dance, R'n'B and much more, who could be seen as 'Rude Girls'. Nadia Rose, MIA, Lava La Rue and Nao are young women whose music is political and focused on contemporary issues facing themselves and their broader communities (La Rue, Rose). La Rue, a young rapper from West London, cites Nina Simone, Erykah Badu, Neneh Cherry and Angela Davis, among others, as her influences. Her youth is lived and observed from within a specifically Black, Black Atlantic female lineage, of women artists and thinkers. She places herself in a broader, Anglo-American politicised musical and literary tradition as well as 'being from' West London. Journalist articles about her in cutting-edge fashion magazines like *Dazed* focus on the sonic geography apparent in her work: 'There's something distinctly London about it, not just in her accent, but in the sound too, as if the deep, dubby basslines of the city's Jamaican sound systems and pirate radio stations have unconsciously seeped into the music' (Bulut, 2018).

When Forman starts his book on race, space and hip-hop, he describes the experience of listening to place, as he drives on interstate highways in and out of cities and hears the racial spaces being mapped in the radio he is tuning in to as he drives. The same thing happens in the UK. As you drive into West London from outside, the main radio channels of the BBC and commercial radio cede to the local radio sounds of London, and of those pirate stations broadcasting music that is not heard outside of it. A similar thing will happen travelling north into the West Midlands and Bhangra stations suddenly become available. You drive into and out of different sonic worlds, depending on where you start from. This is almost too obvious to be remarked upon, but as Sara Ahmed reminds us again, what seems unremarkable is only so due to a consensus, and it is this which should be queried.

TETRA, Lava La Rue's music video, is filmed in the West Side, Ladbroke Grove. This is a famous underpass that runs across The Portobello Road, a street that takes you from Notting Hill to the Golborne Road, from millionaire pads to newly 'cleared' spaces which once housed local people in council housing and the Trellick Tower, a 1972 brutalist tower block, whose flats now also sell for hundreds of thousands. The Westway lies beneath the A40 dual carriageway flyover as it cuts through West London and the Tube. It is a 'site[s] of significance' (Forman, 2002, p. 26) for British punk history and for West London's musical identity in particular. It figures large in the punk imagination as The Clash were photographed against it in 1977 and it figured in the title of the 2000 retrospective documentary about them *Westway to the World* (dir. Letts). (Don Letts has a history with The Clash, having worked with them on the video for 'White Riot' (1977), 'Tommy Gun' (1978) and 'London Calling' (1979), managed The Slits who supported The Clash on the White Riot tour and produced *The Punk Rock Movie* (1978), which partly documented that tour.) The Clash symbolise a sense of, maybe in retrospect, naïve utopianism with regard to multicultural co-production that was also evident in Two Tone. Ladbroke Grove was home to the annual Notting Hill Carnival (1966 onwards), had seen race riots (notably those that inspired The Clash's song 'White Riot') and is now arguably, fissured along race and class lines, according to La Rue. It is a place then whose history La Rue positions herself and her 'crew' within because it is her history.

Filmed in The Westway, she performs against a recognisable hip-hop aesthetic: graffitied walls, skate riders, rapping down to camera. Her crew are multiracial, and in her live shows she gives a shout out to the 'POC LGBT'. When she chatted in between songs in her support slot for Christine and the Queens at Birmingham's 02 Academy on November 26, 2018, she confessed that it was first visit to Birmingham (she was 20 at the time). She asked the crowd if she was pronouncing the name right. She is a tourist in the UK, and, as she sings in 'Widdit', where she has 'three little brothers to feed[and]London city was a mother to me'. That same city she also calls 'Babylon'. She is both linked to and alienated from her home, the place that is her city, London.

The city is both a physical and symbolic (Forman, 2002, p. 35), lived in and imagined. For Black it (Coventry) museumifies her as part of its popular music heritage, for Leshurr it (the generic and the specific city, both Solihull and South-East London) affords her a place to be and for La Rue, lyrically, it is both nurturer and enemy (mother and Babylon) and music video visual rhetoric places her firmly in a recognised West London landmark.

It is worth going back to a distinction that Laurence Grossberg made between place and space in order to position how Black, Leshurr and La Rue can age 'as' Rude Girls. For him, place offers stability; it is affectively invested in whereas spaces are the parameters beyond which people and what they do might move (Grossberg, 1992, p. 295 cited in Forman, 2002, p. 25). Looking at where these three women, aged in their 50s, early 30s and early 20s, are placed, Coventry 1979, the 'city' and 'West London' are the places where they 'stop and act'. Their mobility, the potential for them to reach beyond those parameters, is highly coloured by place, if not curtailed. Black has had a career as an actress, works on national British radio, has penned a memoir; these are the 'spaces' she has moved to, beyond the 'place' with which she is conflated, Coventry and Two

Tone. Leshurr and La Rue, young British Black women, exist in a tense discursive relationship with the city and its streets. Flights into 'space' are afforded by the rich diasporic and Black Atlantic heritage, recalled by La Rue in her live performance, but Rude Girls, young Black British women who have political things to say, are always confined to the city. The only pop moment involving a young woman of colour going 'wild in the country' was Annabelle Lu Win of Bow Wow Wow (1982), managed by Malcolm McLaren, who placed her and her band in a pastiche of Manet's 'Le Dejeuner sur L'herbe', inserting Blackness into white art history and reasserting racist myths around Black female bodies and nature.

In your place

Lefebvre writes of how 'Space is socially produced', of how it is both political and ideological (in Forman, 2002, p. 4). When it is marked out, determined and cordoned off 'as' a place in space (Coventry, Birmingham, London) and in time (Two Tone, grime), it becomes a constraining category shot through with myth and narrative that are hard to unpick. Voices that come 'from' a place (an urban place, a deprived place, a concrete jungle of a place) are always pulled back to that place. Black, Leshurr and La Rue age against a political backdrop that always 'places' them on the margins and in the underpasses of British popular music culture and history.

This relates, in part, back to the idea of the previous chapter on genre age, which noted how ageing might be inflected by intimations of place, specifically generic geographical origin or reification of 'place'. Here I am wanting to think how place inflects age through an alliance to specific musical movements, ska and grime. Pauline Black, Lady Leshurr and Lava La Rue are all ageing (in that they are living out their performing lives) against a generic, 'subcultural' background to which a 'city' is integral. The point of this is to consider a potential skew in how Black British women might be mapped onto places and into histories that pins them as living (and ageing) within parameters that are different to those of white British women. There is a potential tension in the securing of Black British identities to cityscapes, a trend that has been critiqued (Andrews, 2018). There is, in the placement of Black female bodies, young and old, to 'the city' (Black to Coventry, Leshurr to Solihull and South London, La Rue to West London) a degree of containment of the enunciative Black female. Shirley Bassey, not connected to any scene, was always someone who came 'from' Tiger Bay, Cardiff (Jennings in Gardner and Jennings, 2019). Might it be different for women who are white? Ageing female musicians who continue to perform do so as 'singer-songwriters' and unfixed to 'a' place (Kate Bush, Marianne Faithfull, Tracey Thorn, Alison Moyet). When they are (as Shirley Collins is to Sussex) it is due to the particularities of the generic discursive regime within which the narratives of their lives are positioned. Collins was also 'part' of a movement that was about the music of a place (England) and a member of the Albion Band. The question is whether white women are allowed to be *unfixed* to places, particularly to cities and therefore able to travel more widely in the discursive imagination.

In 2018, Marianne Faithfull released a new album, some of it produced and co-sung by Nick Cave. The music video for Gypsy Girl, a track from it has a close-up of Faithfull against a verdant green English pre-Raphaelite typesetting wherein the young 'gypsy girl' of the title dances. Faithfull (born 1946) can be set anywhere – an English forest serves as any forest. In this she is allowed to be placed against a background that can function to be an 'anywhere' whereas Pauline Black in the 'Return to the 80s' gig and the Two Tone museum, Leshurr in her videos and La Rue in hers, live (and age) in a kind of restricted location. They are denied the Englishness of Bush, Thorn, Moyet, the freedom to 'be' extra-national (Faithfull) and are always 'of' the city and all its raced vectors. Black, Leshurr and La Rue are not only creative female musicians, but they are products within a larger industry. And perhaps their USP is where they come from. That 'provenance' may come to (over) determine their presents, as they age through the life course. The problem is that this 'provenance' or mark of authenticity also bars them from moving out of the imagined city. Theirs are bodies not free to roam. As Rude Girls, they are always associated with a Black Jamaican diaspora and with a criminal or deviant masculinity entrenched in that term. They are hooked back to the Rude Boys of Jimmy Cliff and *The Harder They Come* (1972). They are also, by default (and like Paul Weller, the 'angry young man' referred to in Chapter 4), evocative of a time when Rude Boys were fashion icons for Mods, for the 1960s and the promise of an integrated, multicultural forward-thinking youthful Britain. They are also, notably Black, hooked into the history of Two Tone which, in turn, is located in the Midlands. Lady Leshurr and Larue are similarly fastened into narratives around Black women and urban music genres. The positive aspect of placing them as Rude Girls is that it acknowledges their diasporic histories and influences, and the impacts of those on British popular (music) culture. The negative is that these histories are denied the 'freedom to roam'. This locational tradition is both enabling and constricting; it allows both a 'take-over' (Lewis, 1993) of masculinised public space (the 'street') and a containment within it (they are placed and once this is done, that is where they stay). As Black British women, they are conflated with a musical genre or scene that has 'the city' at its centre, and although they take-over those streets in their performances, they are inevitably always conflated with them.

Conclusion

My purpose here has been to illustrate some tensions that I sense are at play in the performances of young and older Black British musicians in ska and grime as they are bounded by the city, be it Coventry, Birmingham or London. This is done in part to consider the places where Black British women, old and young, are expected and allowed to speak from. And it is germane to look at a contemporary example of being 'out of place' to clarify this a little more.

When the 2018 Friday night headliner for the British music festival Glastonbury was announced as Stormzy, a UK grime star, it was greeted by some with comments that point to this idea of 'place'. Similar to the reactions to Jay Z, Kanye

West and Beyoncé, the comments were not about gender, but about genre, and then about genres that have come to be understood 'as' raced (Roy, 2002). So, these three British Black women's bodies and bodies of work are intricately linked to the place-rich narratives of the musical genres within which they work. Provenance secures the subject into one place, and that place (the city, the 'urban') then becomes the dominant discourse within which they are positioned. The 'where they are from' becomes the 'where they can be placed' and disqualifies them from travelling beyond it. Their middle ages and youth are mapped into place, their performances located in the urban, the city and the historical. They voice the politics of disenfranchisement, disillusion and discrimination as well as the politics of the personal. There are competing and contradictory forces running through and from their presence within British popular music culture.

Black can be identified as a successful and appropriate ager as she continues to create and perform and does so as she ever did. Her look and her sound are as they ever were. Her androgyneity allows her more slack as she ages within masculinist space and her place with the national and local popular music heritage of Two Tone keeps her forever young. Leshurr and La Rue live out their youth against a backdrop of urban places linked to crime and to punk history (The Westway). They are all positioned firmly within British places, places that are historicised as diasporic and subculturally aligned places. They illustrate the complex matrices of narratives that weave through them and within which they perform. They cannot age without being referred to where they come from. And that seems to prevent them from being able to escape.

6 'They're not going to give me Stormzy'

Ageing matters behind the scenes

> I didn't play with dolls. I had a Dansette record player.
>
> (Mandy Parnell, 22nd October, 2018)

> How did sound mixer Mandy Parnell make it to the top in such a blokey industry?
>
> (Hutchinson, 2017)

Black Saloon Studios is difficult to get to. It has no house number on it and is set back off the main street in the quiet residential streets of Walthamstow, East London. It sits between an Islamic Cultural Centre and a children's playground and not even the builder working on the house next door to it knows where it is. In it, in the autumn of 2018, Mandy Parnell is mastering Björk's virtual reality album, due for release at Christmas. Parnell is one of a very small handful of women audio engineers working in the British music industry and has mastered albums by Aphex Twin, Daughter and Mica Levi, as well as Björk. She has been working as an engineer for over 30 years and won The Music Producers' Guild's 'Mastering Engineer of the Year' Award in 2015. She was one of two women out of 36 nominees for a Music Producers Guild Award, whose female membership runs at 6% according to their own survey (*The Guardian*, 2017).

So far, this book has focused on the front women. But let's move back a bit, just like Neville Morgan did in his 2014 film documentary *20 Feet from Stardom*. Let's look at the backline, the 'other' band members, the women who EQ the live sets, who sort the production, who manage the bands, and at musicians who are not in the 'big time' but for whom music is their career. These are the women who are part of the music industry, who have had and continue to have careers in it. The stars and performers, the singers and musicians are the ones whose stories are written, published and broadcast, but the women who support them, musically, technically and administratively, have experiences of age and aging that are worth telling for what they reveal of the complexity of ageing across the Anglo-American music industry.

This chapter reflects on Parnell's thoughts on ageing in the music industry as one of 19 semi-structured face-to-face interviews, conversations and questionnaires over email I had between April 2018 and January 2019 with women who were mostly over 50 years old and had been, or still were, working in the music industry as part time musicians, producers, sound engineers, tour managers, tech and stage hands, publishers and journalists. The age range expanded as the research went on as some women were interested in taking part as they had had a long career in the music industry but were between 40 and 50. Participants came via my extended professional networks and were contacted through Twitter, Facebook, phone, email and text message. Six face-to-face semi-structured interviews were held between April 27, 2018 and November 28, 2018. The conversations generated from these interviews and comments received build up a picture that adds to the complex and shifting notion of ageing. Responses via the Sound Girls organisation, a supportive network for women working in audio (https://soundgirls.org/about-us/) that I contacted, were from lot younger women working in tech and highlighted perceptions of ageing in younger women (who see themselves as long-lived within their industry). These different avenues and research trajectories added into the idea of the fluidity of ageing.

Asking women in the industry was something that had developed from a conference paper given to a small audience at Manchester University's 'Troubling Time: An Exploration of Temporality in The Arts', June 2, 2017. Here, one delegate suggested that I might look to women who made up the backline, who were the session musicians, the jobbing musicians whose stories are never heard. The initial sense was to concentrate on women who were not 'up front' or 'in focus' and a snowballing technique combined with internet cold-calling returned 19 respondents in all. It is an attempt to snapshot a small slice of experience with regard to ageing in the contemporary Anglo-American music industry as a counterpoint to the other conceptually and theoretically driven chapters of the book. Haruch asks where all the producers are, where all the studio workers are, and this chapter goes a very small way to try to find some. In the article below in a magazine called *The Nashville Scene*, Haruch describes this inequality whereby contemporary female musicians' visibility is largely enabled by men:

> Women are as visible as ever in music – between them, Taylor Swift, Beyoncé and Lady Gaga have sold over 22 million records since 2008. But look closer at the credits on those albums, and women's names are few and far between. What about producing and engineering? Who's guiding the sound and leading the recording process, and doing the work in the studio that takes the sound waves, electrical impulses and digitized bits of sonic information and shapes them into the music we hear? Those roles are almost all filled by men. Beyoncé was a producer on *I Am … Sasha Fierce*, but she is a rare specimen. By most estimates, women represent less than 5 percent of producers and engineers industry-wide.
>
> (Haruch, 2010)

Research motives and methods

The research for this chapter has been undertaken with similar motives to Marion Leonard's (2007) work on gender in the music industry. It is informed by an acknowledged feminist position, this time concerned with women as they age and how that might inflect their experiences of working in their roles within the music industry. It is also an attempt to consider the idea of ageing within the Anglo-American industry from the viewpoint of women who work in it and so spotlight a small slice of experience. I am not an anthropologist or ethnomusicologist and have limited experience working in the 'real' world beyond text and discourse, and so methodologically, there may be flaws to this part of the project. However, the little experience I have on Erasmus+ funded digital storytelling projects has taught me to listen and to consider issues from the people that experience them. This informs forthcoming work on troubling musical inheritances with Sara Cohen, Andy Bennett, Murray Forman, Jocelyn Guilbault, Line Grenier and Helmi Järviluoma-Mäkelä, based on workshops across Europe, North America and Australia that consider musical inheritances.

The participants were drawn first from a personal network that comes from working in a largely vocational Media School that has three undergraduate music degrees. One of the teaching staff had worked with Andy Franks, a tour manager with years in the music industry, who has worked with Coldplay, Depeche Mode, The Stone Roses and The Rolling Stones and others. Franks had come to speak to undergraduate music students and was willing to give me the contacts for women he had worked with. Two women responded via this route. I met two more women at a book launch at the Houses of Parliament organised by Dr Rupa Huq MP, and one of them was interested in sharing her story of being a live sound engineer. The journalists were contacted directly, as they are known to me through the University and other intra-university groups (notably Birmingham City University). Other women came forward through social media direct invitations via Emily Baker, an academic and musician living in Brighton. Folk musician, Sharron Kraus I met in Zakynthos at a digital storytelling event whilst working on an Erasmus + media project, who then introduced me to Aby Vulliamy. Fran Malyan is an old friend of Mike Smith, an ex-colleague of mine who plays keyboards with Gorillaz and The Good, the Bad and the Queen. Mandy Parnell I cold called.

The women were offered two options to return their thoughts, a face-to-face interview revolving around ten questions, or to respond in writing to those questions. The questions had three closed questions to establish current working status and six open questions to elicit conversations about ageing within their work experience, one of which worked to generate answers about their enjoyment of the industry in order to further a comfortable conversational atmosphere.

By the close of the research process at the end of November 2018, six interviews were conducted. This is an admittedly small selection of women; five more were approached, some of them high profile within the broader British music industry (encompassing radio and music journalism). Those who did respond were interested to know who else had been in touch, and, in one case, wanted to know who else had been invited, before they committed to the interview; the world of women behind the scenes seemed to be small. Five of the women initially contacted chose to respond online rather than face to face. To supplement this,

50 women working in the industry as tech or backline were emailed through the *Soundgirls.org* word Press site on November 5, 2018, with a request to fill in a tweaked version of the questionnaire, where two new questions were added after my experience of interviewing, as these issues were covered in conversations not anticipated in the original questionnaire. These were 'If you are under 50, do you think that age will impact you in your work?' and 'If you are over 50, what are you views on ageing and how other people in the industry view you?'.

The Soundgirls directory is a US-based resource for women working in the American popular music industry and set up by Karrie Keyes and Michelle Sabolchick Pattinato in 2013. It hosts events, supports women in the industry, mentors and offers advice. Their mission statement declares that it exists to: 'inspire and empower the next generation of women in audio. Our mission is to create a supportive community for women in audio and music production, providing the tools, knowledge, and support to further their careers' (https://soundgirls.org/about-us/). It also has a directory where women can upload professional information. This directory lists 508 audio engineers (93 Broadcast, 319 Live Sound and 259 Studio), 38 lighting specialists, 169 women in production and 50 on backline, technical (boom operators, sound design, live monitors). The women who responded from this directory were of all ages (some in their early 20s) and so shifted the initial frame of analysis away from older women reflecting on their time in the industry to younger women thinking about how ageing might affect them, or if their age at the point of return of the questionnaire had any impact on their career. The methodology had to change with the changing circumstances and in so doing, it captures a broader picture of ageing across a number of women at different points on their life course. Women responded in this call from the USA and Italy. The respondents were all pleased to have been asked to take part in the research and wanted to be informed of the book's publication and this was similar to what Leonard found in her 2007 research (p. 16).

Research expectations

Prior to the research being conducted, I had an open mind as to what responses might come in. Having only taken part in the music industry as an amateur keyboard player in the mid-1990s, my expectations were really more or less in line with ones I had formulated as a young woman: that there was sexism (always being assumed to be the girlfriend and not a band member) and that there were no women over 30 to be seen gigging or in the studio. So, women were being discriminated against as young women, and as older women they didn't figure. The story was one of the usual pressures and absences.

There was no expectation at the outset of this research that there would be consistent themes emerging from these women, given that they do such different roles within the industry; writing freelance for The Observer and *The Quietus* is completely different from putting on Robbie Williams' Moscow World Cup gig, or doing backline tech set up for punk bands on American and European tours. And this was the gulf of difference that the work of a music journalist and a production manager reveals. To expect them to experience similar situations with regard to their ageing relies on not only an essentialist approach to their gender, but a false presumption that all of their work places and surrounding personnel would be similar. The 'music industry' is many industries. It is an enormous ecosystem that hosts touring, production, studio management, PR, journalism, performing and engineering. To try to make any generalised claims about women and ageing across it is potentially doomed to failure. The worry that the remit was too great, too unsubstantiated, was starting to figure, but the importance of hearing some voices from within the industry was still paramount.

In her 2007 research, Leonard referred back to Frith and McRobbie's work from 1990 which asked whether 'The music business is male-run; popular musicians, writers, creators, technicians, engineers and producers are mostly men. Female creative roles are limited and mediated through male notions of female ability' (Frith and McRobbie, 1990, p. 373 cited 2007, p. 24). Nearly 30 years on, the experiences of the women interviewed here and whose stories were emailed to me reveal that in some cases not much has changed. When it comes to tech support, studio work and technics, women make up a very small proportion of the workforce. An article on *The Guardian* from October 2017 includes data from Sound Girls, The Music Producers Guild and Ents24.com (a gig listing site). They note that 6% of music producers are women, 5% are sound engineers, 30% of senior executives are women, and that 'Of this summer's festival headliners in the UK, eight out of ten were male' (Larsson, 2017).

Gender disparity is not something consigned to popular music memory, but it is apparent in the second decade of the twenty-first century. Larsson quotes Shay D, a hip-hop artist who reports that 'female performers are still treated as a "novelty" by promoters. "I've had so many issues with promoters who want to book you because 'they need some female energy'," she says. "What's so annoying is that it's only when they need to fill a quota or to look as if they're being fair"' (Larsson, 2017). Larsson reports on female-centred initiatives to readdress the balance to get more women applying for grants or to promote engineers and producers, led by the Performing Right Society (PRS) Foundation and the three-year Leeds-based 'ReBalance' programme (2018–2020). This was an initiative to help mentor, support and give studio time to female musicians (https://rebalancemusic.com).

In the peer review for this book's proposal, the comment on this chapter wondered if a section on women in the contemporary music industry on the subject of gender disparity might date quickly. I wish it would. But it appears that despite the repeated journalistic swathes of copy heralding the 'resurgence' of 'women in rock', what Leonard found in 2007 and what seems to be happening still is that a cocktail of entrenched disparity with relation to gender is still apparent, and that feeds into ageism. The PRS initiative is laudable, but look at the image for its publicity and it would seem that there are no women over 40 on it.

As the project snowballed and returns came in, themes emerged. These revolved around professional ability, longevity, mentoring and motherhood. Indeed, more than one participant referred to the first one, the importance of earning, and maintaining 'their chops', slang that means their ability to do the work to standard in their field. Many of the participants noted how important it was to mentor younger women, or to find female mentors and to create female-centric professional networks to do so.

The interviews

The six interviews took place in six different venues over eight months, from April to November 2018. Venues included my university office in Cheltenham, Gloucestershire, the upstairs room of Patisserie Valerie on Old Compton Street, Central London, a participant's basement café in Cheltenham, a home studio in Walthamstow, East London, Sony EMI's headquarters in London's Golden Square and a café in Wimbledon, South West London.

Participants were sent an email with the questions for interview after the initial invitation so that they could gauge where the questions would be centred. The set of questions was modified for music journalists. The initial email send out had included information on the nature of academic publishing to allay fears about any comments being broadcast far and wide, noting that 'Needless to say, as they [the books] are academic they sell to libraries and universities so the readership is pretty niche…'. The interviews began with an introduction to the project and myself, which included some information about my time in amateur bands, playing a Hammond with a Leslie speaker. This was done to try to ensure a feeling of some kind of shared history in relation to musicianship and awareness of some of the experiences of being in a band and gigging. It was following Hodkinson's notion that to share 'insider codes' (Leonard, 2007, p. 16) was a productive strategy towards successful research interviewing: 'holding some degree of insider status can offer important additional benefits and possibilities, most notably with respect to generating a relaxed atmosphere conducive to open conversation and a willingness to disclose' (Hodkinson, 2005, p. 139 cited 2007, p. 16).

Each interview lasted between one and two hours, depending on the ensuing conversations. All of the conversations were recorded on a 'Voice Recorder' App on my iPhone: an app that apes an old cassette tape recorder and though not as good as capturing sound as a HanZoom 4, it is much easier to operate and download. It also proved a useful conversation starter, and comments were made about tech and mixtapes, comments that enabled the discussion to be primed for the questions that had been sent through prior to the meeting. Depending on the participant, some of the questions acted as prompts, some of them generated no responses and were not followed up and some generated a lot.

There was some initial resistance to talking about ageing from the interviewees, as Helen said that no one really likes to talk about it, and Aby asked why a book project was talking about it with reference to musicians when we all age. So, as Leonard noted, there was a resistance to 'certain lines of enquiry' (2007, p. 16) that were addressed by further discussions about age and ageing that then returned comments around persistence, community and motherhood. This only happened in the face-to-face interviews; on paper, the participants provided full commentary on their views on whether age had ever impacted on their lives, or if they had experienced ageism in their work places. Perhaps women are not used to talking about age in other way than to avoid it (I feel like I'm 18) or to consider it a question about their appearance. I always told the interviewees how old I was (52), and what it was like ageing within an academic context and how students viewed me (usually positively not least for having seen James Brown perform live).

Research findings: writing about music

Three journalists returned questionnaires: Laura Snapes, *Guardian* Deputy Music Editor (late 20s), *Guardian* and *Observer* journalist Jude Rogers (40), and Anna Pointer, course leader for Magazine Journalism and Production at the University of Gloucestershire (where Jude Rogers also worked part time). Their questions were tailored to their profession as journalists. They had differing responses to the first question on whether they had experienced ageism within their sector. Laura replied that she had, because of her youth, 'I got my first job at NME when I was 21 and was routinely dismissed for being young, both in the office and by external publicists'. Anna suggested that 'younger, more "glamorous" types may well catch a commissioning editor's attention'. And Jude commented:

> Not exactly – but I have noticed a few people not considering me for jobs as they used after I had my son at 36, and I wonder if age is a factor here. There is an assumption, I feel, that as an older woman you won't want to travel as much, particularly if you have family.

There was then, among the three, an awareness of the perceptions of age and the expectations wrapped up in those perceptions. They were all in agreement in their responses to Question 2 which asked 'As a music journalist, have you ever been aware of 'age' being a factor in how women musicians might be perceived?'

LAURA: Yes. Older female musicians do not get the same kind of coverage as their male equivalents. Also aesthetically, a profile of e.g. Roger Daltrey will be illustrated with an image of him now, whereas a profile of Kate Bush, Joni Mitchell etc. would feature a picture of them in their 20s.

ANNA: Yes. I'd say that large swathes of the media represent female musicians as 'over the hill' or 'yesterday's news' – and far more readily than their male counterparts. For instance, you might hear journalist colleagues or readers commenting on the age of singers such as Chrissie Hynde, Cher or Dolly Parton in a pointed or derogatory way, with criticism that they are dressing or presenting themselves inappropriately 'for their age'. (Sexism in music is a whole other debate, though.) In contrast, male artists of a similar age are idolised or thought of as 'improving with age.' Case in point: Bruce Springsteen, whose appearance (and therefore his age) is rarely commented on, and hardly ever in a negative way. Yet it appears to be much more of a defining characteristic for female musicians. In fact, it seems that their talent comes *in spite* of their age, rather than it being a positive.

JUDE: Definitely. Madonna, of course. Even if you're not keen on the music she makes, there is an ugly tone of ageism in much of the criticism of her. It must be said that male acts have this too – the Rolling Stones do, for example – but this is rarely linked to age and sexuality. Men are more often than not allowed to be sexual later – perhaps because they could still be fertile? Women aren't, as if fertility was the be-all and end-all of sexuality…

Jude also pointed out that recently older women such as Tracey Thorn and Shirley Collins had had their work positively received, which gave her a degree of hope for the future: 'So I'm positive things are getting better. It helps that journalists' attitudes are expanding, and more women of an "older age" are still writing…'. When asked about what they thought others in their profession's attitudes to older women musicians, they noted that they were 'often perceived as past their prime, a bit tragic, unviable because they're no longer seen as sexy, and often their influence is only acknowledged in a very one-dimensional way – eg Stevie Nicks' style, Joni Mitchell as a "confessional" acoustic songwriter – rather than for the breadth of their achievements' (Laura) and that the 'leaning towards younger women musicians' was possibly a 'symptom of our reality TV era, when every competitor is younger, "sexier" and more marketable' (Anna). Anna also noted that for women journalists, an older woman subject is more interesting to write about than a younger one:

> I would say to anyone starting out in music journalism that there is much to be gleaned from the older woman musician. A woman in her 80s producing new music would be far more interesting to write about than someone in her early twenties who has not seen the industry evolve and change, or who has limited cultural reference points in terms of the music business generally. Age is genuinely no barrier to musical talent, and we as journalists should relish the opportunity to break down social barriers and encourage greater diversity.

Mentoring is also a role that Jude, particularly, has taken on and her comments echo those of the women tech and backline workers from the Sound Girls list. Her advice that: 'Role models are massively important. I'd say, listen and learn lots. Know your stuff. Develop specialisms' is repeated in the returns from the young women working as tech crews on live tours.

There was agreement over the continued lack of women in the industry, with Anna suggesting that new forms of consumption and encounters with music might rejig the balance:

LAURA: Yes, of course. Data shows that men and women enter the industry at roughly parallel rates, but women's participation drops off in their mid-30s: they're not pushed through to managerial positions in the same way that men are, and if they take time out to have a baby, their progress is also often stymied. It's an industry built around men's desires, whims and needs. I have seen some progress but nowhere near enough.

ANNA: Streaming, social media and the internet have irrevocably changed how we consume music, so our listening choices are no longer packaged up and decided for us in the same way. Having said that, I'm sure few of the top-level roles in the industry are occupied by women. And even if they are, we definitely don't know enough about them.

JUDE: Things have definitely improved from there as far as I can tell – I notice more producers in the industry, for example. I interviewed Björk's mixer for Utopia, Marta Salogni, and she said this explicitly too.[]There are many more female music journalists writing too, I think (although I don't have the figures!) – I genuinely think online culture has been a great thing in opening up new spaces for women's voices (Twitter in its early days was amazing for this…before the trolls arrived.) One thing that irks me, though, is that people often say "ah, they are hardly any female music journalists around" when they haven't bothered looking. Kitty Empire has been the Observer's music critic for years, and Miranda Sawyer one of their main music interviewers. Kate Mossman is the New Statesman's music interviewer. Sophie Heawood has done tons for women's mags and music mags on female musicians. Etc. Visibility is a problem sometimes, but so are other people's perceptions of invisibility

Research findings: family, femininity and fitting in

> 'My dad was an engineer, why couldn't I be an engineer?'
>
> (Gerri Frame, April 24, 2018)

Liz (55) has worked in the industry as a production coordinator for 34 years, starting out in 1984 with Everything but the Girl, for whom she made soup, a vegetable lasagne and apple crumble. As a catering student at an FE college in Gloucestershire, UK, she happened to bump into the guy running the SU bar who needed someone to provide a rider for the band. She didn't know then what a rider was but she is still working in the industry. She has toured with Pink Floyd, Genesis, Paul Young, Muse, Take That, Robbie Williams. On the date of the interview, she was just back from having worked on Robbie's performance at the opening ceremony of the football World Cup in Moscow. She is not thinking of stopping work since she doesn't know 'anything else', touring is 'part of' her. The only way in which she considered ageing was in her reluctance to get on another tour bus, about getting a 'bit tired'. This was echoed by others who had had experience touring and called it 'brutal' (Carol) and 'stressful' (Gerri) and how it 'takes its toll', something that the younger women from the Sound Girls list were mindful of in their worries about their future ageing and its impact on their working lives.

The key changes Lizzie had noticed in her working life were that there was now more awareness of the need for separate facilities for women working as part of a crew. 'In the 80s everybody shared rooms', she said, but 'we get girl showers now'. Essential to her notion of herself was her femininity and not trying to be 'one of the boys', so if another woman was on tour with her, they would dress up for dinner, 'go out for a manicure' and try to maintain a sense of a separate feminine space.

The impact of motherhood is something that Gerri, a 'working class girl from Glasgow', also disclosed in interview. Working now as a psychotherapist and trustee with the charity 'Music Support', which supports people in the industry with mental health and addiction challenges, she was live sound engineer and tour manager for Mute Records, Factory and Rough Trade from 1979 to 1989 and worked with Nick Cave and The Birthday Party, Yazoo and Depeche Mode among many others. Part of her job involved being in New York for two years, away from her then young son whom her partner was taking care of and she recalls the 'terrible wrench' that she reflects was coupled with societal shame and guilt which impacted negatively on her well-being. Later on in her career she toured with Depeche Mode on a US and South East Asia tour whilst pregnant with her second child, thinking that she just had to 'keep going'. Gerri also stressed the need to know 'your role as a professional' and not to 'get caught up caring for men' nor to 'try to keep up with them', so the notion of some types of prescribed parameters of 'femininity' and its attendant expectations, and when to adhere to them and when not, seems to be part of the negotiating that was going on for her (and for Lizzie). This is different to how Rochelle, who is on the Sound Girl register with experience in sound and radio, reads gender roles, negotiating her femininity so that it is erased: 'If you're going to work with the boys, you need to think like the boys and meet them halfway'.

Sharron, a recording and touring musician, noted that whilst she continues to record and tour, some of her habits have changed as she has aged:

> My creative practice has changed in many ways over time and some of these changes relate to age: the pace of touring I used to enjoy, staying up late drinking after each gig, has had to give way to a more gentle routine, as I end up feeling like a zombie the next day if I overdo the drink nowadays! I think there's also an urgency that's developed as I get older and mortality looms a little closer.

As a singer, on stage and therefore on display to an extent. She remarks more than any other of the respondents on 'looks' and how their fading is something she has considered:

> Age is something I've started thinking about, and I'm definitely aware of how women start to notice their status lessening as they age and their beauty fades. I'm bloody-mindedly against taking that kind of thing seriously, though, and intend to grow old doing what the hell I please!

Aby, an English musician and music therapist aged 43, also wondered whether women might feel 'less welcome to have a voice' as they aged, and whilst adamant that she had never dressed up for stage (although she did 'like to get changed') and had always refused to 'buy into' the idea of appealing to the male gaze, noted the impact of a young family on touring.

Gerri also talked about some of the positive changes she had noticed since her hiatus from the industry. As part of Music Support's festival 'safe spaces' initiative, she was working at Wireless Festival (2017) and wandered back stage: 'I hadn't been back stage for twenty years', she said, 'and I saw this tech woman jump up with leads – it's not unusual any more'. Reflecting on her time in the industry and her role as a mother, she maintained how important it was to state that 'We're here and we exist and we have the responsibility to tell our daughters that getting older is a good thing'. When she started out, without any A levels and having stumbled into the scene through having some friends who were recording with Crass, the UK anarcho punk band, she now says how important it is to be both 'vocal and be visible'. Having had a father who was an engineer, she had asked herself 'why couldn't I be an engineer?' She found live sound engineering a creative role and loved being behind the desk, saying 'it was an instrument in itself'. She saw herself as part of the band, trying to get them the same live sound that they had produced in a studio, seeing herself as a creator as well as someone in a technical role. The first band she went on tour with was the Resistors and the labels she worked with were part of the post-punk 'alternative' music scene of the early 1980s. She comments: 'We were alternative, we were independent, having a woman doing sound was a bit more of a "fuck you".

Carol Scott, now Vice President of Sales for Tait Towers (a live event equipment company), Verity Studios (indoor drone technology company) and vegetarian café owner discussed how she had got into the industry by preferring to be backstage. She wanted to be a lighting designer[but] 'girls weren't allowed to be technicians' and when she started out, a young woman in lighting design was 'new territory'. She recalls it as being a 'male orientated world' where 'men think women don't understand tech as much as they do' and women had to have their 'Game higher than male colleagues' and where 'women have to buckle their balls to prove themselves'. Again there was the sense that femininity had to be protected or denied.

Now working as a part time University lecturer and giggling musician, Helen McCookerybook started out in music in 1977. 'I was made to join a punk band because they needed a bass player, they were all guys'. She played for seven years and then didn't touch a guitar for 25 years. She worked in music support by running song-writing sessions in housing estates in Southward, South London for the GLC (Greater London Council), made music for film and video (including one for the Millwall Football Club). After funding cuts, and volunteers taking over the work, she turned to lecturing and gradually began to consider writing and playing again. She played to 'students whose work I marked' and now gigs around the country, on bills that include poetry and spoken word. She has also, with Gina Birch, produced and directed a film called *She Punks*, a documentary with recollections of their time in music.

Helen releases songs onto YouTube without looking at them herself. 'If I looked at it I'd lose my confidence....' 'Oh, I look old today. I don't look in the mirror much'. Helen's working life in music is arguably informed by her adherence to a

DIY punk aesthetic and ideology so her thoughts on age and women in her life return to the idea of community: of people valuing each other, of 'making sure that there's an older woman on the bill', of revelling in the practice musiking, of writing songs and rehearsing. She notes that the women she encountered in the making of the *She Punks* documentary were not merely 'survivors' but 'thrivers'.

Mandy Parnell is a senior mastering engineer. She started out in the industry, at SAE, when she was 16, got her first mastering job at 21 and is now 50. She was 'obsessed by records all [her] life' and fell into engineering after spending a weekend at Richard Branson's' studio 'The Manor'. Her friend was the housekeeper there and she had gone down to swim in the pool and get drunk. A visit to the studio made her decided to go to college and study audio-engineering. Starting out as one of ten young women out of one hundred students at the School of Engineering (SAE), where a peer told her 'you're a girl, you shouldn't be here', she was one of two of the three women who completed the course and are still working in the industry. She has never experienced any ageism, feeling now she says 'like I'm 18' and praises the industry for being 'accepting'. She is firm about the cordoning off of the studio 'as' a workplace and mentors younger women on how to operate within that space. Key to her longevity is talent. Both her technical ability and capacity to adapt are obvious from the musicians she works with, and her ability to 'put on this persona, to be strong in that environment'. She now mentors younger women audio engineers, offering them advice and support on call.

Martine McDonagh worked in the industry from 1985 to 2015 in artist management. Prior to that she had worked in music retail and wholesale, and had got into the industry by doing PR for indie labels out of the Rough Trade office in Kings Cross. She set up and ran a merchandise company for James and other bands and did tour management. Later, she also taught music business professional practice to undergraduates at BIMM in Brighton and Canterbury Christchurch University. Reflecting back on whether age has been a factor in her career she says:

> I often thought I might be taken more seriously if I were older, but I think any lack of being taken seriously was also to do with being a woman. For example, at large arena shows, despite wearing a laminate with photo stating my role very clearly, I would often have to get road crew to vouch for me when security men wouldn't let me backstage.

So for her, ageing has been a positive as work got easier for her as she aged. When asked about attitudes towards older women in the industry, she replied:

> I haven't come across that many older women to be honest. The older women at labels I worked with were often very experienced, but rarely got the top jobs, in departments other than PR. The industry was always something of a boys' club and attitudes to women in general were fairly dismissive. I'm not sure how much that's changed. Some of the maleartists (definitely not all) had a real problem giving me credit for my ideas and achievements and would claim them as their own.

When asked about her ideas of the lack of women in the industry, she noted that when she was active, women:

> were predominantly employed in PR roles. There were very few women in management and out on the road in technical roles. I get the impression this hasn't changed too much, but I might be wrong. There seemed to be an intrinsic link between the music industry and the male ego.

Fran Malyan is Senior Vice President for Catalogue A&R at Sony ATV and has been in the industry for 41 years. In all that time she has never encountered either sexism or ageism. She had been good at maths and tried out banking after leaving school at 16, and in 1977, she started in the accounts department at ATV because banking wasn't for her. Seeing Paul McCartney walk through the reception inspired her as she hadn't been aware that there was a music industry that you could actually work in. Now a leader in music publishing, she takes care of the 'Legacy and heritage catalogue', and as a music publisher, she protects her clients' song-writing copyright, in adverts, syncs, media and live. These clients include Depeche Mode, Queen, Kate Bush, Sting, Take That, Oasis and Blur.

Working in the publishing area of EMI Sony ATV she noted that she had been inspired to get on and work by her mother, a teacher. She was aware that there was an 'old boys club' which involved golf and football, but was quite content to not be a part of that and never seeing those as holding her back in anyway. She had been in senior management, and in this role, she had followed in the wake of three former female directors so she wasn't a 'trail blazer'. This side of the music business was full of 'open-minded people' and this sense of a climate of creativity and progressive values comes across in her responses to the issues of gender and age in her industry.

'In publishing I look after the older people', she said, in conversation at her office in Golden Square, London, late November 2018. Her private office is to one side of a busy space which, like many 'creative' enterprises, has its table football game. 'They're not going to give me Stormzy', she remarked. At 60, Fran's point is about connection to artists: 'You have to have an affinity with them'. Her point flags up the idea that shared experience is key for a creative and business partnership to thrive. It might also be extrapolated from this that shared memories may also be part of this, a familiarity. Fran also talked about audiences and ageing and that disjuncture between an artist wanting to 'move on' and produce new material where an audience wants to 'hear the hits'. She narrated her own experience of going to a Billy Ocean concert where she just wanted to hear those hits, and when we discussed the recent album by Marianne Faithfull and the emphasis in a television interview on her past with Mick Jagger, Fran was dismissive of her current output saying that her past was 'the most interesting thing about her' and that 'she wouldn't get any press' if that was not the case. From her comments and experience, age was not a gendered issue, and her own career had been free of any overt sexism or ageism that had worked against her. But it is interesting to consider how now, at 60, she heads up a sector of the music publishing industry that uses the words 'heritage' and 'legacy' to speak to those people who just want to hear the hits again.

Sound Girls: younger voices on getting older

The women who responded from the Sound Girls mail out list were based across the USA and Italy. Mostly technicians, self-employed and young, their responses centre more on physical ability and age. Idaho-based Rochelle has been working in radio, digital mixing and recording, live audio production and live performance for 35 years after winning a prize as a teenager, on a radio station and demanding a tour. She comments on how gender rather than age has impacted her more: 'Being female has seemed more of an issue than my age. I'm lucky to look a bit younger than I am, but fear what will happen when I don't'. In response to questions around the attitude towards older women in the industry, her answer refers to the matrices of audience demographics and 'fit':

> I work in radio and used to work at a station with much younger demographics. I've seen older women shift to older music stations, not sure if it was their choice or out of job necessity. I doubt the younger station would hire me now out of fear I'd sound too old or couldn't relate with people.

Signe has been working in the industry for 18 years, learning how to be a sound technician as venues had none for her own shows. She now works for event set-up companies and the stagehand union (International Alliance of Theatrical Stage Employees (IATSE)). When asked the question about whether she had wondered about the importance of age, she responded:

> how many female artists got "discovered" or "made it" after 30? Do I need to keep my age a secret? Does it matter? How damaging is it to my body to do show setup work – staging, lighting, pushing boxes, lifting heavy stuff, etc.?

Women sound techs are 'cool' and so she has rarely come up against any discrimination related to either gender or age although she does note how few women there are in backline roles. Her fears around ageing are related to physicality: 'the longer one puts physical strain on the body, doing stagehand work: pushing heavy boxes, lifting heavy equipment, putting together stages, etc. – the more difficult it is to do physically, as more wear and tear happens on the body'.

Lindsay is a 25-year-old drummer who works as a drum and backline technician and has been active for six years in the industry. Her view on ageing is a positive one, whereby she sees that more women are joining the industry in technical roles and that discrimination is not apparent:

> I know there's a stereo type of women usually just being a singer or whatever the case may be... But I'm meeting and seeing more girls in the

> audio, Backline, stage hands, lighting field and even just playing instruments. There's not many of us but I do see more and more slowly but surely appearing!

Claire is a guitar technician who runs two companies, van hire company and band equipment storage. She has eight years' experience in the industry. Ageing as a factor is something she thinks about in relation to family and physical health:

> Travelling is very exhausting and the older I get I find that I want to put down more of a base. Travelling and touring when you are younger is more practical as you are less likely to have a family etc.

Ageing is only worrying for her in terms of its impact on her physical health and its potential impact on her maybe not wanting to be on tour and away from home for long periods of time. This is similar to Vanessa, a young Italian woman working in live tech, whose worries circle not around ageing per se, but around the irrelevance associated with older age, because, she comments, 'it will be harder for me understanding young people tastes in music and keeping up with new musical trends'. Similar to Vanessa, she has not encountered any ageism, as there is the perception that the 'older you are, the more knowledge you are perceived to have'. She actively mentors women trying to break into touring via the Sound Girls organisation, offering them shadowing opportunities. Her views on the lack of women in the industry are typical of a woman working in the profession who actively mentors:

> There is a definite lack of women working in the industry. There are more women on tour since I've started but we are a far cry from it being anywhere near equal. I know of only a handful of other female guitar techs on the road, which is just crazy to me. I hope by offering mentoring and shadowing opportunities that we can slowly encourage more women into the industry. It needs to be presented as a viable career option when girls are in school, with more options for education and maybe courses for learning the basics etc.

Aliyah is a young woman in Maryland who does freelance backline for local bands and freelance photography. She has been turned down for work at festivals and with artists because she was too young (she was 15), although she had a 'ton' of experience. She admires 'awesome' older women like Lisa Brownlee (tour manager for Sleeping with Sirens, a post-hardcore American band) and says how she is 'frustrated that there are people who are against older women who are in the industry'. She continues, 'How I see it, as long as she can still lift heavy items and withstand long days on her feet, let her backline', and this sense of ability at an age, not just the age, is a theme running through many of the returns from the Sound Girls responses although she thinks she might have to retire and 'find a less strenuous position'. She is pro-mentoring and recommends the following in order to maintain composure in the industry: 'My advice is to not be intimidated by the men around you, don't be a kiss up'. Her experience of touring is that it can be lonely:

> I definitely think that there is a lack of women in the industry. Whenever I go to shows on my time off and even at work, I try to find how many women are on the tour and at most I've seen 2. When you're the only woman on a tour, it makes you feel a little isolated because you don't have anyone to really relate to. Yeah it's cool calling your tour family your "older brothers" but sometimes you wish that you had another female with you. I haven't seen many changes but I think it's cool how The Wrecks hired a female tour manager and Panic! At the Disco added a female bassist. Little changes here and there but nothing major.

Clare is currently based in New York and is a music technologist whose work includes 'live technology and programming for shows, audio engineering and production for artists, as well as creating material for my own artist project that focuses on electronic music and live performance'. Her entry into the industry is driven by both her passion for technology and electronic music and seeing 'other women and people of colour in the field, especially as a young woman of Asian descent myself'. She has often looked younger than she is and so, like Aliyah, found it hard for people to take her seriously. Like Mandy Parnell, her view is that experience and 'chops' cancel out age:

> I have encountered varying views of older women in the music industry, though most have been positive, especially with regards to how they have a wealth of experiences worth sharing with younger women who are foraying into the industry. The negative views I've heard of are more associated with older people in general as opposed to older women specifically, e.g. that older professionals aren't always abreast of the latest technologies.

She too hopes to be taken more seriously as she grows older but she 'always won-der[s] if there's a certain age that might be a "turning point" of sorts where I am instead viewed as "old"'.

Conclusion

Music is the constant to these women's lives: performing it, producing it, publishing it. If they lose sight of it due to caring responsibilities, they return to it at a later stage in their lives. Depending on the part of the industry where they were working and/or performing, they reinsert themselves back in as musicians, or as musician support. They have a fondness for their industry, seeing it as accepting. This may be to do with the areas of it within which they work (the DIY, punk scene for Helen and Aliyah, the folk scene for Sharron). Any worries over ageing if they are young are related to physical ability rather than discrimination. 'No offence, but everyone ages', said one respondent, relating a conversation she had had with her partner whilst discussing not just the questions and potential interview but the entire book project. The implication here is that ageing is the same for all women: why single out musicians and women working in the music industry in support roles? What, if anything, is different about them? The answers from these 19 women illustrate how the worlds of popular music, the stages and studios, the backline and editorial commissioning meetings are shot through with what might be termed ageist microaggressions. There is no obvious limitation on women's ability to continue performing, but women in certain fields (journalists mostly) may be side-lined or moved to the heritage roster. This, again, may not be a negative move given that it is about 'fit' and ability to both support an act and report on it with authority, but it is delimiting.

Female musicians are still operating within a predominantly visual regime as much as they add to an auditory culture. This is ever more the case with increasing musical visuality and the co-dependence of the music video as promotional tool. They remain the focus of many gazes, gendered, raced and aged. There may also be remnants of what Simon Frith (1996) noted was the erotic function of women within the music video realm (and on stage) where they enact and experience a 'private bliss in a public space' (Gardner, 2015. p. 73). The further away from this potentially eroticised space women work (in the studio, on the heritage portfolio, in punk or folk) so there is less pressure to maintain such a function. And in those places where women continue to perform beyond their erotic potential, so their past acts to remind of their past and deflect away from the ageing present (see Malyan's remarks on Marianne Faithfull).

Furthermore, women in all facets of the popular music industry – performing, writing, publishing, engineering, production – are working in an industry that is itself encountering and negotiating its own ageing process. Artists and A&R women who entered into it in the 1960s, 1970s and 1980s are close to drawing their pensions. Its elder statesmen and women keeling over on stage (Meatloaf collapsed on stage in Canada in June 2016) and singing about the death of their friends (Marianne Faithfull's *Negative Capability* album, 2018). The world that is the popular music industry is growing up, growing old and within it, female musicians, and their support staff, age. How they are talked about, mediated, represented throws up tensions around age and experience. These experiences, as the responses show, are diverse and reflect the different economies of genre and scale that 'the industry' hosts.

There is no singular perception of ageing, no uniform experience of it but it traverses their concerns for the future and their recollections of their pasts. If talking to six women involved in various aspects of the music industry and getting 13 more women to answer questions on offers anything, then it is a small slice of the experiences out there of ageing. As the book's premise was to look at how ageing appears across different performance areas, seeing how it does, and does not figure in the experiences of these women illustrates what? Well, it shows that we cannot talk about ageing as a singular and non-negotiable process and in that respect, we are back with Gullette's (2004) 'aged by culture' notion. It shows that there is prejudice around the ability of women past their youth to be able to talk to and report on pop music and its rising stars. This then in and of itself suggests that intergenerational conversations are not yet seen as possible, in both reviewing popular music and publishing it. Prejudices around expectations, of what women should be doing, ought to be doing, are doing (and how that affects their ability to do the job), seem to be the experiences of some of the respondents. However, as others report, some progress has been made, women's voices are being heard. The experiences are varied, and in the worlds of the Anglophone popular music industry, women are found in positions where they 'fit'. For many of the participants, music was a welcoming space; it had enabled them to perform, to engineer, produce and publish. Back when Mandy Parnell started at SAE, she was told 'you're a girl, you shouldn't be here'. Well she is. And so are many others.

Afterword

Age stages, a reflection

Age haunts popular music. Youth is its primary currency and youth and oldness remain embedded in complex and interwoven formats, in expectations played out across vocal and gestural performance, in memoirs that recall youth and in denial of and fear of it. This book has discussed how we talk about women musicians and ageing. It seems there is incredulity when it is not apparent: that we like to assign women musicians an age marker, and that we want to ignore it altogether. We fix older women in their past, via their heritage and legacy; youth is both revered and returned to and wrapped up in narratives of antiquity. Because old women are too old, young women are too young. And no one really notices the middle-aged.

Three examples illustrate these strategies. There is a popular television programme on British TV called 'Strictly Come Dancing'. It goes out on a Saturday evening, has run since May 2004, gains up to nine million viewers regularly and is a reality TV 'dance off' show. On Sunday, October 7, Twitter was talking about Gladys Knight and her appearance on the show. She had sung the James Bond song 'Licence to Kill'. Comments on Twitter all concentrated on her age. *The Express* and *The Sun*, British tabloid newspapers, ran clickbait headlines asking 'How old is Gladys Knight' (7/10/18) and 'What age is Gladys Knight' (8/10/18). This type of 'entertainment news' goes some way to valorise again, the point of this book. Ageing might be like gender 'boring' (Jehnny Beth, lead singer with Savages, in interview with Sinead Gleeson, 2013) or 'not wanting to be talked about' (interviewee, 2/10/18) but when it is not in the right place, when its 'staging' is unexpected, when it is not visible, it gets commented on. And the idea that women's ages are always marked, their journey through life reported is another way in which ageing for female musicians seems to matter more. Even whilst valuing Smith's talent, this journalist tribute to ageing rockers still picks out Smith 'as' the 71 years old. 'Of course, the Stones, bands such as King Crimson and the 71-year old Patti Smith share a vital ingredient to aid their continuing stage presence: they are consummate musicians and writers of music' (Clark, 2018).

There are, too, other ways to continue one's stage presence. In June of 2018, there was an academic conference in the Music Department of Uppsala University, Sweden about pop presents and pop futures. At that conference, Kai Arne

Hansen was discussing the challenges that face boy bands (Take That) as they age and how they might continue 'as' boys when they are middle-aged men. His conclusion was that irony was a route that enabled them to age and be men, but still be in a 'boy band' (Hansen, 2020).

A month or so before that, Abba had revealed that, after 35 years away from their adoring audience, they were going to go on tour again. Well, 'they' weren't going, facsimiles of their youthful bodies were, 'the band had been digitally scanned and 'de-aged' to look like they were in 1979' (Needham, 2018). The audience could really meet their idols, Benny, Björn, Anna and Frida, as they were, as if no time had passed at all.

In these three instances, age is either remarkable by its absence, ironised as a critical manoeuvre in order to keep on performing or forced aside in favour of 'what once was' (youth). Age is a problem in all of these three spaces and the return to youth, or the masquerade of youth is applauded over and above the present. What I have tried to look at is examples beyond this negative – that is, spaces where (older) age is valorised and is a functional component within a canonical narrative, where it collides with genre and race and place and where it is something other than a kind of curse or blight, something to avoided, erased and made ironic. This has resulted in seeing ageing as a non-linear, complex process, which is encountered in multiple ways.

There have been repeated themes on these journeys through and across age and ageing. Place and how it is encountered on the body has been an important ingredient. Where that body comes from, how that body works within a genre that itself too, is placed temporally and geographically has been an important way in to thinking about women in music. Shirley Collins, Calypso Rose, Pauline Black, Lady Leshurr, The Breeders, The Askew Sisters; all tempered by place. Sometimes those places are somewhere elses, third spaces, future spaces, as they were for Janelle Monáe, Letissier and Anohni. Survival seems to be writ large too on the bodies of the memoirists and subculturalists (Black). And trauma has united a number of narratives (Collins, Rose, Albertine, Tutti). These are not, in retrospect, unexpected, but illustrate the matrices within and against which ageing occurs. The interviews and questionnaire responses threw up comments that might be summarised as fit, or alignment. Supporting or reporting on musicians seems to be partly attributable to this 'fit', through age-related affinity and empathy. Femininity and its relationship to motherhood and caring seemed to be one of the factors that ageing produced.

In writing this book, I have left a lot of musicians out. As Hawkins and Niblock (2011) remark in the preface of their co-authored book on Prince, 'a book…can be organised in countless ways', and this iteration is only one of many possible takes on the subject. I know that when I have talked to colleagues about this, I have always had the 'Oh, (so and so) is nearly 70, have you put her in?' question. Yes, there are many musicians not in this book who could have been. Kate Bush, Françoise Hardy, Björk, Beverley Knight, Vashti Bunyan, Joan Baez, Chrissie Hynde, Debbie Harry; all women over 50 who are recording, producing and performing. Still too there are younger women who could have been considered in the 'Sisterhood' chapter, Staves, First Aid Kit, Haim, Hinds, Goat Girl, Chai. A number of these have been mentioned in Lucy O'Brien's chapter in Adrian and Warwick's 2016 collection about 'girlhood' and I didn't want to replicate her work, or merely add different bands to her roster call. As with any book, decisions are made which are subjective. I wanted to shed some light on women whose work is either new to academic discussion (Letissier, The Rheingans Sisters, The Askew Sisters, Leshurr, La Rue, Collins), neglected (The Breeders, Pauline Black) or arguably niche within an Anglo-American music world (Calypso Rose). I also revisited women whose work has generated academic attention (Monáe) and approached them all from the angle of ageing.

I wanted to talk about ageing differently, to open up the term and play with it, to see what might happen when we consider other trajectories; how genres age, how memory considers the past, how racial politics delimits age, how place informs ageing. Framing contemporary female musicians as canonical grandmothers, Rude Girls, neo-Afrofuturist and memoirists settling accounts gives us some respite from a decline or denial narrative and introduces a dynamism into ageing. After all, ageing is living. The book wasn't meant to be about a roster of women over 'a certain age' who are still going; it wasn't about survival. It wasn't an audit. It was meant to reconsider ageing as it is played out, on and by the bodies and voices, the images and performances, of a selection of interesting, important contemporary female musicians.

Bibliography

Ahmed, S. (2017) *Living a Feminist Life*. Durham, NC: Duke University Press.

Ainscoe, M. (2018) 'The Rheingans Sisters: Bright Field – Album Review', *Louder Than War*, 22nd March 2018. https://louderthanwar.com/rheingans-sisters-bright-field-album-review/ (Accessed 24/10/18).

Ajamu Hutchinson, S. (2017) 'A Review of Calypso Rose's "*Far from Home*" Concert', *The New Black Magazine*, 16th January, 2017. www.thenewblackmagazine.com/view.aspx?-index=3744 (Accessed 13/09/18).

Albertine, V. (2016) *Clothes, Clothes, Clothes, Music, Music, Music, Boys, Boys, Boys*. London: Faber and Faber.

AllMusic. (2016) www.allmusic.com/album/lodestar-mw0002981199.

Anderson, R., and Jones, C. E. (2016) *Afrofuturism 2.0. The Rise of Astro-Blackness*. Lanham, MD: Lexington Books.

Andrews, K. (2018) 'Urban' Sounds: It's Time to Stop Using This Hackneyed Term for Black Music', *The Guardian*, 14th August, 2018. www.theguardian.com/music/shortcuts/2018/aug/14/urban-time-stop-hackneyed-term-black-music

Apolloni, A. (2016) 'Authority, Ability and the Ageing Ingénue's Voice', in Warwick, J., and Adrian, A. (eds.), *Voicing Girlhood in Popular Music: Performance, Authority, Authenticity*. New York, London: Routledge, pp. 143–170.

Aucutrier, J.-J., and Pachet, F. (2003) 'Representing Musical Genre: A State of the Art', *Journal of New Music Research*, 32 (1), pp. 83–93.

Avižienis, J. (2005) 'Mediated and Unmediated Access to the Past: Assessing the Memoir as Literary Genre', *Journal of Baltic Studies*, 36 (1), pp. 39–50.

Baars, J. (2012) 'Critical Turns of Aging, Narrative and Time', *International Journal of Ageing and Later Life*, 7 (2), pp. 143–165.

Bacchilega, C. (1997) *Postmodern Fairy Tales: Gender and Narrative Strategies*. Philadelphia: University of Pennsylvania Press.

Baltes, M., and Carstensen, L. (1996) 'The Process of Successful Ageing', *Ageing and Society*, 16 (4), pp. 397–422.

Bannister, M. (2006) *White Boys, White Noise: Masculinities and 1980s Indie Guitar Rock*. Aldershot, Burlington: Ashgate.

Bascomb, T.T. (2015) '"I'm So Proud to Be Your Queen": Alison Hinds and Queenliness as a Diasporic Resource', *Meridians: Feminism, Race, Transnationalism*, 13 (1), pp. 78–102.

Bayton, M. (1997) 'Women and the Electric Guitar' in Whiteley, S. (ed.), *Sexing the Groove: Popular Music and Gender*. Oxford, New York: Routledge, pp. 37–49.

Beauman, N. (2006) 'Is Violence Holding Grime Back?', *The Guardian*, 6th November, 2006. www.theguardian.com/music/musicblog/2006/nov/06/isviolenceholdin ggrimeback, www.radiox.co.uk/features/x-lists/are-these-the-most-iconic-female-fronted-bands-90s/

Beebe, R., Fulbrook, D., and Saunders, B. (2002) *Rock over the Edge*. Durham, NC: Duke University Press.

Beer, D. (2012) 'Genre, Boundary Drawing and the Classificatory Imagination', *Cultural Sociology*, 7 (2), pp. 145–160.

Bennett, A. (2006) 'Punk's Not Dead: The Continuing Significance of Punk Rock for an Older Generation of Fans', *Sociology*, 40 (2), pp. 219–234.

Bennett, A. (2008) 'Popular Music, Media and the Narrativization of Place', in Peters, G.G., and Luckmann, S. (eds.), *Sonic Synergies: Music, Technology, Community, Identity*. Aldershot: Ashgate, pp. 69–78.

Bennett, A. (2009) '"Heritage Rock": Rock Music, Representation and Heritage Discourse', *Poetics*, 37, pp. 474–489.

Bennett, A. (2010) 'Popular Music, Cultural Memory and Everyday Aesthetics', in de la Fuente, E., and Murphy P. (eds.), *Philosophical and Cultural Theories of Music*. Leiden: Brill, pp. 243–262.

Bennett, A. (2013) *Music, Aging dand Style: Growing Old Disgracefully*. Philadelphia: Temple University Press.

Bennett, A. (2018) '"Heritage Rock": Rock Music, Representation and Heritage Discourse *Poetics*', 37, pp. 474–489.

Bennett, A., and Hodkinson, P. (eds.) (2012) *Ageing and Youth Culture: Music, Style and Identity*. London: New York, Berg.

Bennett, A., and Peterson, R. A. (2004) *Music Scenes, Local, Translocal, Virtual*. Nashville: Vanderbilt Press.

Bennett, A., and Rogers, I. (2016) *Popular Music Scenes and Cultural Memory*. London: Palgrave MacMillan.

Bhatiya, U. (2018) 'Alt-Rock Favourites The Breeders Are Back', *LiveMint*. www.livemint.com/Leisure/oywqkk0HU3lSlWN0r0TE7N/Altrock- favourites-The-Breeders-are-back.html.

Black, P. (2011) *Black by Design*. London: Serpents Tail.

Blake, T. (2018) 'The Rheingans Sisters: Bright Field', *Folk Radio*, 21st March 2018. www.folkradio.co.uk/2018/03/the-rheingans-sisters-bright-field/. (Accessed 27/01/19).

Boak, S. (2016) 'The Female Singer-Songwriter in the 1990s', in Williams, J., and Williams, K. (eds.), *The Cambridge Companion to the Singer-Songwriter*. Cambridge: Cambridge University Press, pp. 257–266.

Bobbio, N. (2001) *Old Age and Other Essays*. Cameron, A. (trans. and ed.). Oxford: Polity Press.

Bohlman, P. (1988) *The Study of Folk Music in the Modern World*. Bloomington: Indiana University Press.

Boland, P. (2010) 'Sonic Geography, Place and Race in the Formation of Local Identity: Liverpool and Scousers', *Geografiska Annaler, Human Geography Series B*, 92 (1), pp. 1–22. Doi:10.1111/j.1468-0467.2010.00330.x.

Borelli-Persson, L. (2018) 'Meet Pauline Black, the Originator of "Rude Girl" Style and Duro Olowu's Latest Muse', *Vogue*, 5th June. www.vogue.com/article/pauline-black-selecter-frontwoman-evolution-of-1980s-rude-girl-look-to-becoming-muse-to-duro-olowu-fall-2018.

Boyes, G. (2010) *The Imagined Village: Culture, Ideology and the English Folk Revival*. Leeds: No Masters Co-operative.

Boym, S. (2002) *The Future of Nostalgia*. New York: Basic Books.

Bradshaw, M. (2008) 'Devouring the Diva: Martydom as Feminist Backlash in *The Rose*', *Camera Obscura*, 23 (1(67)), pp. 68–88.

Braidwood, E. (2018) 'The Best Female-Fronted Punk Bands', *NME*, 20th October, 2018. www.nme.com/blogs/best-female-fronted-punk-bands-2344471 (Accessed 14/12/18).

Brett, P., and Wood, E. (2002) 'Lesbian and Gay Music', *Electronic Musicological Review*, 7, pp. 1–31. www.sidastudi.org/resources/inmagic-img/dd6114.pdf (Accessed 11/12/18).

Brocken, M. (2003) *The British Folk Revival 1944–2002*, Farnham: Ashgate (reissued 2018 by Oxford, New York: Routledge.

Brownstein, C. (2015) *Hunger Makes Me a Modern Girl: A Memoir.* London: Virago.

Bulut, S. (2018) 'Meet Lava La Rue, the West London Rapper Doing Things DIY-or-Die.' *Dazed*, 29th June, 2018. www.dazeddigital.com/music/article/40539/1/lava-la-rue-letra-interview.

Burns, L., and Lafrance, M. (2002) *Disruptive Divas: Feminism, Identity and Popular Music.* New York: Routledge.

Butler, J. (1990) *Gender Trouble: Feminism and the Subversion of Identity.* New York and London: Routledge.

Butler, J. (1993) *Bodies that Matter: On the Discursive Limits of Sex.* New York and London: Routledge.

Calasanti, T., and Slevin, K. (2006) *Age Matters: Realigning Feminist Thinking.* New York, London: Routledge.

Campbell, N, A. (2016) 'Calypso Rose and The Cult of Nostalgia: Far from Home – An Album Review', *iRadio:tt blog*, 28th November, 2016. https://iradiott.wordpress.com/2016/11/28/calypso-rose-and-the-cult-of-nostalgia far from home an album review'/ (Accessed 13/09/18).

Chapman, C. (2005) Theorizing about Aging Well: Constructing a Narrative', *Canadian Journal on Aging*, 24 (1), pp. 3–18.

Charles, M. (2019) 'Are You Grime or Part-Time?! Reviewing Race and "Realness" in Britain's Grime Scene', in Essed, P., Farquharson K., Pillay K., and White E. (eds.), *Relating Worlds of Racism.* Basingstoke: Palgrave Macmillan, pp. 299–328.

Charnock, R. (2018) *Joni Mitchell: New Critical Readings, Music and Sound Studies.* London, New York: Bloomsbury Press.

Chivers, S. (2003) *From Old Women to Older Women: Contemporary Culture and Women's Narratives.* Columbus: Ohio State University Press.

Chivers, S. (2011) *The Silvering Screen: Old Age and Disability in Cinema.* Toronto: University of Toronto Press.

Clarke, P. (2016) 'Shirley Collins – Lodestar', *Clash Music*, 5th December, 2016. www.clashmusic.com/reviews/shirley-collins-lodestar.

Clark, A. (2018) 'The Spice Girls Showed Us How to Party. In Dark Times, They're Back to Remind Us', *The Guardian*, 12th November, 2018. www.theguardian.com/commentisfree/2018/nov/12/spice-girls-touring (Accessed 12/11/18).

Cleto, F. (1999) *Camp, Queer Aesthetics and the Performing Subject: A Reader.* Edinburgh: Edinburgh University Press.

Cohen, S. (1972) *Folk Devils and Moral Panics.* London: MacGibbon and Key Limited.

Cohen, S. (2007) *Decline, Renewal and the City in Popular Music Culture: Beyond the Beatles.* Farnham: Ashgate.

Collins, S. (2018) *All in the Downs: Life, Landscape and Song.* London: Strange Attractor Press.

Connell, J., and Gibson, C. (2003) *Soundtracks: Popular Music, Identity and Place.* London and New York: Routledge.

Connor, S. (2000) *Dumbstruck, A Cultural History of Ventriloquism.* Oxford: Oxford University Press.

Cooper, K. (2018) '15 Female Fronted Bands You Need to Listen To', *BeatMedia.* https://beat.media/15-female-fronted-bands-you-need-to-listen-to (Accessed 14/12/18).

Coventry Live 'The Selecter Announced as Latest Act for Step Back 80s', www.coventrytelegraph.net/whats-on/selecter-stepback-80s- ricoh-coventry-14638859 (Accessed 21/01/19).

Cragg, M. (2016) 'Christine and the Queens: From Soho Drag Club to French Superstardom', *The Guardian*, 7th January, 2016. www.theguardian.com/music/2016/jan/07/christine-and-the-queens-soho-drag-club-to-french-superstardom-heloise-letissier.

Cubitt, S. (1993) *Videography: Video Media as Art and Culture*. London: MacMillan.

Cubitt, S. (2002) 'Visual and Audiovisual: From Image to Moving Image', *Journal of Visual Culture*, 1 (3), pp. 359–368.

Cubitt, S. (forthcoming) *Finite Media: Environmental Implications of Digital Technologies*. Durham, NC: Duke University Press.

Culshaw, P. (2016) 'Calypso Rose: 'I'm Fighting for Everyone, Regardless of Sex', *The Guardian*, 21st July, 2016. www.theguardian.com/music/2016/jul/21/calypso-rose-im-fighting-for-everyone-regardless-of-sex (Accessed 10/09/18).

de Lacy, A. (2015) 'Deeper Than Rap: Grime is Not a Subgenre of Hip-Hop', *Complex*, 3rd November, 2015. www.complex.com/pigeons-and-planes/2015/11/grime-hip-hop.

Deming, M. (2016) 'All Music Review by Mark Deming', *All Music*. www.allmusic.com/album/lodestar-mw0002981199.

De Nora, T. (2000) *Music in Everyday Life*. Cambridge: Cambridge University Press.

Denselow, R. (2016) 'Calypso Rose: Far from Home Review – A Glorious Summer Album', *The Guardian*, 14th July, 2016. www.theguardian.com/music/2016/jul/14/calypso-rose-far-from-home-review-because-music-cd-world-music-review (Accessed 13/09/18).

Diamond, E. (1997) *Unmaking Mimesis: Essays in Feminism and Theatre*. London, New York: Routledge.

Dickinson, K. (2001) '"Believe" Vocoder, Digital Female Identity and Camp', *Popular Music*, 20 (3), pp. 333–347.

Dibben, N. (2013) *Björk*. Sheffield, Bristol, CT: Equinox.

Dillon, K. (2018) *The Spectacle of Twins in American Literature and Popular Culture*. Jefferson, NC: McFarland.

Dishman, M. (2015) 'Sam Lee and Friends, Folk and the Fade in Time.' www.folkwitness.co.uk (Accessed 13/01/2016).

Dolan, J. (2012) '"The Queen", Aging Femininity and the Recuperation of the Monarchy', *Ageing Studies in Europe*, 2 (1), pp. 39–52.

Dolan, J. (2013) 'Firm and Hard: Popular Culture, Gendered Stardom and the Troubling Embodiment of "Successful Aging"', in Prieto-Arranz, J. et al. (eds.), *De-centering Cultural Studies: Past, Present and Future of Popular Culture*. Newcastle-Upon-Tyne: Cambridge Scholars Press, pp. 217–246.

Dolan, J. (2017) *Contemporary Cinema and 'Old Age': Gender and the Silvering of Stardom*. London: Palgrave MacMillan.

Dreyer, E., and McDowal, E. (2012) 'Imagining the *Flâneur* as a Woman', *Communication*, 38 (1), pp. 30–44, Doi:10.1080/02500167.2011.634425.

Driessen, S. (2015) 'Larger Than Life: Exploring the Transcultural Fan Practices of Dutch Backstreet Boys Fandom', *Participations, Journal of Audiences and Reception Studies*, 12 (2), pp. 150–196.

Driver, C., and Bennett, A. (2014) 'Music Scenes, Space and the Body', *Cultural Sociology*, 9 (1), pp. 99–115, Doi:10.1177/1749975514546234.

Dudley, S. K. (2004) *Carnival Music in Trinidad: Experiencing Music, Expressing Culture*. New York: Oxford Press.

Dyer, R. (1993) *The Matter of Images, Essays in Representation*. London: Routledge.

Dyer, R. (1997) *White*. Oxford, New York: Routledge.

Edgar, R., Mann, F., and Pleasance, H. (2019) *Music, Memory and Memoir*. London: Bloomsbury.

Edwards, L, H. (2018) *Dolly Parton, Gender and Country Music*. Bloomington: Indiana University Press.

Elia, A. (2014) 'The Languages of Afrofuturism', *Lingua e Linguaggi*, 12, pp. 83–96.

Ellen, B. (2018) 'Interview Kim Deal: 'Misogyny is the Backbone of the Music Industry', *The Guardian*, 3rd March, 2018. www.theguardian.com/music/2018/mar/03/kim-deal-breeders-misogyny-pixies-cobain-rehab (Accessed 14/11/18).

Elliott, R. (2013) *Nina Simone*. Bristol: Equinox.

Elliott, R. (2015) *The Late Voice: Time, Age and Experience in Popular Music*. London, New York: Bloomsbury.

Empire, K. (2011) 'Mojo Launch Heralds the Age of Heritage Rock', *The Guardian*, 12th June, 2011. www.newsmulti.com/music/2011/jun/12/mojo-launch-heritage-rock (Accessed 24/05/19).

Empire, K. (2017) 'The Breeders Review – Kim Deal's Music Continues to Defy Physics', *The Guardian*, 22nd October, 2017. www.theguardian.com/music/2017/oct/22/the-breeders-electric-ballroom-london-review-kim-deal-music-defies-physics (Accessed 14/11/18).

English, D, K., and Kim, A. (2013) 'Now We Want Our Funk Cut: Janelle Monáe's Neo-Afrofuturism', *American Studies*, 52 (4), pp. 217–230.

Eshun, K. (2003) 'Further Considerations on Afrofuturism', *CR: The New Centennial Review*, 3 (2), pp. 287–302.

Essentially Pop (2018) at http://essentiallypop.com/epop/2018/09/christine-and-the-queens new album-chris-channels-janet-jackson-and-prince-with-a-touch-of- chic-while-maintaining-a-unique-style/

Fabbre, V. D. (2014) 'Gender Transitions in Later Life: The Significance of Time in Queer Aging', *Journal of Gerontological Social Work*, 57 (2–4), pp. 161–175, Doi:10.1080/01634372.2013.855287.

Fabbri, F. (1980) 'A Theory of Musical Genres: Two Applications', in Horn, D., and Tagg, P. (eds.), *Popular Music Perspectives, Papers from the First International Association of Popular Music Conference on Popular Music Research*. Amsterdam: Goteborg and Exeter, pp. 52–81.

Fanfair, R. (2018) 'Calypso Rose Aging Well Like Old Wine', www.ronfanfair.com/home/2018/1/31/calypso-rose. (Accessed 10/09/18).

Finnegan, R. (2007) *The Hidden Musicians: Making Music in an English Town*. Middletown: Weslyan University Press.

Fleming, A. (2018) 'The Breeders: Still a Breed Apart after 30 Years', *The Financial Times*, 22nd February, 2018. www.ft.com/content/af48345e-1661-11e8-9c33-02f893d608c2

Forman, M. (2002) *The 'Hood Comes First: Race, Space, and Place in Rap and Hip-Hop*. Middletown: Weslyan University Press.

Foucault, M. ([1978]1998) *The History of Sexuality: The Will to Knowledge*. London: Penguin.

Fox, K. (2016) 'Happy Birthday Punk: The British Library Celebrates 40 Years of Anarchy and Innovation', *The Guardian*, 13th March, 2016. www.theguardian.com/music/2016/mar/13/punk-1976-1978-british-library-40th-anniversary-sex-pistols-buzzcocks

Freeman, E. (2010) *Time Binds: Queer Temporalities, Queer Histories*. Durham, NC, London: Duke University Press.

Frith, S. (1996) *Performing Rites: On the Value of Popular Music*. Oxford: Oxford University Press.

Frith, S., and Horne, H. (1987) *Art into Pop*. London: Methuen.

Frith, S., and McRobbie, A. (1990 [1978]) 'Rock and Sexuality', in Frith, S., and Goodwin, A. (eds.), *On Record: Rock, Pop and the Written Word*. New York: Routledge, pp. 371–389.

Gaiman, N. (2018) Liner Notes for *All Nerve*, The Breeders, http://thebreedersmusic.com/bio/.

Garde-Hansen, J. (2011) *Media and Memory*. Edinburgh: Edinburgh University Press.

Gardner, A. (2015) *PJ Harvey and Music Video Performance*. London, New York: Routledge.

Gardner, A. (2017) 'PJ Harvey and Remembering England', in Brooks, L., Donnelly, M., and Mills, R. (eds.), *Mad Dogs and Englishness: Popular Music and English Identities*. New York, London: Bloomsbury, pp. 66–82.

Gardner, A. (2018a) 'PJ Harvey, YouTube and Ageing: An Everyday Story of the Erasure of Age', *Convergence, International Journal of Research into New Media Technologies, Sage Journals*, online only, Doi:10.1177/1354856517750367

Gardner, A. (2018b) 'Anohni and Transgendered, Trans-Age Transgression', in Holland, S., and Spracklen, K. (eds.), *Subcultures, Bodies and Spaces: Essays on Alternativity and Marginalization*. Bingley: Emerald Publishing, pp. 133–152.

Gardner, A., and Jennings, R. (2019) *Aging and Popular Music in Europe*. New York, Oxford: Routledge.

Gardner, A., and Moorey, G. (2016) 'Raiders of the Lost Archives', *Popular Communication*, 14 (3), pp. 169–177.

Gill, J. (ed.) (2006) *Modern Confessional Writing: New Critical Essays*. London, New York: Routledge.

Gill, M. (2011) 'The Myth of the Female Dandy', *French Studies*, 61 (2), pp. 167–181, Doi: 10.1093/fs/knm062.

Gilleard, C., and Higgs, P. (2014) *Ageing, Corporeality and Embodiment*. London, New York: Anthea Press.

Gladys Knight Strictly Come Dancing (2018) https://twitter.com/search?q=gladys%20knight%20strictly%20come%20dancing&src=typd.

Gleeson, S. (2013) 'Savages Aren't a Great Girl Band, They're a Great Band', *The Irish Times*, 8th March 2013. www.irishtimes.com/culture/music/savages-aren-t-a-great-girl-band-they-re-a-great-band-1.1320152

Goodwin, A. (1992) *Dancing in the Distraction Factory: Music Television and Popular Culture*. Minneapolis: University of Minnesota Press.

Gordon, K. (2015) *Girl in a Band, a Memoir*. London: Harper Collins.

Greaves, G. G. (1995) 'The Rhetoric of the Calypso of Political Commentary from Therepublic of Trinidad and Tobago: An African-Centered Historical-Critical Analysis', *Howard Journal of Communication*, 6 (4), pp. 324–334.

Grenier, L., and Valois-Nadeau, F. (2018) *A Senior Moment: Cultural Mediations of Memory and Aging*. Bielefeld: Transcript Verlag.

Grosz, E. (1998) 'Bodies – Cities', in Nash, H., and Pile, S. (eds.), *Places Through the Body*. London, New York: Routledge, pp. 42–51.

Guerra, P. (2015) 'Keep It Rocking: The Social Space of Portuguese Alternative Rock (1980–2010)', *Journal of Sociology*, 52 (4), pp. 615–630.

Guerrón-Montero, C. (2006) 'Can't Beat Me Own Drum in Me Own Native Land: Calypso Music and Tourism in the Panamanian Atlantic Coast', *Anthropological Quarterly*, 79 (4), pp. 633–665. www.jstor.org/stable/4150925 (Accessed 27/03/18).

Guilbault, J. (2005). 'Audible Entanglements: Nation and Diasporas in Trinidad's Calypso Music Scene', *Small Axe: A Journal of Criticism*, 17, pp. 40–63.

Guilbault, J. (2007) *Governing Sound: The Cultural Politics of Trinidad's Carnival Musics*. Chicago, IL: University of Chicago Press.

Gullette, M. (2004) *Aged By Culture*. Chicago, IL: Chicago University Press.

Halberstam, J. (2005) *In a Queer Time and Place: Transgender Bodies, Subcultural Lives*. New York: New York University Press.

Halberstam, J. (2011) 'Keeping Time with Lesbians on Ecstast', in Callum, E.E., and Tukhanen, M. (eds.), *Queer Times, Queer Becomings*, Albany: SUNY Press, pp. 333–344.

Halberstam, J. (2013) 'Go Gaga: Anarchy, Chaos and the Wild', *Social Text*, 116, pp. 127–134.

Hall, I. (2018) 'Calypso Rose, So Calypso! Album Review', *Liverpool Sound and Vision*, 29th June, 2018. www.liverpoolsoundandvision.co.uk/2018/06/29/calypso-rose-so-calypso-album-review/ (Accessed 13/09/18).

Hall, S. (1993) 'What Is This "Black" in Black Popular Culture?', *Social Justice*, 20 (1/2 (51–52)), pp. 104–114. www.jstor.org/stable/29766735.

Halperin, M. (2014) 'We Will All Howl: Anthony Hegarty on the State of Transfeminism', *Flavorwire*, 24th November, 2014. http://flavorwire.com/489997/we-will-all-howl-antony-hegarty-on-the-state-of-transfeminism (Accessed 27/04/17).

Hansen, K. A. (2020) *New Directions: Contemporary Pop Music and Post Boy Band Masculinities*. New York: Oxford University Press.

Harrington, C., and Bielby, D. D. (2010) 'A Life Course Perspective on Fandom', *International Journal of Cultural Studies*, 13 (5), pp. 429–450.

Haruch, S. (2010) 'Women Account for Less Than 5 Percent of Producers and Engineers – But Maybe Not for Long', *Nashville Music, Scene*, 3rd June, 2010. www.nashvillescene.com/news/article/13034234/women- account-for-less-than-5-percent-of-producers-and-engineers-but- maybe- not-for-long (Accessed 13/11/18).

Hawkins, S. (2002) *Settling the Pop Score: Pop Texts and Identity Politics*. Farnham: Ashgate.

Hawkins, S. (2016a) *The British Pop Dandy: Masculinity, Popular Music and Culture: Male Identity, Music and Culture*. Oxford: Routledge.

Hawkins, S. (2016b) *Queerness in Pop Music: Aesthetics, Gender Norms, Temporality*. New York, London: Routledge.

Hawkins, S., and Niblock, S. (2011) *Prince: The Making of a Music Phenomenon*. Aldershot: Ashgate.

Hebdige, D. (1979) *Subculture: The Meaning of Style*. London: Methuen.

Hebdige, D. (1987) *Cut 'n' Mix: Culture, Identity and Caribbean Music*. Oxford, New York: Routledge.

Hebdige, D. (2007) 'Posing....Threats. Striking....Poses: Youth, Surveillance and Display', in Gelder, K. (ed.) Second Edition. *The Subcultures Reader*. London, New York: Routledge.

Heritage Lottery Fund. (2015) 'London to Celebrate 40 Years of Punk Culture in 2016', *hlf*, 26th November, 2015. www.hlf.org.uk/about-us/media-centre/press-releases/london-celebrate-40-years-punk-culture-2016.

Hersh, K. (2010) *Rat Girl, A Memoir*. London: Penguin.

Hibberd, L. (2014) 'Grown Up Girls: Newspaper Reviews of Ageing Women in Pop', in Whelehan I., and Gwynne J. (eds.), *Ageing, Popular Culture and Contemporary Feminism* London: Palgrave Macmillan, pp. 121–139.

Higgens, M. (2018) 'The Rheingans Sisters – Bright Field (RootBeat Records)', *Northern Sky*, http://northernskymag.com/reviews/cd-reviews/rheinganssisters-bright-field-rootbeat-records (Accessed 24/10/18).

Hirai, M. (1998) *Sisters in Literature. Female Sexuality in Antigone, Middlemarch, Howards End and Women in Love*. London: Palgrave MacMillan.

Hodkinson, P. (2005) "Insider Research' in the Study of Youth Cultures', *Journal of Youth Studies*, 8 (2), pp. 131–149.

Hogarty, J. (2017) *Popular Music and Retro Culture in the Digital Era*. New York, London: Routledge.

Hubble, N., and Tew, P. (2013) *Ageing, Narrative and Identity: New Qualitative Social Research.* Basingstoke: Palgrave MacMillan.

Hutcheon, L. and Hutcheon, M. (2012) 'Late Style(s): The Ageism of the Singular', *Occasion: Interdisciplinary Studies in the Humanities*, 4. http://occasion.stanford.edu/node/93 (Accessed 20/03/13).

Huq, R. (2013) *Making Sense of Suburbia through Popular Culture.* London, New York: Bloomsbury.

IASPM, UK and Eire Biannual Conference – program https://crosstowntraffic2018.wordpress.com/programme/.

Irigaray, L. (1985) *This Sex Which Is Not One.* New York: Cornell University Press.

Jackson, C. (2017) 'Grime Music Linked to Knife Crime Rise', *The Daily Express*, 3rd July, 2017. www.expressandstar.com/news/local-hubs/2017/07/03/increase-in-knife-crime/.

James, R. (2015) *Resilience and Melancholy: Pop Music, Feminism and Neoliberalism.* Alresford: Zero Books.

Jameson, F. (1984) 'Postmodernism, or the Cultural Logic of Late Capitalism', *New Left Review*, 196, pp. 53–92.

Jarman-Ivens, F. (2011) *Queer Voices: Technologies, Vocality and the Musical Flaw.* New York: Palgrave MacMillan.

Jenkins, C. (2018) 'A New Breeders Album Is Just One Sign of a '90s Alt-Rock Resurgence', *Vulture*, 2nd March, 2018. www.vulture.com/2018/03/the-return-of-90s-alt-rock.html.

Jennings, R. (2015) 'Popular Music and Ageing', in Twigg, J. and Martin, W. (eds.), *The Routledge Handbook of Cultural Gerontology.* London: Routledge, pp. 77–84.

Jennings, R. and Gardner, A. (2012) *Rock On: Women, Ageing and Popular Music.* New York, London: Routledge.

Jermyn, D., and Holmes, S. (2015) *Women, Celebrity and Cultures of Ageing: Freeze Frame.* London: Palgrave MacMillan.

Johnston, M. (2018) 'Breeders All Nerve Review', *Pitchfork*, 2nd March, 2018. https://pitchfork.com/reviews/albums/the-breeders-all-nerve/ (Accessed 16/10/18).

Joy, S.M. (1992) 'Revolution Grrrl Style Now', *Melody Maker*, 10th October, 1992, pp. 30–32.

Kane, S, A. (1996). 'Wives with Knives: Early Modern Murder Ballads and the Transgressive Commodity', *Criticism*, 38 (2), pp. 219–237. www.jstor.org/stable/23118187 (Accessed 26/03/18).

Kaplan, A. (1987) *Rocking Round the Clock: Music Television, Postmodernism and Consumer Culture.* New York, London: Routledge.

Katz, S. (2005) *Cultural Aging: Life Course, Lifestyle and Senior Worlds.* Toronto: University of Toronto Press.

Katz, S. (2013). 'Active and Successful Aging: Lifestyle as a Gerontological Idea', *Recherches sociologiques et anthropologiques*, 44, pp. 33–49.

Katz, S. (2014) 'Music, Performance, and Generation: The Making of Boomer Rock and Roll Biographies', in Lee Harrington, C., Bielby, D., and Bardo, A.R (eds.), *Aging, Media, and Culture.* New York, London: Lexington Book, pp. 93–106.

Katz, S. (2018) 'The Greatest Band that Never Was: Music, Memory, and Boomer Biography', *Popular Music and Society*, Doi:10.1080/03007766.2018.1522234

Keathley, E. (2002) 'A Context for Eminem's 'Murder Ballads', *Echo: A Music-Centered Journal*, 4 (2). www.echo.ucla.edu/volume4- issue2/keathley/keathley_1.html

Keightley, E. (ed.) (2012) *Time, Media and Modernity.* London: Palgrave MacMillan.

Keightley, K. (2016) 'Canned: A Genealogy of Mass Cultural Critique', conference paper at IASPM UK Eire conference, Huddersfield, UK, www.iaspm.org.uk/iaspm/wp-content/uploads/2016/04/IASPM_Brighton_Schedule.pdf.

Kellaway, K. (2019) 'Joan Baez: 'Music Can Move People to Do Things'', *The Guardian*, 24th February, 2019. www.theguardian.com/music/2019/feb/24/joan-baez-interview-whistle-down-the-wind-farewell-tour-folk-music-protest-songs.

Kent, N. (2010) *Apathy for the Devil: A Seventies Memoir.* Philadelphia, PA: Da Capo.

Kidman, D. (2016) 'Shirley Collins, Lodestar', *Folk Radio*, 8th November, 2016. www.folkradio.co.uk/2016/11/shirley-collins-lodestar/ (Accessed 26/03/2018).

Knox, D. (2008) 'Spectacular Tradition: Scottish Folk Song and Authenticity', *Annals of Tourism Research*, 35, pp. 255–273.

Kraus, R. (2017) 'The Breeders are Back, Right When We Need Them More than Ever', *Mashable*, 4th October 2017. https://mashable.com/2017/10/04/the- breeders-wait-in-the-car/?europe=true.

Larsson, N. (2017) 'Live Music Acts Are Mostly Male-Only. What's Holding Women Back?', *The Guardian*, 12th October, 2017. www.theguardian.com/inequality/2017/oct/12/tonights-live- music-acts- will-mostly-be-male-only-whats-holding-women-back (Accessed 08/11/18).

Lee, S. (2014) Sam Lee on the Significance of Shirley Collins, at www.youtube.com/watch?v=5hWHdNRcfbc (Accessed 22/01/19).

Lee, S. (2015) 'Ballad Lands: Jonny O' the Brine – Sam Lee Discovers the Roots of This Ancient Traveller Song', *YouTube*. www.youtube.com/watch?v=B8CwSbsqQE4 (Accessed 29/05/18).

Lefebvre, H. (1991) *The Production of Space.* Oxford: Blackwell Publishing.

Leighton-Dore, S. (2018) 'Janelle Monáe Dedicates Grammy Nomination to Black Queer Community', *Special Broadcasting Service*, Australia, 10th December, 2018. www.sbs.com.au/topics/sexuality/fast-l ane/article/2018/12/10/janelle-monae-dedicates-grammy-nomination-black- queer-community (Accessed 11/12/18).

Lena, J. C. (2012) *Banding Together: How Communities Create Genres in Popular Music.* Princeton, NJ: Princeton University Press.

Leonard, M. (2007) *Gender in the Music Industry: Rock, Discourse and Girl Power.* Farnham: Ashgate.

Leonard, M., and Kifton, R. (2015) 'Engaging Nostalgia: Popular Music and Memory in Museums', in Cohen, S., Knifton, Leonard, M., and Roberts, L. (eds.), *Sites of Popular Music Heritage.* Oxford, New York: Routledge, pp. 160–173.

Lewis, L. (1993) 'Being Discovered: The Emergence of Female Address on MTV' in Frith, S., Goodwin, A., and Grossberg, L. (eds.), *Sound and Vision: The Music Video Reader.* London: Routledge, pp. 111–158.

Little, S. (2018) 'Women, Ageing, and Hip Hop: Discourses and Imageries of Ageing Femininity', *Feminist Media Studies*, 18 (1), pp. 31–46.

Long P., and Collins J. (2012) 'Mapping the Soundscapes of Popular Music Heritage', in Roberts L. (ed.), *Mapping Cultures.* London: Palgrave Macmillan, pp. 144–159.

Long, R. (2018) 'Sexual Subjectivities within Neoliberalism: Can Queer and Crip Engagements Offer an Alternative Praxis?', *Journal of International Women's Studies*, 19 (1), pp. 78–93.

Luciano, D. (2011) 'Nostalgia for an Age Yet to Come: Velvet Goldmine's Queer Archive', in Mc Callum, E. E., and Tuhkanen, M. (eds.), *Queer Times, Queer Becomings.* Albany: State University of New York Press, pp. 121–158.

Lusty, N. (2007) *Surrealism, Feminism, Psychoanalysis.* Aldershot, Burlington: Ashgate.

Mackay, E. (2015) 'Kim Deal Interview: On A New Breeders Album, Keeping It Cottage Industry And Patricide', *NME*, 9th March, 2015. www.nme.com/blogs/nme-blogs/kim-deal-interview-on-a-new-breeders-album-keeping-it-cottage-industry-and-patricide-759788#JcoeISczwc0qYZFp.99.

Mahabir, C. (2001) 'The Rise of Calypso Feminism: Gender and Musical Politics in the Calypso', *Popular Music*, 20 (3), pp. 409–430, Cambridge University Press. www.jstor.org/stable/853630 (Accessed: 10/12/2018).

Marshall, B. (2014) 'Sexualising the Third Age', in Lee Harrington, C., Bielby, D., and Bardo, A.R. (eds.), *Aging, Media, and Culture*, New York, London: Lexington Books, pp. 169–180.

Marshall, B., and Katz, S. (2002). 'Forever Functional: Sexual Fitness and the Ageing Male Body', *Body & Society*, 8 (4), pp. 43–70.

Massey, D. (1994) *Space, Place and Gender.* Minneapolis: University of Minnesota Press.

May, L. S. (2001) *Disorderly Sisters: Sibling Relations and Sororal Resistance in Nineteenth Century British Literature.* Lewisbury: Bucknell University Press.

McClary, S. (2002 [1991]) *Feminine Endings, Music, Gender and Sexuality.* Minneapolis: University of Minnesota Press.

McLeod, K. (2003) 'Space Oddities: Aliens, Futurism and Meaning in Popular Music', *Popular Music*, 22 (3), pp. 337–355.

McRobbie, A. (1991) 'Settling Accounts with Subculture: A Feminist Critique', *Feminism and Youth Culture.* Youth Questions. London: Palgrave, pp. 16–34.

Melina, L. R. (2008) 'Backstage with the Hot Flashes: Performing Gender, Performing Age, Performing Rock'n'Roll', *Qualitative Inquiry*, 14 (1), pp. 90–110.

Meyer, M. (1994) 'Reclaiming the Discourse of Camp', in Meyer, M. (ed.), *The Politics and Poetics of Camp.* London, New York: Routledge.

Mitchell, E. (2015) 'In Excess, Elsewhere and Otherwise: Feminine Subjectivity in Eija-Liisa Ahtila's Multi-Screen Installation if 6 Was 9 (1995)', *Networking Knowledge: Journal of the MeCCSA Postgraduate Network*, 8 (5). Doi:10.31165/nk.2015.85.395.

Moglen, D. (2008) 'Ageing and Transageing: Trangenerational Hauntings of the Self', *Studies in Gender and Sexuality*, 9, pp. 297–311.

Molleson, K. (2017) Shirley Collins Review – A Five-Star Foray into the Darker Depths of Folk', *The Guardian*, 5th February, 2017. www.theguardian.com/music/2017/feb/05/shirley-collins-city-halls-glasgow-review-celtic-connections (Accessed 10/12/18).

Moore, A. (2002) 'Authenticity as Authentication', *Popular Music*, 21 (2), pp. 209–223.

Motley Crüe (2002) *The Dirt: Confessions of the World's Most Notorious Rock Band.* New York: Harper Collins.

Mulvey, L. (1991) 'A Phantasagoria of the Female Body; The Work of Cindy Sherman', *New Left Review*, 1 (88), pp. 137–150.

Munoz, J, E. (2009) *Cruising Utopia: The Then and There of Queer Futurity.* New York, London: New York University Press.

Music Business Worldwide, www.musicbusinessworldwide.com/with1m-album-sales-worldwide-christine-and-the-queens-ready-next-step/.

Needham, G. (2018) 'Abba Announce First New Songs for 35 Years', *The Guardian*, 27th April, 2018. www.theguardian.com/music/2018/apr/27/abba-announce-first-new-songs-for-35-years (Accessed 10/12/18).

Negus, K., and Pickering, M. (2002) 'Creativity, Communication and Musical Experience', in Hesmondhalgh, D and Negus, K. (eds.), *Popular Music Studies.* London: Arnold, pp. 178–190.

Nelson, A. (2002) 'Introduction: Future Texts', Afrofuturism: A Special Issue of Social Text', *Social Text*, 71, Durham, NC: Duke University Press.

Novara, V. J., and Henry, S. (2009) 'A Guide to Essential American Indie Rock (1980–2005)', *Notes*, Second Series, 65 (4), pp. 816–833.

O'Hagan, S. (2016) 'Brix Smith Start: 'Mark E. Smith? He's Complicated'', *The Guardian*, 1st May, 2016. www.theguardian.com/music/2016/may/01/brix-smith-start-interview-rise-fall-rise-mark-e-smith-nigel-kennedy-philip-start-the-extricated.

O'Meara, C. (2003) 'The Raincoats: Breaking Down Punk Rock's Masculinities', *Popular Music*, 22 (3), pp. 299–313.

O'Neill, E. R. (2007) 'The M-m-mama of Us All: Divas and the Cultural Logic of Late Ca(m)pitalism', *Camera Obscura*, 22 (2), pp. 11–37.

Orr, G. (2016) 'We Have A Mission To Make Rock'n'Roll More Equal', *Vogue*, 26th May 2016. www.vogue.co.uk/gallery/girl-bands-2016 (Accessed 04/12/18).

Paier, N. (2018) 'New Report Shows Major Lack of Representation by Women in the Music Industry', Billboard, 25th January, 2018. www.billboard.com/articles/news/8096196/new-report-shows-major-lack-representation-women-music-industry (Accessed 07/12/18).

Passen, H. (2018) 'Welcome to Janelle Monáe's America', *New America*, 10th May, 2018, www.newamerica.org/weekly/edition-206/welcome-janelle-monaes-america/

Pattison, L. (2016) '*Shirley Collins*, Lodestar', *Pitchfork*, 8th November, 2016. https://pitchfork.com/reviews/albums/22587-lodestar/ (Accessed 26/03/18).

Petridis, A. (2016) 'Shirley Collins: Lodestar Review – Austere, Foreboding Music from Long-Silent Singer', *The Guardian*, 17th October, 2016. www.theguardian.com/music/2016/oct/27/shirley-collins-lodestar-album-review-austere-foreboding-folk-music (Accessed 26/03/2018).

Petridis, A. (2018a) 'Janelle Monáe: Dirty Computer Review – Vagina Monologues from a Far-Off Star', *The Guardian*, 27th April, 2018, www.theguardian.com/music/2018/apr/27/janelle-monae-dirty-computer-review-vagina-monologues-from-a-far-off-star.

Petridis, A. (2018b) 'Christine and the Queens: Chris Review – Pop Music That Truly Matters', *The Guardian*, 20th September, 2018. www.theguardian.com/music/2018/sep/20/christine-and-the-queens- chris-album-review (Accessed 12/12/18).

Petrusich, A. (2018) 'The Remarkable Persistence of The Breeders', *The New Yorker*, 9th March, 2018. www.newyorker.com/culture/culture-desk/the-remarkable-persistence-of-the-breeders.

Pickard, S. (2018) *Age Studies: A Sociological Examination of How We Age and Are Aged Through the Life Course*. London: Sage.

Port, C. (2012) 'No Future? Aging, Temporality, History, and Reverse Chronologies.' *Occasion: Interdisciplinary Studies in the Humanities*, 4 (May 31, 2012), pp. 1–19.

PRS Foundation, at https://prsfoundation.com/funding-support/funding-music-creators/all-career-levels/women-make-music-2/background-to-women-make-music/ (Accessed 07/12/18).

Puar, J. (2005) 'Queer Times, Queer Assemblages', *Social Text*, 23 (3–4 (84–85)), pp. 121–139.

Raasch, B. (2018) 'Comments on 'Cannonball' by The Breeders', *YouTube*, www.youtube.com/watch?v=5i76b0OrdIQ (Accessed 30/01/19).

Radiox www.radiox.co.uk/features/x-lists/are-these-the-most-iconic-female- fronted-bands-90s/ (Accessed 14/12/18).

Radstone, R. (2007) *The Sexual Politics of Time: Confession, Nostalgia, Memory*. Oxford, New York: Routledge.

Railton, D., and Watson, P. (2011) *Music Video and the Politics of Representation*. Edinburgh: Edinburgh University Press.

Ratliff, B. (2016) *Every Song Ever: Twenty Ways to Listen in an Age of Musical Plenty*. London: Picador.

Reddington, H. (2007) *The Lost Women of Rock Music: Female Musicians of the Punk Era*. Aldershot: Ashgate.

Reynolds, S. (2011) *Retromania. Pop Culture's Addiction to Its Own Past*. London: Faber and Faber.

Reynolds, S. (2016) *Shock and Awe: Glam Rock and Its Legacy*. London: Faber and Faber.

Reynolds, S., and Press, J. (1995) *The Sex Revolts: Gender, Rebellion and Rock* 'n' Roll. London, New York: Serpents Tail.

Roberts, L., and Cohen, S. (2015) 'Unveiling Memory: Blue Plaques as Intangible Maker of Popular Music Heritage', in Cohen, S., Knifton, R., Leonard, M., and Roberts, L. (eds.), *Sites of Popular Music Heritage*. Oxford, New York: Routledge, pp. 221–267.

Robertson, P. (1996) *Guilty Pleasures: Camp from Mae West to Madonna*. London: I.B Tauris.

Rogers, J. (2015) 'The History of Punk was always His-Story', *The Guardian*, 15th November, 2015. www.theguardian.com/music/2015/nov/15/history-of-punk-was-always-his-story-women-rock-biographies (Accessed 14/03/17).

Rolling Stone (2018) 'Readers' Rock List: The Best Female-Fronted Bands', *Rolling Stone*, 4th March, 2008. www.rollingstone.com/music/music- lists/readers-rock-list-the-best-female-fronted-bands-239858/ (Accessed 14/12/18).

Roy, W. (2007) 'Aesthetic Identity, Race, and American Folk Music', *Qualitative Sociology*, 25 (3), pp. 459–469.

Rozanova, J. (2010) 'Discourse of Successful Aging in *The Globe & Mail*: Insights from Critical Gerontology', *Journal of Aging Studies*, 24, pp. 213–222.

Russo, M. (1999) 'Aging and the Scandal of Anachronism', in Woodward, K. (ed.), *Figuring Age: Women, Bodies, Generations*. Bloomington: Indiana University Press, pp. 20–33.

Samuel, R. (2012[1994]). *Theatres of Memory: Past and Present in Contemporary Culture*. London: Verso.

Sandberg, L. (2008) 'The Old, the Ugly and the Queer: Thinking Old Age in Relation to Queer Theory', *Graduate Journal of Social Science*, 5 (2), pp. 117–139.

Schilt, K. (2004) '"Riot Grrrl Is…": The Contestation over Meaning in a Music Scene', in Bennet, A., and Peterson, R. A. (eds.), *Music Scenes: Local, Translocal and Virtual*. Nashville, TN: Vanderbilt University Press, pp. 115–130.

Scovell, A. (2017) *Folk Horror, Hours Dreadfull and Things Strange*. Leighton Buzzard: Auteur.

Schütze, M. (1922) 'The Fundamental Ideas in Herder's Thought. IV', *Modern Philology*, 19 (4), pp. 361–382.

Segal, L. (2013) *Out of Time: The Pleasures and Perils of Ageing*. London, New York: Verso.

Shah, R. (2017) 'Hail The Queen', *Trinidad and Tobago News*, 24th February, 2017. www.trinidadandtobagonews.com/blog/?p=9939 (Accessed 10/09/18).

Shamas, L. A. (2007) *"We Three": The Mythology of Shakespeare's Weird Sisters*. Bern: Peter Lang.

Shumway, D. (2016) 'The Emergence of the Singer-Songwriter', in Williams, K., and Williams, J. A. (eds.), *The Cambridge Companion to the Singer-Songwriter*. Cambridge: Cambridge University Press, pp. 11–20.

Sisario, B. (2018) 'Gender Diversity in the Music Industry? The Numbers Are Grim', 25th January 2018, *The New York Times*. www.nytimes.com/2018/01/25/arts/music/music-industry-gender-study-women-artists-producers.html (Accessed 07/12/18).

Siverskog, A. (2015) 'Ageing Bodies that Matter: Age, Gender and Embodiment in Older Transgender People's Life Stories', *NORA - Nordic Journal of Feminist and Gender Research*, 23 (1), pp. 4–19, Doi:10.1080/08038740.2014.979869.

Smith, P. (2010) *Just Kids*. London, New York: Bloomsbury.

Smith, P. (2015) *M Train*. London, New York: Bloomsbury.

Snapes, L. (2018) 'How Robyn Transformed Pop', *The Guardian*, 28th September, 2018, www.theguardian.com/music/2018/sep/28/how-robyn-transformed-pop-music-honey (Accessed 13/12/18).

Sontag, S. (1984) 'The Double Standard of Aging', in Rainbolt, M., and Fleetwood, J. (eds.), *On the Contrary: Essays by Men and Women*, Albany: State University of New York Press, pp. 99–112.

Spencer, N. (2016) 'Calypso Rose: Far from Home Review – The Calypso Queen Dazzles', *The Guardian*, 10th July 2016. www.theguardian.com/music/2016/jul/10/calypso-rose-far-from-home-review (Accessed 13/09/18).

Steinskog, E. (2008) *Voice of Hope: Queer Pop Subjectivities*. http://trikster.net/1/steinskog/1.html.

Step Back Concerts, at https://stepbackconcerts.co.uk/product/stepback-80s-coventry/

Stosoy, B. (2016) 'Anohni on Art, Corporations and the Music Industry', *The Creative Independent*, 10th October, 2016. https://thecreativeindependent.com/people/anohni-on-art-corporations-and-the-music- industry/ (Accessed 08/10/18).

Strong, C. (2011a) *Grunge: Music and Memory*. London, New York: Routledge.

Strong, C. (2011b) 'Grunge, RiotGrrl and the Forgetting of Women in Popular Culture', *The Journal of Popular Culture*, 44 (2), pp. 398–416.

Strong, C. (2019) 'Re-Calling Grunge: Seattle, Anniversary Journalism, and Changing Narratives of a Genre', in Lashua, B., Wagg, S., Spracklen, K., and Yavuz, M. (eds.), *Sounds and the City. Leisure Studies in a Global Era*. London: Palgrave Macmillan, pp. 15–32.

Tambling, J. (1990) *Confession, Sexuality, Sin: The Subject*. Manchester: Manchester University Press.

Taylor, J. (2012) *Playing It Queer: Popular Music, Identity and Queer World Making*. Bern, Berlin: Peter Lang.

Thorn, T. (2013) *Bedsit Disco Queen: How I Grew Up and Tried to be a Pop Star*. London: Virago.

Tinker, C. (2012) 'Âge Tendre et Têtes de Bois: Nostalgia, Television and Popular Music in Contemporary France', *French Cultural Studies*, 23 (3), pp. 239–255.

Troughton, R. (2016) 'Carnival Queen Calypso Rose Interviewed', *The Quietus*, 21st April 2016. www.thequietus.com/articles/20097-calypso-rose-intreview (Accessed 10/09/18).

Tutti, C. F. (2017) *Art, Sex, Music*. London: Faber and Faber.

Van Dijck, J. (2007) *Mediated Memories in the Digital Age*. Stanford, CA: Stanford University Press.

Vaziri, A. (2018) 'The Breeders Return, with Classic Line-Up and Punk Spirit Intact On 'All Nerve'', *The San Francisco Chronicle*, 28th February, 2018. www.sfchronicle.com/music/article/The-Breeders-return-with- classic- lineup-and-punk-12716906.php.

Vernallis, C. (2004) *Experiencing Music Video: Aesthetics and Cultural Context*. New York: Columbia University Press.

Vernallis, C. (2013) *Unruly Media: YouTube, Music Video and the New Digital Cinema*. Oxford: Oxford University Press.

Vroomen, K. (2004) 'Kate Bush, Teen Pop and Older Female Fans', in Bennett, A., and Peterson, R. (eds.), *Music Scenes, Local, Translocal, Virtual.* Nashville: Vanderbilt University Press, pp. 238–265.

Wade, P. (2000) *Music, Race and Nation: Musica Tropical in Columbia.* Chicago, IL: University of Chicago Press.

Wald, G. (1998) 'Just a Girl? Rock Music, Feminism, and the Cultural Construction of Female Youth', *Signs: Journal of Women in Culture and Society*, 23 (3), pp. 585–610.

Waldrep, S. (2016) *Future Nostalgia: Performing David Bowie.* London: Bloomsbury.

Warner, M. (1994) *Managing Monsters: Six Myths of our Time.* The 1994 Reith Lectures. London: Vintage.

Warwick, J. (2007) *Girl Groups, Girl Culture: Popular Music and Identity in the 1960s.* New York, Oxford: Routledge.

Warwick, J., and Adrian, A. (eds.) (2016) *Voicing Girlhood in Popular Music: Performance, Authority, Authenticity.* New York, London: Routledge.

Webb, P. (2004) 'Interrogating the Production of Sound and Place: The Bristol Phenomenon, from Lunatic Fringe to Worldwide Massive', in Whiteley, S., Bennett, A., and Hawkins, S. (eds.), *Music, Space and Place: Popular Music and Cultural Identity.* Farnham: Ashgate. pp. 66–88.

Whelehan, I. (2013) 'Ageing Appropriately: Postfeminist Discourses of Ageing in Contemporary Hollywood', in Gwynne, J., and Muller, N. (eds.), *Postfeminism and Contemporary Hollywood Cinema.* London: Palgrave Macmillan, pp. 78–95.

Whelehan, I., and Gwynne, J. (2014) *Ageing, Popular Culture and Contemporary Feminism.* London, New York: Routledge.

Whiteley, S. (2000) *Women and Popular Music: Sexuality, Identity and Subjectivity.* New York, London: Routledge.

Whiteley, S., Bennett, A., and Hawkins, S. (eds.) (2004) *Music, Space and Place: Popular Music and Cultural Identity.* Farnham: Ashgate.

Wilkins, W. (2018). 'The Rheingans Sisters- Bright Field', *Bright Young Folk*, http://brightyoungfolk.com/records/bright-field-the-rheingans-sisters (Accessed 24/10/18).

Williams, J. (2014) *Rhymin' and Stealin': Musical Borrowing in Hip-Hop.* Ann Arbor: University of Michigan Press.

Williams, J., and Williams, K. (2016) *The Cambridge Companion to the Singer-Songwriter.* Cambridge: Cambridge University Press.

Wilson, S. (2003) *Oprah, Celebrity and Formations of Self.* London: Palgrave MacMillan.

Winters, T., and Keegan-Phipps, S. (2013) *Performing Englishness: Identity and Politics in a Contemporary Folk Resurgence.* Manchester: Manchester University Press.

Wiseman-Trowse, N. (2013) *Nick Drake: Dreaming England.* London: Reaktion.

Womack, Y. (2013) *Afrofuturism: The World of Black Sci-Fi and Fantasy Culture.* Chicago, IL: Lawrence Hill Books.

Woodward, K. (ed.) (1999) *Figuring Age, Women, Bodies, Generations.* Bloomington: Indiana University Press.

Woodward, K. (2006) 'Performing Age, Performing Gender', *NWSA Journal*, 18 (1), pp. 162–189. www.jstor.org/stable/4317191.

Worley M. (2011) 'One Nation under the Bomb: The Cold War and British Punk to 1984', *Journal for the Study of Radicalism*, 5 (2), pp. 65–83.

Ylanne, V. (2012). *Representing Aging: Images and Identities.* Basingstoke: Palgrave MacMillan.

Young, R. (2010) *Electric Eden, Unearthing Britain's Visionary Music.* London: Faber and Faber.

Zuberi, N. (2001) *Sounds English: Transnational Popular Music.* Urbana, Chicago: University of Illinois Press.

Filmography

The Ballad of Shirley Collins (2017) Directed by Rob Curry and Tim Plester [Film]
The Blood on Satan's Claw (1974) Directed by Piers Haggard [Film]
The Brother from Another Planet (1984) Directed by John Sayles [Film]
Calypso Rose, Lioness of the Jungle (2011) Directed by Pascale Obolo [Film]
Desperately Seeking Susan (1985) Directed by Susan Seidelman [Film]
Ginger Snaps (2000) Directed by John Fawcett [Film]
Hannah and Her Sisters (1986) Directed by Woody Allen [Film]
The Harder They Come (1972) Directed by Perry Henzell [Film]
Kill Bill (2003) Directed by Quentin Tarantino [Film]
Natural Born Killers (1994) Directed by Oliver Stone [Film]
The Punk Rock Movie (1978) Directed by Don Letts [Film]
Sense and Sensibility (1995) Directed by Ang Lee [Film]
She Punks (2018) Directed by Gina Birch [Film]
Soul Food (1997) Directed by George Tilman [Film]
Thelma and Louise (1991) Directed by Ridley Scott [Film]
This is England (2006) Directed by Shane Meadows [Film]
Throne of Blood (1957) Directed by Akira Kurosawa [Film]
Turning (2006) Directed by Charles Atlas [Film]
The Virgin Suicides (1999) Directed by Sofia Coppola [Film]
Westway to the World (2000) Directed by Don Letts [Film]
Whatever Happened to Baby Jane (1962) Directed by Robert Aldrich [Film]
The Wicker Man (1973) Directed by Robin Hardy [Film]
Witchfinder General (1968) Directed by Michael Reeves [Film]
20 Feet From Stardom (2014) Directed by Neville Morgan [Film]

Music videos

Anohni, 'Marrow' (2016) dir. Unlisted. Rebis Music
Björk, 'Oh so quiet' (2005) dir. Spike Jonze
Calypso Rose, 'Calypso queen' (2016) dir. Pascale Obolo
Christine and the Queens, 'Christine' (2014) dir. J.A.C.K
Christine and the Queens, 'Girlfriend' (2018) dir. Jordan Bahat
Christine and the Queens, 'La marcheuse' (2018) dir. Colin Solal Cardo
Christine and the Queens, '5 Dollars' (2018) dir. Colin Solal Cardo
Lady Gaga, 'Telephone' (2009) dir. Jonas Akerlund
Lady Leshurr, 'The queens speech – Episode 1' (2015) dir. Lady Leshurr and Wowa
Lady Leshurr, 'The queens speech – Episode 2' (2015) dir. Lady Leshurr and Wowa
Lady Leshurr, 'The queens speech – Episode 3' (2015) dir. Lady Leshurr and Wowa
Lady Leshurr, 'The queens speech – Episode 4' (2015) dir. Lady Leshurr and Wowa
Lady Leshurr, 'The queens speech – Episode 5' (2015) dir. Lady Leshurr and Wowa
Lady Leshurr, 'The queens speech – Episode 6' (2016) dir. Lady Leshurr and Wowa
Lady Leshurr, 'The queens speech – Episode 7' (2017) dir. Lady Leshurr and Wowa
Lava La Rue, 'Tetra' (2018)
Janelle Monáe, 'Tightrope' (2010) dir. Wendy Morgan
Janelle Monáe, 'Dirty computer' (2018) dir. Andrew Donoho and Chuck Lihgtning
Janelle Monáe, 'Pynk' (2018) dir. Emma Westernberg
Janelle Monáe, 'I like that' (2018) dir. Lacey Duke
Janelle Monáe, 'Make me feel' (2018) dir. Alan Ferguson

Robert Palmer, 'Addicted to love' (1986) dir. Terence Donovan
The Breeders, 'Spacewoman' (2018) dir. Richard Ayoade
Robin Thicke, 'Blurred lines' (2003) dir. Diane Martel

Discography

Anohni, *Hopelessness* (2016) Produced by Hudson Mohawke, Oneohtrix Point Never and Anohni, Secretly Canadian. [Vinyl, LP album, CD]
Calypso Rose *Far From Home* (2016) Produced by Manu Chao, Because Music. [Vinyl, LP album, CD]
Christine and the Queens, *Chaleur Humaine* (2014) Produced by Christine and the Queens. Because Music [CD, LP album]
Christine and the Queens, *Chris* (2018) Produced by Cole MGN (Vocals), Because Music. [CD, LP album]
Ewan McColl and Peggy Seeger (1962) 'Bonnie Annie' on *Popular Scottish Songs* Smithsonian Folkways FW 8757 [LP album]
Janelle Monáe, *Dirty Computer* (2018) Produced by Chuck Lightning and Janelle Monáe, Atlantic. [CD, LP album]
Lady Leshurr, *Queen's Speech 1* (2016) Not On Label (Lady Leshurr Self-released) [File, EP]
Lady Leshurr, *Queen's Speech 2* (2016) Not On Label (Lady Leshurr Self-released) [File, EP]
Lady Leshurr, *Queen's Speech 3* (2016) Not On Label (Lady Leshurr Self-released) [File, EP]
Lady Leshurr, *Queen's Speech 4* (2016) Not On Label (Lady Leshurr Self-released) [File, EP]
Lady Leshurr, *Queen's Speech 5* (2016) Not On Label (Lady Leshurr Self-released) [File, EP]
Lady Leshurr, *Queen's Speech 6* (2016) Sony Music [File, Single]
Lava La Rue, *Letra* (2018) Produced by Tariq Dissu, #Nine8Collective# [File, MP3]
Marianne Faithfull, *Negative Capability* (2018) Panta Rei, BMG. [CD, LP album]
Nick Cave and The Bad Seeds, 'Jubilee Street', Track 4 from *Push The Sky Away* (2012) Produced by Nick Cave and The Bad Seeds and Nick Launay, Bad Seed Ltd. [CD, Single]
Nirvana, *In Utero* (1993), produced by Steve Albini, DGC Records. [CD, LP album]
Patti Smith, *Horses* (1975), produced by John Cale, Arista Records. [LP album]
Pixies, *Surfer Rosa* (1987), produced by Steve Albini, 4AD. [CD, LP album]
Shirley and Dolly Collins, *Love, Death and The Lady* (1970), produced by Austin John Marshall. [LP album]
Shirley Collins, *Lodestar* (2016), produced by Ossian Brown, Stephen Thrower (pre-production) and Ian Kearey, Domino Records. [CD, LP album]
The Askew Sisters, *In The Air of The Earth* (2014), produced by Andy Bell. [CD, LP album]
The Breeders, *Pod* (1990), produced by Steve Albini, 4AD. [CD, LP album]
The Breeders, *All Nerve* (2018), produced by Steve Albini, 4AD. [File, MP3, CD, LP album]
The Rheingans Sisters, *Bright Field* (2018), produced by Anna Rheingans and Rowan Rheingans, Root Beat Records. [CD, LP album]
The Selecter (1980) *Too Much Pressure*, produced by Errol Ross and The Selecter, Two-Tone Records. [LP album]
The Selecter (1981) *Celebrate the Bullet*, produced by Roger Lomas and The Selecter, Chrysalis. [LP album]
The Selecter (2011) *Made in Britain*, produced by Arthur Hendrikson, Neil Pyzer and Pauline Black, Vocaphone Records. [CD, LP album]
The Selecter (2013) *String Theory*, produced by The Selecter, Vocaphone Records. [CD, LP album]
The Selecter (2015) *Subculture*, produced by Neil Pyzer, DMF. [CD, LP album]
The Selecter (2017) *Daylight*, produced by Neil Pyzer, DMF. [CD, LP album]

Index